D1130492

GOLDSWORTHY
LOWES DICKINSON

G. L. D.

From the portrait by Roger Fry.

GOLDSWORTHY LOWES DICKINSON

BY
E. M. FORSTER

HARCOURT, BRACE AND COMPANY

NEW YORK

PRINTED IN THE UNITED STATES OF AMERICA
BY THE POLYGRAPHIC COMPANY OF AMERICA, NEW YORK

FRATRUM SOCIETATI

PREFACE

DURING the last twelve years of his life Dickinson wrote a quantity of autobiographical matter. He told me that it was not to be published in its entirety, but might be used at my discretion, so I have used it in writing this book. It will be referred to under the general title of 'Recollections'; indeed all quotations may be assumed to come from this source, when they are not otherwise assigned. I have also worked part of the 'Recollections' into the substance of the narrative; for instance, the details about his childhood and his various states of mind are not guesses of my own, but rest on his authority.

How good is that authority? To what extent can a man be trusted to review his own past? Something must always be discounted, and in Dickinson's case we must discount a thin veil of melancholy which interposed between him and the paper as soon as he sat down to type. He was aware of this and tried to neutralise it, and it is, I think, his only defect as an autobiographer. For when he tried to look back at himself he was at the height of his power as a prose writer; his mind was active and clear, his outlook fearless and humane; intent on the truth, he never exalted himself, and even resisted the more congenial temptation of self-depreciation. Such a breadth of outlook would have been impossible for him in his pre-war days, such detachment would have been impossible during the war. It was only at the close of his life that he was fitted to record his life, and—except for the tendency to write it down as rather sadder than he felt it to have been—his record may be accepted.

After the 'Recollections' my chief source has been his letters, a number of which I have read, thanks to the kindness of his family and friends. He was not, in my judgment, a great letter-writer, but he always provides interesting views, terse sentences, relevant information, and I have quoted frequently. His books have also helped, and though I have not attempted detailed criticism of them I have referred to them all in passing, and have also described the contents of his privately printed works and of some unpublished MSS. Most of his books are now published by Messrs Allen & Unwin. 'The Greek View of Life' is to be had from Messrs Methuen, 'Goethe and Faust' from Messrs Bell, the 'Life of McTaggart' from the Cambridge University Press. 'From King to King' and 'The Development of Parliament in the Nineteenth Century' are out of print.

I have not tried to exclude facts about him with which I am not in sympathy or which might be held to decrease his reputation. To do so would be to pay him a poor compliment, for neither did he care anything for his reputation, nor was he dazzled by the reputations of others. He admired a biography not when it treated its subject in a reverent spirit but when it made it come alive. I should like to adopt his own standard here. I should like to make him live for people who never met him in the flesh, and to whom his voice when he broadcast was sometimes the first indication of his existence. It is for the general public rather than for his friends (who need no words of mine) that I write this book, and for that reason he will be oftener referred to as 'Dickinson' than as 'Goldie'. He was not merely intelligent, affectionate, charming, remarkable; he was unique. But how is this to be conveyed?

I knew him for thirty-five years, and knew him well for twenty, so feel qualified to write about him from the personal, and perhaps from the literary, point of view. But there my qualifications end. I can discuss him neither as a philosopher nor as a publicist, and these sections of the book are bound to be unsatisfactory. I thought indeed of asking others to undertake them, and to deal in particular with his League of Nations work. But it seemed better that one person should be in charge, however obvious his limitations. Collaboration leads to thoroughness but not to consistency, and it is only through unity of treatment that the underlying unity of Dickinson can be stressed.

The arrangement of the book has been rather a problem, for his life was not dramatic and does not divide into strongly marked periods. I have aimed at a narrative but a halting narrative, which is interrupted by Chapter xi (his extra-European interests) and to some extent by Chapter vii. I have tried to write simply. Some of his friends, who do not know foreign languages, have suggested that quotations in them should be translated, but I was unwilling to interrupt the flow of his prose, and think that the few words of Greek, Latin, French and German which occur in it will be explained by their contexts.

My thanks are due in the first place to his sisters, Miss May Lowes Dickinson and Mrs Lowes. Although the responsibility for the book is mine, it would not have been begun without their approval, and it could not have been completed without their help. In the second place I desire to thank the Provost and Fellows of King's College, Cambridge. They have given me every possible facility, and I want, in this connection, particularly to thank Mr R. E. Balfour, Fellow of the College, for his bibliography. Mr Balfour has done a lasting service to future students. In the third place special acknowledgment is due to Dickinson's main publishers, Messrs Allen & Unwin, for the assistance they have so willingly given. In the fourth place comes the list of those who have lent letters, supplied information, given photographs, and helped in other ways, a list which includes the names of:

Mr H. G. Alexander, Lord Allen of Hurtwood, Mr and Mrs C. R. Ashbee, Mr Julian Bell, Mr E. K. Bennett, Mr Bernhard Berenson, Mrs Bridges (for Robert Bridges), Mrs O. W. Campbell, Mr H. Corner, Mr J. J. Darling, Lord Dickinson, Mr Bonamy Dobrée, Mr O. P. Eckhard, Mr Leonard Elmhirst, Mr C. R. Fay, Mr Elliott Felkin, Professor Roger Fry, Professor A. J. Grant, Mr Gerald Heard, Mrs E. B. C. Lucas,

Mr Edward Marsh (for Rupert Brooke), Mr J. H. Mason,
Mr R. J. G. Mayor, Professor H. O. Meredith, The Misses
Moor (for Mrs Moor), Lady Ottoline Morrell, Mr W. A. R.
Munro, Mrs Newman, Mr Robert Nichols, Lord Passfield,
Lord and Lady Ponsonby, Mr Dennis Proctor, Mr D. H.
Robertson, Mr D. K. Roy, Mrs C. P. Sanger (and for C. P.
Sanger), Mr Peter Savary, Mr F. N. Schiller, Professor G. C.
Moore Smith, Mr Dominick Spring-Rice, Miss Melian Stawell,
Mr Cecil Taylor, Mr N. Teulon-Porter, Miss Cecilia Townsend,
Mr and Mrs R. C. Trevelyan, Mr Stanley Unwin, Miss Webb
(for Mrs Webb), Mr N. Wedd, Mr H. G. Wells, Colonel E. J.
Wighton, Mr and Mrs Leonard Woolf, Professor W. Perceval
Yetts.

CONTENTS

LIST OF ILLUSTRATIONS

> Here, where the dews of sorrow
> Drop from a sky of lead,
> I set myself to fashion
> A garland for thy head.
>
> Perhaps on that tomorrow
> When we are counted dead
> By some diviner passion
> It will be perfected.

(There is no satisfactory portrait of him in middle life.)

GOLDSWORTHY
LOWES DICKINSON

CHAPTER I

FAMILY

GOLDSWORTHY LOWES DICKINSON (Goldie) was the son of Lowes Cato Dickinson and Margaret Ellen Williams.

On the father's side the family was Northumbrian, and has been traced back to the great-great-grandfather, Jacob Dickinson, of Whitfield (d. 1773) and his wife Alice Alexander (d. 1800). There is a story that this Jacob and his brother were foundlings, who were dropped off a coach on the moors, nicely dressed, and that a farmer of the name of Dickinson adopted them, but no one can vouch for the truth of the story. The great-grandfather, William Dickinson (1738–1819) had a farm near Bardon Mill; he married Jane Lowes (1749–1811), and there are other instances of marriage between these two families.

Goldie's grandfather, Joseph Dickinson (1782–1849), came to London at the beginning of the nineteenth century, and set up a print- and lithograph-shop and photographing business in Bond Street. He was gentle, sensitive, artistic, considerate of others, and what one may recognise as the family type emerges with him. His wife, Ann Carter, was from Devonshire, and claimed connection with Sir Humphrey Gilbert; Goldie always felt more in sympathy with this Devonian strain in him than with the Northumbrian. The children could just remember their grandmother and thought her formidable. She was certainly a woman of character, if I may judge by her entries in the family bible: 'Hope this will be the last', she writes opposite the birth of one of her babies, and opposite the next birth 'This must be the last'. As it was. Some of the babies were christened out of Plutarch, for whom Joseph Dickinson had a great admiration, Cicero

and so on, and about half-way down the long list comes
Goldie's father, Lowes Cato Dickinson, born in 1819.

Lowes Dickinson (he dropped the Cato) grew up in the
Bond Street shop, and was earning his living by the age of
sixteen. He began as a lithographer. In 1850 he was sent by
some friends to Italy to study art, and the charming letters
which he wrote during his three years' tour have been printed
for private circulation. In his day, to travel meant to live
with the people of the country, and his delightful personality
gained him a warm welcome from them. He made some
attractive water-colour drawings of the scenery, which have
been preferred by some critics to his more professional work
as a portrait painter. On his return from Italy he came into
touch with F. D. Maurice and the Christian Socialist movement, and, together with Charles Kingsley and Tom Hughes
and others of that group, he set himself to transform society
in the intervals of his work, and if possible by means of his
work. He helped to found the Working Men's College—
which was then not the trim municipalised institution up in
Crowndale Road but a lodge in the wilderness of Great Or-
mond Street. Here he taught drawing for many years, in the
midst of discomfort and enthusiasm. Ruskin was a fellow
teacher. Although never a fashionable painter, he was in
steady demand among the intellectual middle classes, and
many London clubs and Cambridge colleges possess examples
of him. He specialised in posthumous portraits; the picture
of one of his heroes, Gordon, now hangs at Khartoum, a re-
plica of it being in the Gordon Boys' Home.

He married Miss Williams in 1857, and lived at first in a
studio at Langham Chambers, where the four elder children
were born. Then he moved out to Hanwell. His relations with
them all, until school intervened, were perfect. He would go
up to his work and return in the evening to play, or to read
Scott, Shakespeare or Coleridge aloud, while Goldie and his
sister May perched together on a stool by the wood fire. In
1877–9 he built a London house close to his old studio—1 All

Souls Place, a tall dark red wedge-shaped house all windows and hospitality, and it was there that I saw him once or twice towards the end of his life. He was then nearly ninety, and he walked round the rooms with a candle to show some pictures which he thought would give me pleasure. His courtesy and intelligence left a deep impression. Perhaps, like many happy natures, he was better suited for affection than for intimacy; Goldie, though he loved him, never felt that they knew each other well. Father and son were alike in one respect, they were both subject to fits of gloom. But whereas the son could give reasons for his depression which are only too convincing, the father was vaguer about it; he would write a despairing letter, and be puzzled when a consolatory answer was returned. Despair in the nineteenth century was a male prerogative; there was held to be something noble and authoritative about it. The twentieth century has had to take a less romantic view.

When we turn from the father's side of the family to the mother's, we find much the same tradition of decency and sensitiveness. There seems to have been no notable clash of types in Dickinson's make up and he experienced none of the dangers or thrills which may be traced to war within the blood. His grandfather on his mother's side was William Smith Williams. Mr Williams was for many years literary adviser to the publishers Smith Elder & Co.; he discovered Charlotte Brontë, and welcomed her when she made her famous first visit to London. His correspondence with Charlotte has been printed in Clement Shorter's Life. He was incapable of self-advertisement. After his retirement, he lived quietly at Twickenham, where he died in 1875. His wife, a Miss Hill, possibly had Jewish blood in her and this would preserve Dickinson from the stigma of pure Aryan descent; otherwise the ancestry seems to have been English. The Williams had several daughters, one of whom, Anna, became a famous singer. Another, Fanny, is said to have had an even finer voice.

The marriage of Ellen Williams to Mr Lowes Dickinson was
supremely happy, and perhaps that is why their son came to
regard marriage as the best attainable earthly state—a risky
state, like any other, but promising a union of emotion and
companionship which cannot be found outside. Mrs Lowes
Dickinson was a woman of sweet but firm character, with
strong opinions as to what is right and wrong, and with a
narrow vein of piety running through the abundance of her
natural goodness. She died when her son was only nineteen,
so he never developed with her the close relationship which
often exists, for good and evil, between a mother and a
grown-up son. He looked back on her as he did on his
father: with love and admiration, but with the feeling that
there had never been any intimacy. There certainly was
nothing which can be described as an exchange of ideas.

There were five children to the marriage: Arthur (now Sir
Arthur Lowes Dickinson), May, G. L. D. himself, Hettie (now
Mrs Lowes), and Janet. Arthur was three years older than his
brother, and they were so different in outlook that they never
became intimate, though there was friendliness and respect.
On the other hand, Dickinson remained in close touch with
his three sisters. His earliest companion and friend was his
sister May. In their childhood May was 'rather precocious,
she acted and sang and danced, and to the best of my remembrance flirted'. The 'little ones', Hettie and Janet,
seemed then to be separated by a great gulf of years, and he
and May were anxious lest they should intrude. 'However,
we were all very friendly together, and unless the sentiment
of the past deceives me we were all very happy.' He was in
many ways well fitted for domestic life, and he never knew
real misery until he was wrenched away from it.

He took his name Goldsworthy from Sir Goldsworthy
Gurney, one of the Cornish Gurneys, who were related to the
Carters. Sir Goldsworthy was an inventor, and considering
how his namesake denounced motor cars it is ironical that he
should have invented the first steam carriage and should have

driven it to Bath and back at the rate of fifteen miles an hour. After his death, a stained glass window was put up to him in St Margaret's, Westminster, which window is not as well known to visitors as it should be. Most of it is occupied by saints, but at the bottom of its central light two very graceful angels hold up a plaque on which is the little steam carriage itself, traversing an undulating landscape in grisaille. Sir Goldsworthy Gurney is aboard driving a party of passengers in top hats, while some gentlemen admire him from an adjacent hill. In a separate compartment to the left of the angels he reappears on a large scale, thinking out something in his study, and to their right is a lighthouse amid a stormy sea. The inscription says: 'He invented the steam jet and the oxyhydrogen blowpipe'. Who could wish to trace the name of Goldsworthy back any further after this? though a Miss Goldsworthy, ancestor to the Gurneys, is said to have been maid of honour to Queen Anne.

The origin of his second name, Lowes, has already been indicated; it came from his great-grandmother on the father's side, and it has been adopted by all his branch of the family.

CHAPTER II

THE SPRING COTTAGE
1862–1872

DICKINSON'S 'Recollections' begin as follows:

The earliest thing I remember—or rather remember to have remembered; for that is how it now presents itself to me—is looking out of a pointed window, opening like a door and filled with small diamond panes of glass, at the people coming home from church through the little gate of our garden. I may have been two years old and my nurse was holding me. This was in our cottage at Hanwell, then a little country village, now part of the suburbs of London. One or two other memories seem to float vaguely at this threshold of consciousness. Once, for example, stars looked large, with points all round them, as they used to be painted on the roof of the old St James' Hall in London. For I remember one night, later, looking up and feeling surprised and disappointed to see nothing but pale tiny points of light. That seems all I can recover of those earliest days. After that, memory proper begins, treacherous, complicated, stratum piled on stratum, reflection and comparison vitiating experience.

He had been born in London (Aug. 6th, 1862), and his family moved to The Spring Cottage soon afterwards. It was first thought to be 'Spring Cottage', and associated with the vernal season, but this proved a mistake; it took its name from a neighbouring residence, 'The Spring', whose grounds contain a spring, and its note paper had to be altered. All his early memories centred round it. It was—or rather is, for it still exists—the sort of house which excites and charms a child, for it was small, and completely surrounded by a garden. When the family arrived there were only two sitting rooms, two bedrooms, a kitchen, and a verandah covered with white roses, but they added a dining room on the ground floor and nurseries above it, and since the new dining room was connected with the old drawing room by a greenhouse, no conceivable delight was lacking not even panes of coloured glass. Then there was the furniture: the library table and the Hepplewhite chairs which followed him finally to Cambridge; the black clock; the Collard piano in a boxwood case, 'sweeter in tone, I think, than pianos have since become'; the Sheraton sideboard; the green velvet chairs; a vase supported by two little cherubs; the books, dark in colour, and including 'Curiosities of London' where a boy was blinded by tying across his eyes two shells in each of which was a live beetle.... The children dashed quickly up to bed past the books. And above the white roses on the verandah grew a wistaria, which his mother, leaning out of her window, plucked to put in her hair. The whole picture, as he recalled it, has the graciousness and the solidity of a woodcut belonging to the period. It is a childhood of the 'sixties.

The garden hangs in my past like a vision of light. Flower beds are brighter than they have ever been since, shrubberies more mysterious, spaces larger, storms and rain more exciting. How I recall at this moment the oncoming of a storm, the black sky, the still air, and us in the twilight garden running and screaming with delight. And the lightning hour after hour, the sky opening and closing like an amazing flower, as I lay and watched it from my bed, till at last some elder pulled down the green venetian blinds and there was nothing to be seen but the flicker of light at their edges.

The various trees in the garden had their characters. The fir tree was smothered in ivy, the chestnut commanded a view of the road, the sycamore dropped seeds on to the fernery, the cherry was covered with double white blossom, and under it his mother sat and sewed while they read aloud to her; to the end of his life this particular image recurred whenever he saw the double cherry in the Fellows' Garden at King's. There was also a kitchen garden, a shed, and a swing in which he and his brother and his sisters would impersonate the broad-

gauge engines of the Great Western Railway. And outside
the garden began in easy processes the world, reached by
the trains, or by the new village cab upholstered in purple
velvet, or on foot, or in a perambulator.

When Emma their nurse took them into the world, the expedition usually ended at a cemetery. Hanwell was happily
placed for cemeteries: there were two large ones, besides the
churchyard, and Emma liked to see the hearses come slowly
down from London. Under her supervision, the children
watched the interments from a distance, and spelled out the
inscriptions on the tombs, and observed that the hearses called
at a public-house on the return journey, and then proceeded
less sadly. A young grocer who was courting her sometimes
took them for rides in his cart. This was a great delight, and
they gained lessons in deportment too, and learnt to refer to
people mysteriously and by initials only: Mr A., Mrs C.—
a method to be extended later to royalty. They learnt
too that tea should be drunk with a loud smacking sound.
Emma married her grocer, and Dickinson kept in touch
with her until her death, which occurred a year before his
own. She was a most warm-hearted and affectionate
woman.

The children were by no means left to run about with servants. They moved in the first circles of Hanwell society as
soon as they could move at all, for although their father was
not rich he was an artist of repute and position. 'There were
the people you knew and the people you only knew about,
and the tradespeople who were outside the pale, and the poor
who sat in what were called free seats in church, and were
visited and helped if they were good.' Their chief friends were
at The Spring—Sir Alexander Spearman and his family—but
they were constantly at the rectory too, and this is important
in view of later developments. The rector of Hanwell, Derwent
Coleridge, was a son of the poet. He was a learned old gentleman, with a shaven chin and white side whiskers, who knew
several languages, and preached an annual sermon beginning

'Reading Plato the other night...'. He had a son Ernest, a daughter Christabel, and a niece Edith, who knew Greek, and taught the children's mother, who, in her turn, taught them. The most interesting feature of the rectory was not the Coleridges but the long succession of young Americans, who came to be initiated by them into English niceties; seated upon the knees of one of these kind young men, Dickinson asked him why his face was so spotty—a piece of innocence which it horrified him to recall, yet it was not uncharacteristic. There was also an ecclesiastical crisis. Mr Coleridge took to turn east during the creed and this involved him in a dispute with the squire, who turned west as a counterweight. The Dickinsons took the rector's side, and their father, who was fond of writing letters, sent one in which he rebuked the squire for 'straining at the gnat of turning to the East while swallowing the camel of unchristian feelings at the communion table'. But the children visited at the squire's house too—if indeed he was the squire: there was a little doubt, he was melancholy and had an organ. And there were other figures who seemed, in retrospect, almost too fantastic to have lived; the lady who sang but could not shake until she heard Grisi sing The Nightingale, 'and then I shook and shook and have shaken ever since'; the lady who was shocked because work was done on the new railway station on Sunday, and cried: 'Be sure Mr Dickinson, God's blessing will never rest upon it', and the rector calling to his wife in the middle of a party: 'Mary, my dear, we must have a little Poe in the drawing room'. The chief drawback to all these kind people was that they were elderly and had no little children. For purposes of play, less eminent families had to be commandeered.

'In this place and society I passed my earliest years', and then follows a long list of little memories. Among them are 'Lying in bed in the dusk, listening to the Moonlight Sonata played below; lying in bed in the morning; playing at fairies with my father which meant stealing up and tickling his bald head while he pretended to be asleep; singing in a little piping voice a song about a little fish; singing hymns on Sunday evening'; composing a hymn of his own

> Woe unto ye Pharisees
> Woe unto ye Scribes
> Walking in the darkness
> Of your darkened eyes

and reciting it to his mother; being sent to bed, and crying for hours; being spanked, once only. And then lessons, based on Little Arthur's History and other text-books of the period, and not at all interesting, though not repellent.

My mother with infinite patience conducted us through this routine, as well as running the house, providing her little dinner parties, learning her Greek and adoring my father who also loved her but not I think as she loved him. Then every year a month or so by the sea, sands and donkey rides, sea anemones, bathing, blackberries and cream. A happy life as I look back on it, and the happier because it was followed by such misery. For the time came when I was sent to school.

CHAPTER III

THE MISSES WOODMAN'S MORNING CLASS
1872–1874

THE first school was not alarming, indeed it was only an extension of his home life. It was a day school kept by two sisters called Woodman at 13 Somerset Street, Portman Square. He never forgot the address because he got a prize every term, and on its cover was stamped the Misses Woodman's monogram surrounded by their address and by the words 'Morning Class for the sons of gentlemen'. Tom Hughes' sons, Pip and Plump, went to the same school and it was evidently the best that Christian Socialists could provide for their young. Tradesmen were excluded, except when they were definitely rich, like Tab, afterwards Lord Brassey, and vice should have been excluded too, but it crept in and there was an appalling scene one morning during geography when a red-headed boy was detected telling a lie. 'William Watson!' said Miss Woodman in terrible tones, 'You have told a lie!' 'I thought', said the assistant mistress afterwards, 'that Miss Woodman would have fainted.'

To this snobby, conscientious, and harmless establishment the child went up daily, taking the early train from Hanwell to Paddington, and returning in the afternoon, to be welcomed at the garden gate by his nurse. He had a pleasant time, and was 'well grounded'. Education, as we understand it to-day, was scarcely attempted. Everything was learnt by heart. His mother had taught him Greek and Euclid by heart, and the Misses Woodman continued on her lines. Before long he could repeat a number of sentences like 'Common are to either sex, Artifex and opifex', and 'Syllaba longa brevi subjecta vocatur iambus'—sentences to which neither he nor the Misses Woodman attached any meaning. In geography, when a country was outlined on the blackboard and round blobs were put for its towns, he could name the blobs as long as he looked at the board. No one suggested to him that 'iambus' had to do with poetry, Greek with literature, and geography with Hanwell or Paddington. They were incantations which his preceptors desired him to memorise.

There were two Miss Woodmans, Miss Woodman proper, who was stern and ironical, and Miss Maria with a cast in her eye, who was violent and ugly. When we said our irregular verbs to Miss Woodman she would repeat 'Yes. Fatiscor. Fatiscor, I am weary, I am weary of you boys'. Meanwhile from the room above, out of the floor of which a circular hole opened into the room below, would come the smack smack of Miss Maria boxing some one's ears. Miss Woodman would pause with a sigh and then resume operations: Fatiscor, I am weary. About these two great goddesses the lesser mistresses revolved deferentially. Later on a man was introduced as an experiment. He was called 'the graduate', but he was not a success, I can't remember why. At any rate one term saw the end of him and at the prize giving Miss Woodman remarked with caustic wit that should the graduate turn up it would be as an uninvited guest.

Miss Woodman was a remarkable character. His sister Hettie taught in her school some years later and got the same impression of her love of the dramatic and her disciplinary power; 'lay not this flattering unction to your soul' was a favourite and a mysterious exclamation.

Once his parents went to America, the Hanwell cottage was shut up for a term and he was sent to board at the school. He became a favourite, and the mistresses cosseted him. He enjoyed scripture and breakfast in the morning, for he was a pious and hungry little boy. In the afternoon there were walks in Hyde Park, where a steam engine was seen, not Sir Goldsworthy's but an object in a vermilion box. Midday dinner was served in the gas-lit basement:

We were expected to provide the Miss Woodmans with what they wanted without their having to ask for it, and terrible it was when I heard a voice 'Goldie, I have had to *ask* for the salt'. I learned to say thank you instead of please, and became conscious of a much improved style. A curious thing is memory! For now there comes back to me a picture of Miss Maria, in the water closet, trying in vain to flush it, and screaming 'Someone has been using much too much paper'. Many years later Miss Woodman married and Miss Maria separated from her....

The term passed rather slowly and he was glad to be back at The Spring Cottage again. He found that his sisters had grown out of all recognition, and he felt much more important himself. His childish outlook continued. He still loved playing at engines, he still thought education meant learning by heart, and, instigated by his mother, he was still very 're-ligious'. Every night he read a chapter of the bible, sitting in his night-gown out on the landing under the gas jet and wishing someone would come and see how good he was. He must have been at the same time a charming and a morbid child. The charm was immense. All the visitors loved him and tried to spoil him. The morbidity may have been fostered by misguided training. The piety of his parents was, in his later judgment, unhelpful. It checked his instincts for enjoyment and gave him nothing with which to take their place. Yet how delightful life was—until the age of twelve. Then came the last childish holiday, at Croyde in Devonshire, and the news that he was going to a 'real' school. His heart sank, but there was nothing to be done. The Misses Woodman and The Spring Cottage itself faded away, and he was carried off by his mother and left by her in a large newly scrubbed room, there to await the arrival of real boys.

CHAPTER IV

BEOMONDS
1874–1876

DICKINSON once took me to see his old preparatory
school. It is at Chertsey, not far from the poet Cow-
ley's house, and stands with its flank to the road. It
is still a school, but for girls. We rang the bell on the chance,
and were let in. He told the young mistresses how unhappy
he had been there once, and how cold, and how he had
scrambled in the morning for hot rolls, and they patronised
him, but they were impressed when he told them that Charles
Kingsley had once attended a prize distribution in the room
where we were all standing. It was the room on the right of
the entrance, and perhaps it was here that his mother left
him to face the world. Frail, distinguished, and in the eyes
of the mistresses doubtless somewhat absurd, he looked sadly
round his former prison, which had become romantic because
it was so far away. Then he thanked them with his usual
gentleness, and returned to the world—a place which, for all
its horrors, had never quite fulfilled the preliminary threat.
'One suffers more later, but one has at least experience to
correct it and character to fight it. At school a timid boy
like me has no aid and no hope.'

When he went to the school it had just been started by
Ernest Coleridge, the son of the rector of Hanwell. He was
a pompous fattish man, 'who later found his proper work as
an editor of Byron', and his letters to Mr Lowes Dickinson
about his pupil make ironic reading, when one thinks of the
black pools of misery beneath—decent prim letters, such as
schoolmasters always will be content to write and parents to
receive. He likes Goldie and reports that he can be taught
anything, 'and has more or less mastered the style of Horace',

Age 14

Age 6

Photo by Dickinson Bros.

but is inaccurate, and 'not an ascetic in regard to his dinner'. The housekeeping was first done by Mr Coleridge's sister, Christabel. Then he took to himself a wife, whom he was said to have courted for years. There was rather an awkward silence when he brought her into the schoolroom to be introduced. None of the boys could think what to say. At last Charles Kingsley's son, who had a certain amount of savoir-faire and had previously been at Harrow, said, 'I am sure sir we all congratulate you very much', and the situation was saved.

The wretchedness began at once. When it is recorded it looks like nothing at all, and seems to constitute no real indictment of the boarding-school system. There was no physical bullying to speak of, and no revolting orgy; indeed to the normal boy and the complacent grown-up Beomonds must have seemed quite a sound place. But, like most boys who have any imaginative contribution to make, Goldie was not normal. He suffered from torments which assail the spirit, from moral bullying, of which there was a great deal, and from his own timidity. Sometimes he gave in to schoolboy ethics as in the crisis of the potatoes, which shall be recorded presently, and then he was tortured by remorse. Sometimes he held out, but at great nervous expenditure and with none of the glow of martyrdom as a reward. He managed to get the worst of both worlds, to appease neither his darker angel nor his brighter, and for the reason that the third world —the world of Ariel—was excluded. Instead of the Moonlight Sonata, floating up through the floor of The Spring Cottage, sounds like these assailed his ears:

Sitting round the table in the evening, supposed to be preparing unintelligible 'work', I was disturbed and perplexed by the talk of older boys. 'Bitches.' What was a bitch? Did I know? 'It's a female dog isn't it', asked Kingsley, and I said yes, and thought perhaps it was. But then why talk about it? Then someone put something cold down my back. Then prayers in the hall, all the servants trooping in and Mr Coleridge in great form. Prayers I think always ended with 'For so he giveth his beloved sleep'. That sounded soothing. But then one went up to a bedroom with three other boys, one older and inclined to bully, and there were many pains before sleep was given to one who I fear was not his beloved.

What with the sinister hints, what with his top hat, which had belonged to his brother and turned Sunday into a catastrophe, and what with his habit of washing thoroughly at night and only a little in the morning, whereas the other boys washed only in the morning and not at all at night, he was instantly reduced to despair, and before a week had elapsed he wrote home and asked to be taken away. Very characteristically he wrote on a postcard. It was intercepted, much to his surprise, and he was summoned by Miss Coleridge to the drawing-room. Buxom and effusive Christabel took him on her knee, cosseted him, talked to him like a mother, and ended with: 'And now we will destroy this unlucky postcard'. It went into the fire, and with it his last hope of escape. His letters home were henceforward read by the masters, indeed he no longer thought of escape: after the unlucky postcard had been burnt, there was nothing to be done, and time stretched forward endlessly, without a gleam to vary its monotony. The gloom was increased by Mr Coleridge's attempts to deal with what was still termed 'the mystery of sex'. Serious and incompetent, he had summoned Goldie to the rectory at Hanwell before school opened, and had made some vague remarks that had no meaning whatever. Later on, hearing that he had had a bath with another boy, he called him to his study and cross-questioned him. The child was absolutely bewildered, he had no idea what the conversation was about, and Mr Coleridge soon became scared at the absence of response, and then dismissed him with the words 'I don't know whether you are more fool than knave'. He never heard one sensible word from any grown-up person on the subject. Once at home he had noticed that the cat looked larger than usual, and hazarded the guess that she had kittens inside her—not that he really believed anything so preposterous. His grandmother, who heard him, became humorous and sly, and changes in sleeping arrangements were the only answer.

His parents loved him and they had good instincts. But it was an age in which principles, not instincts, were valued, and they harnessed their love to the chariot of a narrow morality. The boys at Beomonds, for instance, were forbidden to buy sweets from the tuck shop in term time; they all did it, so did he, and he referred to it in the holidays. His mother was deeply distressed, she spoke to his father, there was a painful lecture, and he returned to school with the feeling that it was definitely 'wrong' to buy sweets or break any rule whatever. 'Wrong', and at the same time 'right'; he felt for the first time the fascination of disobedience for its own sake.

The effect was far greater than might seem probable. It formed a kind of complex which haunted me all through my school life. Perhaps it was at the root of my impatience now of most current rules of conduct. But now I have reason and character to justify myself to myself. Then it was a mere fetish which got hold of me to my undoing. *Why* though did it get hold of me when most boys would have let it pass indifferently? That, I suppose, goes deep into my character. At any rate a confusion of conscientiousness timidity and hypocrisy seized upon me and held me for many years. I emerged from it ultimately as a rebel, and at bottom have been so all my life. But by what strange and devious routes the approach was made!

We can see from the above passage (if indeed its evidence were necessary) that he was not the ordinary sensitive boy. He was sensitive, but he was not ordinary, for he had the power of turning his unhappiness to account. There was something pretty tough in him—something which he consciously developed in later life. He could draw strength from the most unpromising objects. And though he regrets the 'strange and devious route', and the apparent waste of energy and time which the fuss about the tuck shop caused

him, we may surmise that he could not have reached his
final position by any other route, so that his parents were
guiding him better than he knew.

The immediate consequences were, no doubt, most ener-
vating. Here is a letter which reveals them in all their force.
Note that he is writing not from Beomonds but from Charterhouse, some months later.

> Charterhouse,
> Godalming,
> Oct. 22nd, 1876.

My dearest Mother,

I want to tell you of something wrong that I did at
Mr Coleridge's. I only remembered it the other day and
thought that I should like to tell you. We used to cook
things in the school room on Saturday evening and once or
twice they sent me to get potatoes out of the stables and I
did not like to refuse and so I went and I suppose it was as
bad as stealing as they were Mr Coleridge's and I took little
things like slate pencils too but I suppose that didn't matter.
Please write to me soon.

> Ever your affec<u>ate</u> son
> Goldie.

His mother evidently dealt with this letter as a parent in
the 'seventies would, and she seems to have declined to distinguish between potatoes and pencils. Anyhow she elicits
a second agonised confession in which the boy assures her
that he is suffering over his wickedness quite as much as she
can suffer and prays God to pardon him. A parent of to-day
would have been bright and brief, and, without condoning
theft, would have managed to censure self-consciousness.
Though even to-day has the recipe for handling sensitive
children been formulated?

Beomonds had its pleasanter moments. He spouted Tennyson's 'Dora', and Miss Coleridge said, 'Well done, little
Goldie'. He acted Mrs Bouncer in Box and Cox amid great
applause, though when he cleaned himself up one of the
guests remarked: 'What! Was it that little whippersnapper!'

There was skating, and walking, and bathing in the Thames without costumes—the middle classes had not yet adopted this fetish. And, occasionally, though more rarely than before, he caught sight of the glory of literature. 'I have seen the sea', said Mr Boyd, a much admired master, meaning by those words that he had seen Salvini in Othello, and the words thrilled Dickinson, and in after years he echoed them. And when he had to translate Horace into verse—even if it was not the Horatian style it was not so bad for a boy of thirteen:

Why love the pine and poplar white
With mingling boughs sweet shade to spread,
Why does the murmuring brook delight
To hurry down its zigzag bed?

But these amenities lay at the edge of his life. Its centre was covered with rubbish and worry. And at its opposite edge lay an imbecile boy whom he sometimes kicked in order to ingratiate himself with his schoolfellows. He made no special confession to his parents about this; it was not a crime like the potatoes, nevertheless it haunted him.

CHAPTER V

CHARTERHOUSE
1876–1881

OF Charterhouse he writes:

> I was there the other day, an elderly stranger, and still
> had the remembrance of prison and the joy of one released.
> It was the same thing as Chertsey, only longer and worse....
> The House was left to the monitors, who had power to
> punish by boxing the ears (called 'Swingeing') and beating
> with sticks (called 'cocking up'—from the attitude as-
> sumed by the victim). The house in my time was what
> would be called a 'Hotbed of vice'. The odd thing is that
> though in a sort of way I knew this I wasn't interested in
> it and didn't attend to it.

There follow some mournful and bitter reminiscences. He
was worried by sex and by the evasions of his elders on the
subject, and he was still more worried by the fetish of rules.
One Sunday, Dr Haig Brown preached a sermon about the
importance of keeping rules, and revived the tuck shop
trouble in Dickinson's anxious mind. What rule had he
broken last? He had been guilty of talking in the dormitory
after dark. The dormitory was divided into cubicles, and the
boys used to chat over the partitions although they were told
not to. That night, half dead with terror, he announced that
he would talk no more, then he put his head under the clothes
expecting martyrdom. Nothing happened. When he listened
again, the dormitory chattered as usual, on other topics,
though later on one boy did remark, 'funny him saying that',
and another replied 'yes'. Nor was he persecuted next day.
He felt both relieved and disappointed, and before long he
resumed talking himself. All that emerged from his effort was
the feeling that he was alien, and that whether he talked or
was silent the rest of the dormitory belonged to another world.

'I have never lost this feeling. Indeed in my old age I feel it as never before. Men become to me simply unintelligible.'

Then there was another address from Dr Haig Brown on the mysterious subject of Collecting. 'I pity that boy', boomed the authoritative voice, 'who has never been a Collector', and Dickinson, who was that boy, felt ashamed. 'But I pity still more that boy who has remained a Mere Collector', and he felt he must be that boy too.

Then there was Confirmation, for which he was prepared on a manual drawn up for domestic servants. Another vague and alarming sex-talk accompanied it. He became more devout and attended Holy Communion with unreal but conscientious religiosity, liking to feel good, and sometimes longing to be bad. He was in a complete muddle, without any standards except what were imposed from outside and even his rebellions were conventional. Left to himself he would have escaped into the lost world of Ariel, where neither obedience nor disobedience existed, and the only sacrament was beauty. And on one occasion that world was rediscovered. He was doing a dead language, Greek. Suddenly the smut, the moral tension, the meaningless lesson vanished, and

> At length in the dreary chaotical closet
> Of Erebus old was a privy deposit
> By night the primaeval in secrecy laid;
> A mystical egg that in silence and shade
> Was brooded and hatched; till Time came about,
> And Love the delightful in glory flew out,
> In rapture and light, exulting and bright,
> Sparkling and florid, with stars in his forehead,
> His forehead and hair, and a flutter and flare
> As he rose in the air triumphantly furnished,
> To range his dominions, on glittering pinions
> All golden and azure and blooming and burnished.

What had happened? Why, Mr T. E. Page, the Sixth Form master, was reading out to his class a passage from Frere's translation of the 'Birds' of Aristophanes. Yes, but what had happened? What was this new existence? These words which came in the middle of Greek and had nothing to do with it, this magic which had nothing to do with chapel, this music which kept its measure apart from rules or the breaking of rules? Mr Page stopped reading, Greek was resumed, the door shut. But Dickinson had had a glimpse of the land which was his home.

One wonders, sharing his exultation, and knowing that in later life he could enter that land at will: one wonders why he did not stay there constantly, always with Ariel and Love the delightful, and rapture and sunlight and the Moonlight Sonata, where sorrow is transformed into grace. Here was his home, and he admitted as much. Yet he entered only to withdraw, and to return to the anarchy whose dark premonition had been shown to him at school. Was it that school, acting on his raw character, had warped him? Or was it, as he came to maintain, that the world of Ariel will not satisfy us until Caliban is tamed, Antonio reformed, and Prospero restored to his kingdom? Perhaps the difference between his boyhood and manhood was that as a boy he could not escape from the horrors of existence, and that as a man he would not escape from them. To a man of his character this constituted a profound difference, and he was never again to be as unhappy as at Beomonds and Charterhouse.

His social career was obscure. He made only two friends—W. A. R. Munro and T. H. Bowlby. Munro was moved by the great protest in the dormitory, came up next day, congratulated the hero on his courage. 'The reward of virtue, I suppose.' Later on Bowlby joined them. They formed one of those alliances which are not uncommon between unpopular boys, and which spring largely from circumstances. In any community it is necessary to have someone with whom you can consort and who will not turn against you when you are attacked, and it is most necessary in the community of school, where attacks are so capricious, and so relentless when they start. Dickinson, Munro, and Bowlby clung to each other through the perils of Charterhouse, played fives together, looked on at games, which were not at that date compulsory, and shared a study where they sat up with cold feet till past midnight, doing work which they did not understand. They were all highly good boys, they worked hard and rose from form to form till they were made monitors, and the school showed them what it thought of them by calling them the Three Graces. Munro is now Rector of Lincoln College, Oxford, Bowlby became headmaster of Lancing and is now a canon at Chichester. Dickinson kept in friendship with Munro, who has preserved several sympathetic memories of him, and thinks that his own memories are somewhat too pessimistic. He lost sight of Bowlby.

Another slight alleviation was acting. His sister May acted well, and he himself had performed with applause, at Hanwell and Chertsey. At Charterhouse the visit of a Miss Volkes developed in him a passion for the stage which, subsiding into an interest, was maintained all his life. Miss Volkes was a professional actress, who had come down with a company of old Carthusians, and her rendering of 'My Johnny was a shoemaker' threw the lad into unusual agitations. He mooned about the court in the hope of seeing her again, and even wrote out by heart the play which she had given, with a view to performing it during the holidays. She echoed as it were the chord struck by the Aristophanes passage, 'sparkling and florid, with stars in his forehead'. She had 'a wonderful laugh, a sort of ripple', and the boys declared she got a little tight while stopping with the Haig Browns. She went, and her gaiety with her, but she had shown him the way to the footlights, and a tendency in that direction which never proved fatal gathered strength after her visit. His music developed also: a more permanent possession. Munro still remembers his Mozart and Beethoven on the piano. He took up the violin for a time and performed in the school orchestra. And there were anemones and bluebells on the hill in spring, but he couldn't feel they belonged to him, for he did not yet belong to himself.

In this dim and unsatisfactory fashion the years wore away. Of course there were the holidays, but they were overshadowed by the masses of the departing and of the approaching terms, they were like a valley between high cliffs, into which the sun has no time to penetrate. No sooner had he got rid of Charterhouse than he had to get ready for it. Some pleasant things happened: one year his father took him and Arthur and May to Switzerland. It was the first time he had been abroad. He enjoyed himself, but he could not remember much afterwards except that they had argued about the names of mountains, and that his father, when trying to pinch his ear in the hotel, had pinched a young lady's by mistake. Other holidays were spent in London; when he was sixteen they left The Spring Cottage and moved into the house in All Souls Place. Memories of the 'Messiah' and better still the 'Elijah'...excerpts from a queer new thing, 'The Ring', and the composer embracing the conductor afterwards.... May liked 'The Ring', he could make nothing of it...the Bancrofts in 'Caste'...Irving in the 'Lyons Mail', and, most moving of all, a play (name forgotten) in which a steamer ran down a row boat on the stage. But each day nearer came the fortress on the hill above Godalming, ready to imprison him, and that was really happiness, people told him, he could never hope to be as happy as at school.

I curse the time as I look back on it. It seems to me all evil and no good. Cut off from home life and they from me, without a root to hold that really sprang from myself, yet tormented by external ties of mere superstition, with none of those passionate friendships or loves which redeem school for many boys, despised, and as I think rightly, yet by people who themselves were despicable, with no intellectual interest and no moral conviction, alone as I have never been since, physically unfit, mentally undeveloped— was ever a sadder drearier more hopeless entry upon life? And no one knew. And so, of course, no one cared.

It is interesting to compare this indictment with that of Robert Graves, who was at Charterhouse thirty years later, and has said what he thought about it in 'Good Bye to All That'. There is no reason to suppose that Charterhouse either was or is worse than our other leading educational hotels, but as generation after generation of sensitive boys record their experiences in them, one marvels why the boarding house system continues at all, and why the middle classes still insist on so much discomfort for their children at such expense to themselves.

CHAPTER VI

CAMBRIDGE
1881–1884

O Cambridge! Cambridge! small the need
Of plighted faith to honour thee;
Thine is the hand that sowed the seed,
The gathered fruit thy guerdon be;
'Twere wasted breath to bid thee take
The creature thou thyself didst make.

G. L. D. (written in 1887).

DICKINSON went up from Charterhouse to Cambridge in the autumn of 1881. Since he was in the popular estimation a typical don, it is curious to reflect that only by chance did he go to the university at all. His father could not afford to send him up unaided, and he was only 'proxime accessit' on the list for entrance scholarships at King's. But one of the successful candidates went elsewhere, and he was given an exhibition of £40 a year. Unobtrusively and indifferently he began a connection which lasted over fifty years. He had no idea what Cambridge meant—and I remember having the same lack of comprehension about the place myself, when my own turn came to go up there. It seems too good to be real. That the public school is not infinite and eternal, that there is something more compelling in life than team-work and more vital than cricket, that firmness, self-complacency and fatuity do not between them compose the whole armour of man, that lessons may have to do with leisure and grammar with literature— it is difficult for an inexperienced boy to grasp truths so revolutionary, or to realise that freedom can sometimes be gained by walking out through an open door. The door had been opened before, to be closed. People, music, books and scenery—the four gifts he loved most—had been shown to him tantalisingly in childhood, and then withdrawn. Now he saw them again, all filled with a new vigour, they beckoned to him, they were all four alive, and their recapture fills the next years of his life. He was often to be exquisitely happy. He was always to have a choice before him which alleviated his miseries. To be a man was, in itself, a satisfaction to him, and he set himself to occupy, so far as he could, our heritage.

When he went up to King's there were only sixty undergraduates and a few resident dons. The Eton connection was still very strong; indeed it was not many years since the college had been open only to Etonians or since its members had had the right to claim a degree without sitting for an examination. King's was, and one hopes still is, a peculiar place. Eton, its twin foundation, gave it a tradition for which all non-Etonians must be grateful: a genuine instead of a faked tradition. And mingling with this were the oddities and the crudities—people who had not enjoyed their public schools or had been to the wrong school or even to none. They too contributed, and though the college tended at times to divide into what has been called the smart and the smarting set no fatal split occurred. Brains are not everything, as we all keep telling one another, still they do counteract social silliness, and the fact that all undergraduates at King's have to read for Honours has ensured a certain level of intelligence, upon which mutual comprehension can seize its chance to build.

His brother Arthur had preceded him to King's, was kind, and launched and lunched him at once, but 'some of his friends were with him, and everything still breathed the wearisome air of the public school. I wasn't at home with that kind of man, and I hardly knew there were other kinds'. Healthy, practical, and destined for worldly distinction, his brother's friends could only intimidate him, and he was slow to find friends of his own. For a year or more he didn't really know what he wanted, and was dazed 'like a boy recovering from a long illness'. One of his friends, Graham, afterwards told him that he had been a very insignificant freshman, 'and

I am sure he was right'. He worked ahead in the torpid, pseudo-industrious way he had acquired at school, taking classics because he was advised to, making notes, keeping lectures, counting hours. He went down to the river to be tubbed because it was the proper thing, and writes to his mother (Oct. 22nd, 1881): 'I am getting on pretty well with my rowing but it is much more difficult than I thought, the coaches are very nice and don't blow one up nearly as much as I expected'. The letter continues on a more genuine note: 'I am getting on beautifully with my bicycle'. He loved the bicycle even in its penny farthing edition, and when the wheels became equal in size he was constantly astride. On this occasion he got no further than Newmarket, where he arrived 'after several falls just too late for the train', and bathed in mud.

By the age of nineteen his desire to serve humanity was already strong, but it took inappropriate forms, like his work and his exercise. We find him, for instance (Feb. 13th, 1882), joining the Cambridge University volunteers. 'What, would you shoot your superior officer, sir?' is the legendary exclamation of the sergeant at whom he had pointed his rifle; and anyhow he was struck off the strength on June 8th, 1884. Then he practised bell-ringing; he took a class of poor boys at Barnwell; he decided to reform prostitutes and asked freshmen for subscriptions for that purpose; he tried to reform his equals, and invited an atheist who had been drunk to join the Church of England Temperance Society. The atheist was headachy and polite, 'but he declined the siren's voice'. In all this activity we can trace the tradition of the Christian Socialism in which he was brought up, and he was in his own way to continue that tradition, though Frederick Denison Maurice would disown him, and Charles Kingsley turn in the grave. After several failures he realised that he could not serve humanity by the old methods, so he turned to new methods, and sometimes they were revolutionary, but he never abandoned the notion of service.

His rooms as a freshman were in Bene't Street. Here he was able to escape and be alone, and the experience was so delightful that he began to wish for company. Undergraduates interested him very little during his first year, but he was impressed by two of the dons. One of them was his tutor, J. E. C. Welldon, who exercised on him an influence which he could not define. 'I was at once shy and hero-worshipping.' Welldon performed his duties conscientiously, but made no attempt to draw his admirer out. 'I doubt whether he deserved the hero-worship. At any rate he and I have moved too far apart since then for any mutual comprehension.' He remained a burly and enigmatical figure, uneasily balancing on a bicycle along the Ely road, and his subsequent career as Headmaster of Harrow, Bishop of Calcutta, Dean of Durham, and critic of the working classes, provoked little enthusiasm.

The other don was a very different story and a longer one. In the letter to his mother quoted above, he goes on to say that he is hearing and playing music at O.B.'s. This is the famous Oscar Browning, friend and enemy to so many generations of Kingsmen. Some people loved him—and Dickinson was to join their number. Others have disliked him so much that they have denied his greatness, and indeed the adjectives describing him do produce a confused effect in their totality. 'Falstaffian, shameless, affectionate, egoistic, generous, snobbish, democratic, witty, lazy, dull, worldly, academic' is Dickinson's list, and he might have added that his hero could be a bully and a liar. He does add that he had 'the Socratic gift of maieusis'—the gift which he himself was to combine with selflessness. O.B. was never bothered with that, still, whatever his make up, he did manage to educate young men. His information might be erroneous, his method of conveying it intolerable, but he did lead them to discover themselves, and to bring to birth what would have lain in embryo. It was he who brought Dickinson out of the seven years' darkness, and set him upon his proper road. The

'Recollections' have much to say about this, and I quote from them with the more pleasure because I agree with what is said. I came towards the end of O.B.'s glory, nor was I ever part of its train. But he shines out with a magnificence which has been withheld from his admirable detractors, he remains as something unique in the history of the University, a deposit of radium, a mass of equivocal fire.

I will set down some things I remember of him. He came to my brother's room, which was on the same staircase as his, when I was a freshman of only a few days. He came rollicking in, already stout, already middle-aged, but with an air of equality, of youth, which I could not then comprehend. Then I spoke at a debate at which he was present. It was about ghosts. He was interested in my speech, came up to me afterwards and said 'I didn't know you were such a clever fellow'. This was characteristic, for his principal gift was his power of making men believe in themselves....After that, I remember playing duets with him on his grand piano, how his bulky form crushed me into a small corner of the seat and the tempo was judiciously manipulated to suit his not too agile fingers. We played I remember the slow movement of Beethoven's 7th sonata [symphony?], and it became very slow indeed when we reached the demi-semi quavers.

He always had some boy or young man as a secretary, and for many boys and youths he did much to start them in life. His interest was in the young aristocrat on the one hand and the obscure struggler on the other. His rooms at that time and for many years were the centre of all that was most sociable, stimulating and genial at Cambridge. Sunday evening he was at home, and I heard at that time really great music....Later he got together some curious kind of harmoniums supposed to represent the different instruments of the orchestra. Undergraduates called them O-B-ophones, and I cannot pretend that I ever heard anything from them except cacophony.

O.B. was secretary of innumerable clubs, including the swimming club, where his corpulent person was constantly to be found in the state of primitive nudity which, in those early and happy days, was characteristic of Cambridge bathing. For even in the meadows open to view, where the members of the town bathed, they ran quite naked in crowds over the green grass. O.B. conducted at that time the Political Society, which he had founded and of which I, though then studying classics not history, became a member. A paper was read, during which the president reclined in his armchair, a red pocket-handkerchief of enormous size covering his face. Then we all spoke in turn, according to an order dictated by lots drawn out of a bag. I have passed many dull evenings there, but some that were interesting. And interesting or dull, O.B. produced his usual effect. We felt that we were men, and history a serious subject. Mr Browning's ambition was to produce statesmen. The only one I remember as emerging from his hearth rug is Mr Austen Chamberlain, perhaps not the most intelligent of men, but always, so far as I knew him, friendly and honorable....Later, when I became a teacher at King's, Mr Browning was my senior colleague. I cannot honestly say that I found it easy to work with him, for I often disagreed with him, and never was there a man more incapable of seeing another man's point of view.

And then comes a picture more appropriate to the Italian Renaissance than the age of Victoria.

I found him once in his inner room, where he slept behind a screen, in the act of getting up. On one side of him was a secretary writing letters to dictation, on the other another playing the violin. O.B. was seated in dishabille between the two, and he began to speak on a subject always congenial to him, himself. Once, he said, he had his horoscope taken. He was born in the ascension of the planets Capricorn and Saturn, the one elating, the other depressing. But however much crushed by Saturn, he always knew that Capricorn would toss him up again to the sky.

One speculates, in passing, whether it was Oscar Browning or Dickinson who termed Capricorn a planet; either was capable of it. Their friendship is pleasant to remember. O.B. always liked 'Gouldie' as he insisted on calling him, and regretted that he had not become more influential. And Goldie, as a rule so fastidious, could thank, with more than usual gratitude, the Silenus who had awakened him from nightmare.

How many young men did he stir to life who afterwards turned against him! They were wrong, though not without excuse. The man was more than his foibles, and I greet him here, as many others might greet him, as one of those who discovered me to myself.

Since he wrote the above there has been a biography of O.B., by his nephew H. E. Wortham. He admired it greatly, and indeed it is one of the best biographies of the last few years—quite unsparing and completely sympathetic.

At the end of his first year at Cambridge (May 1882) a tragic event occurred which moved him deeply and finally marked his transition from the alien life to the real one. It shall be told in his own words.

One day, returning from a bicycle ride, I found a telegram telling me my mother was dead. She had long been ill, but I was expecting no change. The effect of this telegram perhaps I do not justly recall. But, as it seems to me now, it was a curious blend of conventional and real feeling. The incredible had happened—for is not death always incredible?—and I had not come across it before. There was something about that that stunned. Then there was the effort, as it were, to feel more than one did or could, a curious sense of the melodrama of the position. And grief? Yes, I think so, and yet that not prominent and exclusive, as I supposed it to be. I rushed across to my tutor, showed him the telegram and burst into tears. He was very kind, came back with me to my rooms, and helped to send me off to town. I see myself now ringing the bell, my sister coming downstairs in tears, my own tears, the whole distressing scene. I remember my mother, lying on the bed, looking calm and beautiful. I remember my father's grief. Yet after the funeral I remember also sitting at one of our drawing room windows with my sisters in a state of almost hysterical laughter, and one of my aunts remarking coldly that we had better not laugh so much as people might think it heartless. Then I remember lying on the sofa, trying desperately to realise the 'never again', the indubitable and yet inconceivable fact. I returned to Cambridge to finish my term, oscillated between the grave demeanour I felt to be appropriate and the natural forgetfulness and cheerfulness produced by the company of my friends. I had to stay up late to keep my term, and there comes back to me a long solitary expedition to the fens. With this event (the death of my mother) I connect my definite passage to a new phase of life.

It is difficult to analyse more fully than he does himself this very intricate experience. Love, rather than knowledge, had bound the boy to his mother, he had never desired to be frank with her, and perhaps that is why the emotions of the man were so conflicting. His laughter is easily explained—it is a common safety valve. But why the enhanced feeling for Cambridge? From that time he tended to inhabit the University spiritually. The interests and emotions acquired there began to fill the vacations, although the house at All Souls Place remained his headquarters for many years.

From now on my mind was in a ferment, a kind of ferment however which would hardly I think be intelligible to a contemporary undergraduate. It was as though at last a door that had once or twice swung ajar now opened and let me out. What I saw was a dim and moonlit scene, exciting, perilous, full of adventure. It presented itself to me as the problem of existence, at once felt and thought about—if indeed what one did then can be called thinking. It was exciting, to a degree which no modern young man of intelligence could comprehend, to discover that Christianity was not as it were an inextensible box, very small, in which the whole world was packed, but that an immense world extended quite outside of it. That world I began to try to grasp in ways that now seem ridiculous but that had nevertheless an intensity a passion and a romance that it is only given to youth to experience. It was exciting then to conceive that perhaps Jesus was not God but only an exceptional Being. It still seemed shocking at first that anyone should conceive him as only man. Then interest in him—(such a poor ignorant interest as it had ever been)—began to fade. Shelley suddenly gripped me....

With the arrival of Shelley the door swung wide and never closed again. Shelley's influence was so important, it so dominated Dickinson till the day of his death, that it will have to be described in a separate chapter, and the same applies to two other arrivals from the world of books, Plato and Goethe. 'Books' is an inadequate word to use in so personal a connection. It was rather that three people who knew his language proved willing to speak to him in it and to say sentences which he could not have framed for himself. He entered a world which was an extension of his own heart. The habit of awe and reverence was always suspect to him, and he did not humble himself before his great writers, or exclaim (except in the first excitement of his youth) that he was not worthy to unlace their shoes. The world into which they called him was the world of freemen, where there is no bowing down before thrones or chanting outside shrines. What joys did he find in it? He communicated them as well as he could. But we can best share them if we have known his identical longings and pains. The 'Prometheus Unbound', the close of the 'Phaedo', Galatea and the Homunculus—they are only sounds in the air and marks on a page unless we have learnt their language and been preparing to speak with them from childhood. And one of my limitations in discussing Dickinson is that the three writers who meant most to him have never particularly appealed to me, so that I can only divine by analogy what he found in them. One fact at all events emerges: he discovered these writers and human beings at the same time.

While the mists were thus drawing up before religion, poetry, politics (like curtains of gauze on the stage) I was gradually finding for the first time real friends. We feasted on ideas, on speculations, on poetry, music, what not. The best of our life was long talks in our rooms, or in summer pacing the grounds of King's, still as I think one of the loveliest spots in the world, and open still all night to talk as well as to more noisy enterprises. The dedication to my unpublished volume of poems recaptures the feeling of those hours better than anything I can say now, when I pace the same ground half a ghost and more haunted by memories than realities. But always the same beauty, as perhaps may be the case even centuries from now.

Then he recalls the friends of this early period: A. J. Grant (afterwards professor of history at Leeds), 'with whom I associate a moonlit evening spent in the grounds of Trinity after we had climbed a locked gate to get in'; J. W. Graham (afterwards principal of Dalton Hall), 'older than the rest of us, believing so ardently in progress that he would not have it doubted that art too must have progressed'; A. P. Laurie (now principal of the Heriot-Watt College), 'then the most speculative and bold of that little sect, a chemist, a Henry Georgite, a perpetual talker'; and C. R. Ashbee, afterwards an architect and designer. Ashbee is recalled as 'a long youth, enthusiastic, opinionated, schärmerisch', who jumped into a college eight and made a hole, and started a 'Speculative Society', which was to spread through the world but collapsed after its first term. Ashbee had a gift for practical organisation and for sympathetic contact with the working class which Dickinson admired but could not emulate. With him, as with Grant and Graham, he kept in touch all his life. The greatest of his Cambridge friends, Roger Fry and Ferdinand Schiller, become important at a later date, and mention of them must be postponed.

As Cambridge filled up with friends it acquired a magic quality. Body and spirit, reason and emotion, work and play, architecture and scenery, laughter and seriousness, life and art—these pairs which are elsewhere contrasted were there fused into one. People and books reinforced one another, intelligence joined hands with affection, speculation became a passion, and discussion was made profound by love. When Goldie speaks of this magic fusion, he illumines more careers than his own, and he seems not only to epitomise Cambridge but to amplify it, and to make it the heritage of many who will never go there in the flesh.

Others of that set have gone almost out of my mind and some of them out of the world. But still their forms appear in the golden mists of dawn and almost I catch their voices through talk of younger generations, heard under the same chapel walls and the same chestnut groves, on the same great lawns, under the same stars reflected in the same sluggish yet lovely stream that will hear perhaps for centuries yet the same voices at the same budding time of youth; unless—who knows? they fall silent even before the eternal silence closes upon me.

In a meditation such as this the old dry little upper-class notion of an Alma Mater vanishes, and the University becomes for a moment universal.

CHAPTER VII

SHELLEY, PLATO, GOETHE

I

IN an early sonnet to Shelley, Dickinson compares him to a song, floating out of an attic at dusk over a sultry city, and transporting the listener into a land of streams. The sonnet exemplifies what he required from poetry. He did not care for pure poetry; that is to say perfection of expression brought him only a passing pleasure. Nor did he care for poetry which conveyed a view of life hostile to his own. What he wanted was a song which would transport him out of the world in the right direction, wings that would carry him out of the body into a region where good and evil are more clearly opposed than on earth, and where good triumphs everlastingly. Sincere, enthusiastic, and fired with the same social hopes, Shelley provided him with exactly the right pair of wings. It was possible, in that enchanting company, to shake off the flesh. It was possible to shake it off in the company of many other poets, but Shelley remained unique because, however high he soared, he never rejected humanity.

Dickinson loved humanity—so far as the phrase has any meaning; and it still has some meaning, though not as much as it promised in the nineteenth century. He believed, furthermore, in something more definite; in love between two individuals. And it is because Shelley welcomed both sorts of love into the white radiance of eternity that he desired to follow him there. Beyond, or beneath, the human he was reluctant to travel; and it is significant that, while adoring Shelley, he should on occasions have maintained a stiff upper lip towards Walt Whitman. Whitman's mysticism sometimes repelled him, like D. H. Lawrence's later on. It tended to obliterate boundaries which he felt should be preserved. To

'let oneself go' under the stress of emotion is all very well, but,
O my brethren, in which direction? Towards 'Kingless con-
tinents sinless as Eden'? or down into a uniform orgy where
anything is everything, and blackberries and pismires in-
distinguishable from Socrates? Escape is only the first step
towards salvation. It is useless, unless we take the right turning after opening the door. Now, Shelley knows the way.
Shelley is sustained in his airy quest by human love. Hence
his supremacy.

> ...Shelley suddenly gripped me, I don't think as a poet
> but as a visionary about life. His landscapes always shim-
> mering with moonlit streams, his loneliness, his passionate
> and ideal love were what seized me—Alastor and Adonais
> and the more ethereal and musical lyrics of Prometheus.
> I read Hogg's life of him (still in my deliberate judgment
> one of the most fascinating biographies in existence) as
> though it were a new gospel. Shelley at Oxford especially
> appealed to me. And then his political ideas! I thought
> with rapture and reverence of the youth of 19 dropping his
> leaflets among the crowd from a balcony in Dublin. I
> leapt with indignation and contempt at Godwin's solemn
> cry 'Shelley you are preparing a scene of blood'. No one
> who has not felt Shelley once like that can know, I think,
> what Shelley is. I still recover those first feelings when I
> turn to him. And I still resent (rightly as I believe) the
> elderly view of him as a man of genius gone astray, ignorant
> of life, wild and Utopian. He had in fact a clear logical
> mind, a courage of conviction almost unique, and a burning
> passion for truth which is only not appreciated because it
> is of all passions the rarest. If there were indeed that world
> beyond of which the Platonic Socrates used to dream, there
> is no one I would sooner meet; of all men of letters he is I
> think the most lovable humane and genuine.

Shelley's immediate influence was enormous. It operated
in two ways. In the first place it turned Dickinson to politics
and schemes of social reform. Turning from his crude missionary attempts, he began to study conditions, particularly the
problem of the land, as set forth in the work of Henry George.
Henry George—a free-lance economist who is almost for-

gotten to-day—was then a living force among the young men, and the transition to his 'Progress and Poverty' from 'Prometheus Unbound' was not as abrupt as it may appear. George was a sincere man, with a simple view of social disorders and their remedies. He came and lectured at Cambridge with success, and though Dickinson was never a fanatic follower, he hoped for a little that the World's Great Age might begin anew through the taxation of land values. He never re-read 'Progress and Poverty' in later years, but he remembered it as a genuine piece of work, and it led him to make the agricultural experiment which will be described in the next chapter.

Shelley also influenced him in a more obvious way. He began to write poems himself. 'Certainly they had no value. But nothing I have written since has filled me with such excitement, such a sense of being inspired.' The first of these poems, 'Doubt', was sent to the 'Carthusian', of which his friend Bowlby was editor. Many others followed, he improved in technique, and in 1884 he won the Chancellor's Medal 'for a poem supposed to be about Savonarola'. The necessary facts about Savonarola were supplied by Mrs Oliphant, but all else by 'Adonais,' and the monk's fate is celebrated with a pagan melancholy which would not have consoled him and would have been more intelligible to his persecutors:

> But all too brief thy triumph, all too soon
> Thy heavenly kingdom perished, all in vain
> Thou climbedst to the splendour of thy noon
> To sink in night eternal....

Dickinson rightly remarks that the poem was hardly about the subject; 'a way prize poems have, and no doubt a good way'. It is really a tribute to Shelley, at whose photograph he gazed while composing it. In accordance with the University regulations he was obliged to read it aloud in the Senate House, wearing his dress clothes for the occasion and addressing an audience largely composed of his own relatives.

With this bizarre scene his public career as a bard came to an end. He wrote poetry subsequently, but as a vehicle for his private emotions, and, severely self-critical, he has not chosen to give much of it to the world.

> The other day I looked through a collection of my early verses with very curious feelings. Some I had quite forgotten and could not recall having written them, even when I read them. Some brought back an immediate vision of the place and circumstances and time they were written. Though they have, I think, no merit as poetry, they are interesting as biography, as most young men's verses are.

Few of us have felt Shelley's fascination as he did, or else we have outgrown it and taken to 'business or Keats'. But, granted that that strange poetry and ever stranger prose keep in touch with human beings, the fascination is easy to understand. Even when he was afraid of human beings, as at school, or bewildered by them, as in the War, he refused to escape from them, and it was only by a poet who maintained an earthly connection that he could be lifted into the empyrean. All through his life the devotion continued. Here is a typical extract from a letter to May (August 1893):

> Deep down under the beefiest and brutallest disguise there lies the same tragedy which was the essence, unveiled and undisguised, of Shelley. I think one is always in love with something or other; the error consists in seeking in a mortal image the likeness of something which is perhaps eternal. Hinc illae lacrimae—divorces and all the rest of it. 'The desire of the moth for the star, Of the night for the moon' is the epitome not only of Shelley but of all mankind.

And there are many other references, all grouping round the idea that though Shelley was exceptional he was not uncanny, and interprets the average man, if only the average man had eyes to see.

In some correspondence exchanged in 1906 with his friend

Mrs C. R. Ashbee he goes further than this, and emphasises the bodiless quality of his god:

> Shelley never got incarnate. That's what gives him his unique quality, which people either love or hate according as they are more or less incarnate themselves.

Mrs Ashbee replies with vigour that she must certainly be incarnate herself, for she cannot stand Shelley at all:

> I am poles from him, and that is probably why the elusive soap-bubble quality—spirit—does not find any ring of answer in me. He was supernatural I think. It is very astonishing women were so fond of him: it must have been I think the physical fascination and charm, for though women are attracted by intellectual power I don't think they ever get into line with the 'children of the spirit' idea. I believe it is outside their range of consciousness: they can only look on in silent wonder.

Somewhat concerned, he replies:

> About being incarnate—what I had in my mind was that spirit has to enter into matter to create, and in so doing loses its own purity and essence. And Shelley, as I feel him, never *did* enter into matter—which is what fascinates me, and what, in your case repels. All women I think have more need of and love of matter than men. Men are the idealists. That's why they so often make a mess of things. Women would run the world more sensibly, but then so *deadly* sensibly. A woman's first cry is: 'How will it affect the children?' A man says 'How will it affect the soul or the race or God?'—What rot! Pray forgive me.

She forgives him.

He edited the 'Prometheus' but Shelley's real apotheosis is postponed until 'The Magic Flute' (1920) where he appears as a morning star in the Castle of Sarastro—the castle from which Dante had been excluded, because he preferred authority to truth. Shelley is the poet of freemen. He helped to free Dickinson at Cambridge and he gives one more denial to the accusation so foolishly brought against poets, that they are not practical. If they are not practical, how is it that they have accomplished so much? And why have legislators and officials from Plato onwards kept such a watchful eye on them?

2

If Shelley rose like the morning star, Plato was heralded by the dubious twilight of Esoteric Buddhism. Like many young men who are discovering themselves and the world, Dickinson wondered whether there may not be a supernormal path to knowledge. He was by no means credulous or unable to sift evidence, and he had taste and humour, so that Esoteric Buddhism could not detain him long, but for about a year he was intrigued with it. 'My idea I believe was that one must first discover absolute standards of good and evil, and then descend to govern mankind.' So he attended the meeting of the Society of Psychical Research to hear Colonel Olcott describe how he had once been visited by a mahatma who had dematerialised through a closed door, but had left his turban behind him as a proof. 'And here', said the Colonel passing it round, 'is the turban.' This sort of thing does not go down at Cambridge. More impressive than the Colonel and the turban was an Indian called Mohini. For a short time his letters are full of Mohini; 'if he were proved a humbug, I would hide my face and believe in nothing no more', he writes to Grant. He was diffident of approaching, but finally begged for an audience, which was majestically accorded. Mohini refused to shake hands with a creature so gross, but was understood to approve the study of Plato and to recommend meditation upon the One. 'I retired feeling that I had got nothing, but unwilling to admit as much to myself.' Ashbee wearied of Mohini and suggested that a little work for other people might be a good thing. 'To which I find myself replying that living for others is a means to mysticism, not vice versa, and continue to speak of Esoteric Buddhism and mahatmas.'

This being his state of mind, he approached Plato not as a writer of dialogues, or as a depictor of Athenian society, or a logician, or politician, or a publicist, but as an adept who was in the possession of absolute truth, which he had concealed in his writings, probably in his myths. At any moment the universe might open. And though he modified this view, it tinged his future studies with poetry. Here is a letter to Grant describing his original attitude—though 'attitude' is too cool a word to use for the fervour and the ecstasy which filled him. He had just taken his degree at Cambridge, and gone to Germany with Ashbee; at the time he writes to Grant, he was alone at Heidelberg, radiantly happy, and living upon vegetables. The date of the letter is August 1884—that is to say he was just twenty-two. After some preliminary gaiety he says:

I've just descended from a seventh heaven, so to speak, i.e. from something considerably above my ordinary grovelling existence. That is to say for the last two hours I've been sitting on the slope of a hill, looking out over the town and the Schloss and the mountains and the river, with a 'whispering wood' all about me, reading and meditating on Plato's Symposium. Never again will I regret that I've spent years over Greek. I'm 'sitting at Plato's feet' at present, and have really never experienced such 'ecstasy' in the literal sense: why I can't tell you, but so it is. I seem to have got a new light for reading him, and it seems all clear and quite necessarily and incontrovertibly true. And moreover in the 'Phaedrus' is much palpable 'Esoteric Buddhism': do read it again, if you haven't lately, and there you will find the indestructibility of life, and the successive incarnations, and the one great consciousness, or ψυχή and the joys of the adepts, and many such like. I'm getting desperate; I must discover somehow how to keep up to the highest point in the midst of all these necessities of eating and drinking and sleeping and conversing, and I must discover what is αὐτὸ τὸ καλόν, and οἷα ἐστὶν ἡ ψυχή, else how can I ever deliver a respectable set of lectures? How can I explain, for instance, why Shakespeare's characters are natural and marvellous, and Jonson's aren't, unless I know what character is, and all about it. Now, being much at peace and in perfect surroundings, I can see clearly that until one has learnt perfectly to control oneself, and to understand those mysterious laws that give rise to different opinions and passions, one has no right to expect to do any work that shall be necessarily wise and good; therefore if indeed an 'Adept' would speak with me and give me hope, I would vanish to India, at least I hope so. I suppose, otherwise, all this will pass and I shall come down and muddle along, doing a little accidental good among much accidental harm, and cursing as fools all who don't agree with me. This isn't mere talk: I can't tell why, but parts of the Phaedrus and Symposium have come to me in this week like Revelation, and just for an hour or so a day everything has seemed 'stale and unprofitable' except somehow or other to follow out Plato in the paths he hints at as leading to 'the life of the gods'. It's worth having felt, if it all subsides to nothing.

Forty years later, his memory of the Heidelberg experience was still vivid, and he describes it in the 'Recollections' in much the same words as he uses to Grant at the time. It was not the only experience of the sort, for we shall find that he was visited several times by similar intimations of reality. Except perhaps once, at the very end of his life, he never had the mystic vision claimed by his friend McTaggart and by some of the saints. But he often went beyond those vague feelings of awe which represent the furthest most men go from the track of common sense.

Such being his approach to Plato, it is natural that he should be involved in Plotinus. There he found mysticism slab upon slab, without any alloy of Athenian dinner parties. He began to read Plotinus that same summer, and the first work of learning composed by him is a dissertation in which the doctrines of Plato and Plotinus are compared and harmonised. On the strength of the second version of this dissertation he was given a fellowship at King's in 1887. He never published it, and it remains in MS. in the college library. In later years he regarded it as of little critical value, because it made no attempt to discuss the mystic experience upon which the assertions of Plotinus rested. 'Plotinus claims to have had this experience, I daresay he did. The question is what value has it as truth.'

Since however Plotinus is a thinker as well as a mystic, and reasons from his assumptions, there was plenty to say about him, 'and granting my standpoint, the dissertation is, I expect, pretty good'; Dean Inge asked for the loan of it when he was preparing his Gifford Lectures on the same subject.

What I recall now is the curious state of mind in which I was when I wrote it. It was written mainly in the reading room of the British Museum, in one sense not a bad environment for this Oriental-Italo-Egypto-Greco writer. But I really think that for the time being I was almost abstracted from the actual, and mooned about the wintry and foggy London with the feeling that it was all an illusion, and that some day, any day, I should awake into the 'real' world. From the moment I finished the dissertation, to the present time, I have hardly looked into Plotinus. I wonder whether I ever shall again, and if so what I should make of it.

He lost interest in Plotinus, but not in Plato, to whose non-mystical side he then turned. From about 1890 on, he began to care about education, politics and conduct. The Greeks had also been interested in these subjects, and Plato was the most intelligent of the Greeks, and, at all events in his earlier dialogues, the most human. If Shelley dashed and splashed through the country of Dickinson's mind like a mountain stream, Plato was, so to speak, responsible for the irrigation system. He saw to it that the study of modern institutions and conduct should be fertilised by knowledge of the past. He provided breadth of treatment and aptness of comparison, and that subtlest help which comes from affinity of style. Two of the latest books are about him and he also dominates 'The Greek View of Life'. He was also responsible for the dialogues, and the 'dialogue' with Dickinson does not merely mean 'A

Modern Symposium' and 'Justice and Liberty', but all the
unprinted and sometimes unprintable occasions on which he
talked. In his talk, as in writing, he had the evenness of
temper, and the power to state the other side fairly which are
supposed to characterise Socrates. Indeed, to a Goth like
myself he seems much more Socratic than Socrates. Socrates
—as Plato presents him—would have emptied any modern
room at once. Dickinson kept every room full, never nagging,
never setting traps, never reducing the company to silence
while he demonstrated the supremacy of his intellect, the
justness of his opinions, the aptness of his wit, the profundity
of his vision. Even without Plato, he would have known how
to converse, and how to handle life, but he was strengthened
and confirmed by the presence of his companion—less beloved
than Shelley, but more serviceable, for in this world there are
many mansions, and a guide through them is needful. The
Greeks—and Plato particularly—understand our political and
social confusion, but they are not part of it, and so they can
help us.

3

His love for Goethe dates from the same fruitful summer of
1884 when he read Greek in the pine woods above Heidelberg.

> Oh Grant [he writes at the time], I've begun Faust, of
> which indeed I will not speak, for is it not as yet unspeak-
> able? such a rush of music and passion and thought as I
> have not known for long takes me out of this miserable self
> into heaven. Just suits me now; Faust with his weariness of
> books and all things does appeal so *strongly* to a bit of me;
> he's studied everything 'und leider auch Theologie' frustra;
> and then the earth spirit who 'sits at the roaring loom of
> time' (you'll remember in Carlyle). But have you not read
> Faust? yea, I remember thou hast.

The 'rush of music and passion and thought' was, he discovered before long, not continuous. He was soon confronted
with the immense boringness of Goethe, and few Englishmen

have faced it so frankly, and so successfully outstared it. After a forty years' interval he writes to Grant again:

I continue to be intrigued by Goethe and to think him a man of vision in spite of the disquieting fact that there is very little of him I can read. Only a German, perhaps, could manage to be at once a pedant and a genius, an official and a poet, a novelist and a preacher, etc. etc. He achieved anyhow the greatest of all triumphs, which is continuing to live to the last moment instead of dying prematurely at forty and then lingering on as a rather malicious and obstructive ghost, as most of us do.

At the very end of his life he paid homage in 'Goethe and Faust' and in an unpublished Faust translation, and all his last utterances and letters are full of allusions. These will appear in their course. Here I would indicate three reasons for the attraction. In the first place there was Goethe's acceptance of science—acceptance in the sense of willingness to approach the riddle of the universe by any path which is available, scientific or otherwise. Goethe belonged to the tradition of the early Greek philosophers and of the Renaissance humanists, and was closely akin here to Leonardo da Vinci. His own scientific work, his theory of colour, for instance, might be as absurd as the attempts of Voltaire to weigh heat, for it was not to be supposed that he, or any other untrained worker, could perform laboratory experiments of value. But he could direct the spirit in which science could be used; he had not only curiosity but imagination and the capacity for wonder. Dickinson thought that this was an attitude which the modern man should try to share. He himself, though superficial observers dismissed him as dreamy and wistful, was constantly striving to decrease the dark. He hoped for a small circle of light which science would gradually enlarge; beyond this circle stretches a region which, so long as it is unconquered, belongs to imagination and poetry.

In the second place, he admired Goethe's many-sidedness. He was aware of his own limitations, and here was a man of congenial character, who had been not only a poet and scientist, but art critic, theatrical director, courtier, administrator, financier, soldier, philosopher, &c. He never wasted time in regretting that he was not equally various, for he knew that to measure oneself in this way against one's hero is futile, and is indeed a form of conceit. But Goethe was certainly his ideal as far as worldly conduct and scope of practical activities were concerned. Had he been permitted to take a leading part in European affairs, he would have worked in his spirit.

In the third place, Goethe had managed to grow old properly, and the older he grew himself the more he valued this. Most men—though not most women—become intolerable in old age, but here was a sage whom experience never ceased to make wiser, and whose very love-making remained free from senility. It is heartening to remember such a man; he has escaped the shadow of death—and it is the advancing shadow of death, not the actual blackness, which is such a disgrace and terror. Dickinson himself escaped it. Though the fates were to be unkind to him in many ways, they allowed him to keep his strength and sanity to the end.

This admiration for Goethe was connected with a general tolerance for the Teutonic. He liked in the Germans the qualities which endear them to the average Englishman, their good temper, their frankness and their romanticism; and he pardoned, as the average Englishman cannot, their heaviness, pedantry and docility. If his instincts yearned for the Mediterranean, his sentiments still clung to the forests and streams of the North, and in this dual allegiance he recalls that child of Helen and Faust, Euphorion, who symbolised the modern world.

CHAPTER VIII

THE WORLD OF MATTER
1884–1887

I

BETWEEN 1884, when he took his degree, and 1887, when he was elected to a fellowship, Dickinson was in an uneasy state. A first in classics, following on the Chancellor's Medal and other distinctions, gave him an excellent academic record, but what should be the next step? He wanted to support himself, since his father was not well off, and he wanted to help the human race and to impart to it the truth and the beauty which he had discovered. How should he begin? how, and also when? He writes to May that it is a shocking thing to have reached the age of twenty-one without knowing what to do, and to Ashbee at a later date that 'we're all too anxious to begin "doing something" before we've learnt even to shape our characters'. If his education was finished, how should he utilise it, and if it was incomplete what should he learn next?

Connected with this problem was a second one, which arose out of his desire to help humanity. If he held aloof from ordinary people, how could he help them, and if he threw himself into their lives, should he not become like them? He did not want to become like ordinary people. Here he was definite, and he remained, in this sense, an aristocrat to the end. To abandon culture and blunt sensitiveness in the hope of breaking down barriers always seemed to him a desperate expedient. He solved this particular problem in later life by developing the power of entering into other people's positions while he retained his own, but it is impossible for a young man to have this power: he must either abandon himself or hold aloof, and consequently there is a slight touch of arrogance in his dealings with average humanity which does not wear off until he has visited and endured America.

He spent the three years of uncertainty partly in Cambridge, and partly at home or in the provinces, and there were visits abroad. It was a period of experiment and his general state of mind at the beginning of it can be seen in the following letter to Grant (January 10th, 1885).

> ...At Cambridge it was as if we stood all in the light and shook hands bravely and cheerfully and then went out into the night, each on our different paths. And the old myth of meeting again in the light expresses a real need whatever its underlying truth may be. You see I find it rather necessary to cultivate a hard outside in order to keep alive my fire within. Men are so sceptical, so essentially 'faithless', and one has such tendencies that way oneself. For the sad thing to discover is that there is so little *conscious* vice, that the evil is done (or at least the good undone) by men whose position is absolutely logical and righteous in their own eyes; there is a gradual dropping away of the Truth until it becomes impossible to conceive even of a higher Right...Argument loses force and sympathy becomes impossible; one falls back on dogged and apparently unconvincing assertion. All this is very vague, but expresses somehow what I feel about 'people in general', and the danger of assimilating their ideas.

He needed above all things to defend his newly won individuality, and although he desired to help and understand 'people in general' his sympathy with them was still in abeyance. This comes out clearly in the three experiments now to be recorded.

The first experiment is a most fantastic one, and takes him quite outside his usual beat. Full of Henry George, of the social question, of the general ferment of things, he determined to go and work on a co-operative farm.

The farm had recently been started by Harold Cox, afterwards an uncompromising champion of individualism, but at that time a socialist. He had acquired some acres of barren heath in Surrey, which were to be reclaimed, and he had imported from Kent a family of farm-labourers by name of Gibbs with whom he lived in a newly built cottage. It was a strange establishment, which the arrival of the B.A. from Cambridge did not make less strange, for Goldie had no turn for manual labour, and only a theoretical affection for the working classes. However, he did not arrive with great expectations; there were some lectures which he hoped to prepare between the plough and the cow; also he was studying Plotinus. The economic position of Cox's enterprise was already desperate, but he was not interested in economics; he came because he had half a hope that he would now begin to lead the right life—physical work on the one hand, and intellectual creation on the other. The walk up from Farnham station to the farm, the scents of the country—how vividly he remembered them! 'the great commons with fern owls sounding upon them in the dusk, the Frensham ponds, the bracken and the heather were silent witnesses of much passionate brooding in those short weeks'. It was on the human side that he failed to get into touch, because he was choosing an inappropriate method.

He wrote long letters about Craig farm to his sisters and to Ashbee. Here is the letter to Ashbee, who was then in Germany:

Craig Farm
Dear Ashbee,   May 5, 1885
    I've been waiting to write till I was a bit settled, otherwise I should have sent some scathing remarks to your last, and now alas it's too late. Things are good here, especially for working purposes (8 hours pretty easy to get in) but with a distinct tendency to dulness. Cambridge talk &ct was very distracting, but stimulating too, and the conversation and ways of the rustic are a poor substitute. You would laugh to see me solemnly seated at meals in the kitchen talking ineffectually to George, Will and Tom about them there peas and how the dung rotted them, but 'Arold would 'ave 'is way, and how there ought to be hops there and beans there, etc. etc., with jokes about Annie's suitors

and Paget's debts. ('Paget calls 'isself a genleman, I dun call 'im no genleman. What does 'e go for, etc. etc.)

A slight interval in which I've been fetching beer from the pub in an enormous brown jar; the men all sowing soot for manure, and no one to get the beer, so I had to go. It's really very funny. If there were someone to laugh with, I could laugh all day. The family is George Gibbs, silent and humourous (at times) fond of grumbling and hard work: details to me Harold's little mistakes and has a habit of making the same conversation several times over, in which case I of course make the same remarks with as much interest as possible. Mrs Gibbs deaf as a post with whom I communicate mainly by signs: she however converses much, being answered in dumb show.

Then there's Will, fat, stupid, and Alick silently devoted to Annie, who pities him, and Tom cute and self-assertive, with a dormant propensity to Lying and a juvenile fondness for a gun: and then there's Annie! Suffice it to say that she is superior in culture to the rest, and considered by some very pretty. I've just had the sweetest good night chat with her, but then she is so Catholic. For instance, a minute ago I saw her reclining in Alick's arms. . . .

Harold I like much at present, and admire. We get some decent talk over our hoeing and digging, but don't agree much I think at bottom. He is a socialist (Dem. Fed.), but not violent or unreasonable, seems to think they won't do much, but 'anything better than this'. Says it was a great drawback to Mazzini that he believed in a God, which will again show you how much we differ. Rather tired of the farm, I think, that is to say has learnt from it all he will do. Very doubtful if it will pay, all new ground and bad ground which he has just brought to cultivation. Says it isn't possible to combine agricultural and student life unless you take your agriculture as you do your exercise, for an hour or two a day, as I'm trying to do now.

Good God Ashbee (as Stone would say) there came here the other day one Dr Elizabeth B . . . ! All my ideas of higher education for women and the like are pushed back at least a century by the event! How that woman talked! flowing periods, elaborate parentheses, scarcely a pause for breath, words articulated like the snap of a pistol, gratified smack of the lips at each semicolon! Unfortunate female companion reduced to positive deafness and imbecility by constant association: should think she was paid listener in chief. 'Come here my dear and sit by me. Can you give her a low chair?' And we did and there she sat poor wretch at the feet of the monster! Miserablest of females! 'It is my profound conviction—though mark you I profess myself a land nationalist—that it is idle nay injurious to advocate extreme reform before public opinion has duly matured, etc.' Ach Gott! Talk of mental diarrhoea!... As to Annie's opinion of her, that you may imagine. 'These people have evidently not in any degree developed their intellect', quoth the learned Dr. Thank goodness, no, one felt inclined to say.

Mrs Gibbs is becoming painfully friendly. She bursts at all hours into my studious retirement, crying 'Mr Dickinson, I've cut open that chicken and its liver's all diseased. Come and see. Now what would *you* do with it?' I, good heavens! And the woman is deaf. No getting at her. There's no denying that the family quarrels a good deal. Tom for instance 'is such a little beast! I do 'ate 'im'. This alas from a sister. And then Will. He will talk so freely at dinner about kicking your ass. But these drawbacks will occur. I've tried my hand at ploughing with signal success. What a hardy son of the soil I should have been if I'd been born to it! As I wasn't, I remain a puny son of the pen, much in need of a sleeping draught. But I can't milk the cow. No, it may look simple, but I assure you there is an art in manipulating the teat of a domestic cow not easily fathomable. It will ever be sorrow to me, but the fact remains, I can't milk a cow!

O mein Lieber, how I would like to hear that nightingale. But I know 'em of old, and how the chapel sleeps in the moonlit water, and the limes are steeped in fragrance and all the world asleep.

He stopped at Craig farm for a couple of months. Endowed with a sense of humour rather than a zest for comedy, he did not abandon himself fully to its absurdities. Plotinus claimed him. In a cottage hard by vegetated the Salts—Henry Salt had been a rebellious master at Eton, and was to write a book called 'Seventy Years among the Savages'. Salt and Cox were both magnets for cranks, and queer people would call on a Sunday, amongst them young Bernard Shaw. The Gibbs mingled freely in this company, but without pleasure, and became obstreperous and critical. There were musical parties at the Salts, where culture demanded one sort of song, and agriculture another. There was a Homeric meal at the farm where Will Gibbs routed Dr Elizabeth B. by chanting that there were worms in the soup. Dickinson's own table manners were called in question. Then he left, the experiment collapsed, the Gibbs were re-imported into Kent, the desert resumed its own, and Harold Cox went to teach mathematics in India. 'I have met him since, and found he still retains the personal charm he always had. But over the farm experiment a great ox sat upon our tongues.'

About a year later, he wrote a story about this little experience, which still exists in manuscript form. It is a naïf transcript of events, where Gibbs becomes Biggs, and it is not surprising that Kegan Paul, to whom it was submitted, should have declined publication. But in the last few pages it sails into twilight and poetry. 'Crankie Farm' has been a failure, and the two young men who have been muddling there sit by the edge of the great Frensham pond, and watch the moon passing slowly down through heavy clouds and out again into clear sky. Their talk drifts towards immortality, and they agree that it exists here and now, and the trouble of an hour ago becomes nothing; 'we knew it had been, and it was not: while we stood there complete without it'. The night is filled with little sounds, not only the birds but the trees and the water seem to speak, the moon sets behind the trees opposite, and the Surrey landscape, without losing its own beloved and homely character, is absorbed into the cosmogony of Plotinus. All through his life Dickinson had this hope that, at a touch, the world of matter would be—not annihilated but transformed.

> No, not the hand of death! some other power
> Summon to aid thee in the day of doom;
> Earth shall reveal in one immortal hour
> More than was ever garnered in the tomb.

The hope was both a support and a distraction to him during the period of his immaturity.

2

The lectures on which he had been working during his stay at the farm were delivered during the winter of 1885–6 at various provincial centres under the auspices of the University Extension Scheme. They were on Carlyle, Emerson, Browning and Tennyson. For all these writers, except Tennyson, he had unbounded admiration. His idea was that he should reveal their beauties to enthusiastic working men, who would be grateful for any crumbs from the academic banquet. It is an idea which other Extension lecturers have shared, and it seems even to have flitted through the minds of the originators of the scheme. His audiences were actually composed of women of the middle classes, women who had read their Tennysons and compared them with their Brownings for years, and who pointed out his shortcomings with provincial mercilessness.

I had no notion how to speak, and no idea at all how ordinary people felt and thought. I had my lectures written out in full and learned them by heart. They naturally fell very flat, and I still remember the cheerful schoolmaster who was my chairman at my first remarking at the end that we ought to be very grateful to Mr Dickinson for 'even trying' to communicate his ideas on these great authors. Worse however than the manner of my lecture was the matter, for I did not conceal the unorthodox nature of my opinions, also dressed very badly, and was still involved, whenever I had a chance, in my philosophic and mystical studies. The travelling from place to place was fatiguing, and altogether, looking back on myself, I seem a sad outlandish stranded and alien figure. I had no notion how to get into touch with ordinary people, and no desire to do so, for I thought I was the bearer of a message which transcended all actual life.

The message was sometimes inaudible, and according to one

of his friends he would turn his back on the audience when he became interested and toddle away over the platform on his heels, patting himself meanwhile with both his hands behind. Si ce n'est pas vrai c'est bien vu; one endorses the gesture. Nor was he more successful with the weekly classes, the question-papers and the personal contacts which are an important part of University extension. 'My sister has a bone to pick with you, Mr Dickinson: you wrote *Fool* on her paper!' Perhaps he had written 'Good', but it was too late; his handwriting was already getting him into trouble. For the first term, his lecturing centres were Mansfield, Chesterfield and Stamford; for the second term Chester and Southport. He writes to May 'it is all very disgusting, and I'll never talk about poetry again. It's difficult to say which annoys me most, the people who don't like it or the people who do'. And to Ashbee: 'going to lecture now, to which I am gradually becoming calm and indifferent. Life is so much bigger than anything one does in it'. Such language suggests that a crisis is approaching. It came at Chester. He began by affronting the bishop, Stubbs the historian, to whom he addressed a letter as 'The Rev. Dr Stubbs'. His lordship deigned not to reply. Then he quarrelled with his local secretary, daughter to another bishop, who disapproved of his views on Tennyson. His first lecture could not be heard on account of a musical meal which was being given next door to six hundred poor of the city. But the Emerson lecture was heard only too plainly for he quoted two lines of a poem by his author called 'The Initial Love':

> . . . kiss and couple and beget
> By those roving eyeballs bold—

and gave terrific offence. It was more than the cathedral mind could stand and portions of it left the room. The ladies of Chester were prepared to hear about Emerson, but not what Emerson said, the local secretary forwarded their complaint to headquarters, his impropriety was censured, Tom Hughes his defender was ignored, his fate was sealed. Things do not alter much. I remember, thirty years later, a lecturer upon Euripides at Weybridge having to defend himself against the charge of condoning the conduct of the Bacchae.

It is characteristic of Dickinson that, even when appearing to fail, he should gain something of permanent value. This dingy incursion through the Midlands resulted in two life-long friendships. One was with Edward Carpenter, the other with Mrs Webb, wife of the rector of Mansfield Woodhouse. Mrs Webb attended his course at Mansfield, and saw through the badness of its matter and manner to the sincerity behind. Though she was twenty-five years his senior, they quickly became intimate, he poured out his difficulties, a correspondence ensued, and after her husband's death she and her daughter moved to Cambridge. Although he was never drawn to women in the passionate sense, all his deepest emotions being towards men, his life would have been empty and comfortless without them. He found in them —that is to say in a few women—a patience and a nobility undiscoverable elsewhere, and his tribute to Mrs Webb must be quoted here as paying tribute not only to her. He speaks of the illnesses troubling her old age, and then continues:

But all this leaves her as it were unsullied, uncomplaining, the most beautiful soul perhaps I have known or shall know, except it may be my sister Janet and Mrs Moor. She has also a strong and sincere mind, which prevents her swallowing any humbug. She is a member of the Church of England and the widow of a parson. But what she believes now I do not know, nor I think does she. But she has 'faith', in the sense of courage, love, and hope. Those are the last three qualities that abide when all things go, and we can but wait our passage to annihilation or whatever else there may be.

3

His failure as an Extension lecturer led to a most extraordinary reaction. He concluded (which one can understand) that he had no gift for speaking or teaching. But what is so startling is the alternative which he adopted. After his failure at Chester he went for a holiday in Wales. He climbed Snowdon alone. Great torrents of mist came rolling up over the summit, revealing and hiding by turns the precipices and valleys below. The scenic greatness of life—never far off in his outlook—now took a new form. He still desired to discover reality and help mankind, but was it only through literature that this double goal could be reached? In the pinelands of Heidelberg or of Surrey he had thought so, but was there no other path? Abruptly, and not on the grounds of felt inclination or capacity, he decided to be a doctor.

Science always attracted him, and he had, like many men of letters, hopes from it which are seldom cherished by scientists themselves. In his later years he tried to follow Eddington and Jeans and was in close touch with the popularising work of Gerald Heard—work, he considered, as valuable as any which has been done in our day. In 1886 his outlook was cruder, and he regarded science as a sort of Buddhism; it was to illuminate and confirm a positive view of the world, and culminate in a mystic revelation. And if science led to reality, one branch of science—medicine—enabled him by a happy coincidence to help mankind. Two birds of his desire could be killed by one stone, and in deciding to be a doctor he felt surprised that he had not thought of this before.

On descending from Snowdon, he wrote a long letter to his father (April 17th, 1886), explaining the position. He says that although poetry and philosophy seem to him the best in life, he does not find in himself the creative gift which would make him a real artist. He has thought, therefore, of medicine, both for scientific and humanitarian reasons, and has hoped to make enough money by lecturing to support himself while he studies it. But lecturing is unsatisfactory, and prevents him from thinking; so would his father finance him for four years, on 'business principles', until he has got his medical degree, when he will pay the money back. The letter—like all he wrote—is both straightforward and considerate; he makes it clear what he wants, and makes it easy for his father to refuse. His father assented, and in the autumn of the year he returned to Cambridge, and began to study for the M.B. degree.

He was instantly seized with panic. Cambridge seemed dead, his friends had gone down, he was no longer in college. He saw that he would never make a doctor, and that the arguments influencing him had been unreal, and he wrote to his father saying that he wanted to abandon the enterprise. Next morning he breakfasted with his contemporary, Headlam (afterwards Sir J. W. Headlam-Morley of the Foreign Office), and told him what he had done. Headlam persuaded him that he had made a mistake, and he wired to his father telling him not to open the letter. Presumably the letter arrived before the wire, and had already been read, but his father never said anything about it, and he entered duly upon the course. It is a queer little display of wobbling, and in his opinion (not in mine) it is typical of his character; he also comments that it shows 'the uselessness of taking up definite work merely because one thinks it good; there can have been few people less gifted for scientific research (as distinguished from speculation) than myself, and few less qualified for the observation and manual dexterity that profession requires'. This is no doubt true.

He then settled down quietly, and worked hard, but without any feeling of vocation. 'I've begun dissecting and it's not so bad as it might be, has even a certain kind of geographical interest', he writes to May; 'but I can't arrive at the "artistic" view of it which the professor and others seem to take; "it's *beautiful* dissection" is the phrase'. Later on: 'corpses are not repulsive, merely dull' or 'I don't regard anatomy as serious work'. He informs Ashbee the physiology interests him more, 'but it's such an infant science and consequently a chaos of incomprehensible and contradictory facts', a true enough description of physiology fifty years ago.

Roger Fry—whom he now began to know—was also doing medicine though with neater fingers, and would sometimes extricate him from the frog or worm with which he was involved. He passed his first M.B. examination in 1887, his second in 1888. But by that time his fortunes had taken another and a more appropriate turn, and his career as a doctor came to a close.

Medicine was certainly the strangest of his incursions into the realm of matter, but as one looks back at a friend's youth, or indeed at one's own youth, there is always a good deal which seems strange. The personality is then freer, because it is inexperienced, and it starts this way and that, down avenues which will never be explored, without feeling self conscious. Dickinson came to realise that his attempt to be a doctor, though mistaken, was not ridiculous: 'I still think that that profession is the best, and does combine the possibilities of that combination of learning and of life which I wanted then and want now, and have very imperfectly achieved as things are'.

He gave it up because, contrary to any reasonable expectation, Plotinus had turned up trumps. Though the fellowships at King's were then only worth £80 as against their present £300, there were various advantages attaching, so that he became financially independent of his father. His father was disappointed at his change of profession, but as usual never said one word of blame. From 1887 onward, Dickinson made no more false starts, but settled down to a life which, in his opinion, was not the best sort of life but the best which his capacities allowed.

CHAPTER IX

FROM MYSTICISM TO POLITICS
1887–1893

I

TO the north of the front court of King's rises a precipitous wall of stone and glass: Henry VI's chapel, tending by its very size to nullify itself when it has become familiar and to enter but little into the general consciousness of the college. On the south of the court the chapel is acknowledged by some presentable buildings of the Gothic revival, containing the Hall, lecture rooms, the undergraduates' reading room, the dons' combination rooms and so on. Westward, the early eighteenth century speaks; Gibbs's Building, or Fellows' Buildings, almost closes that side of the court: a solid three-story block, graceful, grave, and grouping with its precipitous and perpendicular neighbour into a harmony peculiar to England. There are compliments outside the rules of etiquette, and perhaps they are the only compliments worth receiving. Gibbs is pierced midway by a cavernous entry, known to initiates as the Jumbo House, in whose sombre recesses are usually to be found a ladder, a hand-cart, and a small heap of sand. These too are peculiar to England. The range from them to the soaring chapel-buttresses, pinnacled in the intense inane, is the range of the English mind. They are the unexplained, balancing the inexplicable. Above the arch of the Jumbo House rides a fine semicircular window, above that is the chief architectural feature of the block, a classical pediment, topped in its turn by a couple of chimneys and by the flagstaff from which, on days of commemoration, the dark blue flag of the college depends. Most of Dickinson's academic life was spent in various rooms of Gibbs, and he would recall with amazement how he had wanted it pulled down when he was an under-graduate, on the ground that it had no soul.

On the further side of Gibbs a new world opens: the façade of Clare; an enormous lawn sloping towards the Cam; a bridge over the Cam; the trees of Scholar's Piece; the trees of the Backs; the trees, flowers and tennis courts of Fellows' Gardens. Here we return—and indeed to most visitors the whole expedition has been superfluous. Nearly everyone knows what King's College, Cambridge, looks like; it has been depicted and described since curiosity began. But as we return, as we recross the bridge, as we ascend the gentle slope of the lawn, note how the buildings of Gibbs dominate, how they set their seal upon the composite beauty of the scene. It is they, not the chapel, who would reign in the last resort, but they are too moderate and too civilised to declare their power. What colour are they? It is simplest to say 'grey' and to leave the initiate in the course of years to memorise the exquisite modulations into black, into white, which have been caused by the weathering of the Portland Stone.

There are four staircases in the block, lettered E, F, G, H. Each gives access to six sets. Most of the sets contain three rooms, a large one in front and two small ones behind, looking over the Backs, but this disposition is not invariable.

2

Such was the framework. Although he was to remain in it all his life, he was elected to a fellowship in the first instance for six years only. During this period he is still a recluse, who has not yet realised his teaching powers. He is moving into the open, and, as he does so, four main points may be noted. Firstly, there is the development of his private life—affectionate, emotional, disciplined, idealistic. Secondly, connected with this, is his poetical output. Thirdly, there is a changed attitude towards the world, which leads him away from Plotinus and mysticism and towards Hegel and politics. Fourthly, connected with this last, come his early prose publications.

This period is to be dealt with in the present chapter, and the following letter shall serve as an informal preface to it.

To A. J. Grant

1 All Souls Place
Langham Place, W.
July 16th, 1887

I am not unawaie, O Grant, that you have probably been cursing me; yet I hope not overmuch, being a reasonable man and aware that friendship does not depend on correspondence. I believe I've a good deal to tell you too. The end of term and of a year at Cambridge is always an excitement; even to ancients like me. People dissolve then as at no other time and it becomes evident that there is no good like friendship; which indeed may be termed love; which love, it seems to me, is the one thing to be cherished if there is to be any purport in life; cherished as the fundament of all one's conduct and opinions—much deeper and more important than they. That one should take a diametrically opposite course to other men is to be expected; but that one should cease therefore to love them is 'anathemamaranatha'—n'est-ce pas? Of which things indeed it is good for the most part to be silent; but also occasionally to speak. I've just returned from Durham where I've been staying with Headlam. I shall miss him awfully. I'm going into his rooms and he'll haunt me like a ghost. He's the best man possible; you'll see his soul in his eyes, if you look; lovely eyes. He has an Oxford brother who appears to have no πνεῦμα and therefore has no eyes; otherwise he is clever and epigrammatic—rather wearisomely so. He is naturally going into the church. You should have seen me going to church at Durham in a top hat, with prayer book and hymn book complete. Headlam took me to Tynemouth, and I wrote this.

'Far in the north beside a lonely shore
    A priory crowned the cliff; its little bell
    Morning and evening sent a drowsy°knell
Across wide waters; and above the roar

Of booming tempests oft the wild wind bore
Deep misereres seaward, greeted well
By pious mariners, who when darkness fell
Marked the rich light from painted lancets pour.

'This was: now, thick with smoke and din, the land,
Mile upon mile of brick, is populous,
Save where three arches, black with traffick, keep
A frowning watch to seaward. Men discuss,
Passing in haste to business, why they stand
Thus idly eloquent of an age of sleep.'

That art is the best thing man has, the reward and crown
when his social state is settled, is becoming my conviction.
Whether at present art is the thing is another matter.
Having got himself comfortable it remains for man to 'see
the world and behold it is very good'; and that is what the
artist does for him. Meantime, however, he has to get himself comfortable—with infinite labour, and destroying all
his beauty in the process; at which, I suppose, no wise man
will unduly repine.

I've made various plans for myself this long; among
others the reading of some Hegel. I don't know if that'll
come off; just now I'm a little sceptical of metaphysics,
but without more reason than other people. To be sceptical
of metaphysics means, as often as not, that one is too lazy
to read them; it means that with me at present. I'm going
away with my people to Thursley at the foot of Hinde
Head, near Tilford (do you remember) for August. Can't
go to Cambridge; there's no one up that I know. Or is it
really a fact that Berry is going up for August? Tell him
to let me know.

Are you enjoying Germany much? I don't feel as if
Göttingen is an exciting place. You ought to go to Heidelberg and see Ord. Are you reading Der grosse Goethe at
all yet? Or what are you reading in special? I should like
to have come to see you; but I'm going to stay and work
like a good boy. When do you come back?

I've seen Laurie to-day. He's been trying (in top hat
and black coat) for an Edinburgh professorship, but is
pilled. He has got a post however, at the 'People's Palace';
£150 a year. I saw Stevenson at Newcastle. He's coming
up to live at Toynbee in October.—It's very wrong of you

not to be keener over 'Lohengrin'. You must hear 'Tann-
häuser' before you leave Germany; and go in a duly
solemn frame of mind.—Headlam, Ashbee, Fry and I had
a most delicious 4 days on the river, rowing from Oxford
to London; I think the best time I ever had; a glimpse
of the ideal possibilities of life. This summer has been
glorious to me; to you too, I hope. England is so lovely
it seems idle to go abroad. Even for pictures there are
enough in the National Gallery to last one a life-time.
I suppose I don't much deserve for you to write to me;
but I would be awfully glad if you would. My love to
Berry.

Yours ever,

G. L. Dickinson.

The people mentioned in the above letter are contemporary
Kingsmen. Headlam is Headlam-Morley; Arthur Berry, a
senior wrangler, afterwards became vice-provost of the college; Roger Fry, the painter and critic, is now Slade Professor
of Fine Arts at Cambridge. The sonnet about Tynemouth
was printed with a few variants in the 'Cambridge Fortnightly', a magazine which Fry edited. The letter, as a whole,
is the sort of thing which Dickinson turned out when he was
feeling easy, and in its unpretentious way it introduces various
points which must now be considered: friendship; poetry;
intellectual development; prose.

3

Shortly before becoming a fellow, he had been elected to one
of those discussion societies which still flourish at Cambridge
and play an appreciable part in its mental life. The charac-
teristics of such societies vary but little. The members are
drawn from the older undergraduates and the younger dons,
they meet of an evening in one another's rooms, a paper is
read, lots are drawn to determine the order of the speeches,
the order is observed or ignored, there are developments and
digressions, and finally the reader replies to his critics, handing
round as he does so some such refreshment as anchovies on

toast or walnut cake. Some of the discussions are logical in
their tendency, others informative or whimsical, but in all
cases formality is avoided, presidents and secretaries are reduced to their minimum, and there is no attempt to be forensic
or even parliamentary. The young men seek truth rather than
victory, they are willing to abjure an opinion when it is proved
untenable, they do not try to score off one another, they do
not feel diffidence too high a price to pay for integrity; and
according to some observers that is why Cambridge has
played, comparatively speaking, so small a part in the control
of world affairs. Certainly these societies represent the very
antithesis of the rotarian spirit. No one who has once felt
their power will ever become a good mixer or a yes-man.
Their influence, when it goes wrong, leads to self-consciousness and superciliousness; when it goes right, the mind is
sharpened, the judgment is strengthened, and the heart becomes less selfish. There is nothing specially academic about
them, they exist in other places where intelligent youths are
allowed to gather together unregimented, but in Cambridge
they seem to generate a peculiar clean white light of their
own which can remain serviceable right on into middle age.

Dickinson's life as a young don was more intense than as
an undergraduate, and under this white light he entered upon
what may be regarded as the second cycle of his friendships.
His intellect and his affections were more closely connected
than most men's, and discussion for him was not a cerebral
exercise but an agitation which went deep into his being.
His severely logical mind did not tolerate humbug or hazi-
ness, and in most cases such a mind either atrophies the
emotions or functions independently of them. In his case it
reinforced them. He was attracted to people in the first
instance because they shared or seemed to share his interest
in intellectual problems. Other and more important links
might be forged, but a mutual desire for truth must precede
personal intimacy. Thus he, Roger Fry, J. E. McTaggart and
Nathaniel Wedd were originally drawn together by their

Age 23

passion for philosophy, and they were fired by a belief which McTaggart at all events never abandoned: the belief that philosophy explains the universe. It never did that for Dickinson, but it established relationships which lasted till death.

Since then I have seldom been out of love, if the word love may be used of a feeling continually thwarted on the physical side. That question I leave to casuists and medical men, though without much expectation that they will have anything important to say about it. For emotion, which to me is the determining fact, lies outside their province, and usually outside their competence.

Fry and McTaggart had come up from Clifton together. Goldie's relation with Fry soon became the more profound, and they 'lunched and breakfasted together every day' in the academic year 1887–88. Fry went down with a science degree, but determined to become a painter. He lived for a time in the dignified house of his father the judge. Dickinson visited him, but did not at first make a good impression on the establishment: he was unobtrusive and untidy and forgot to bring his white tie. 'Have you any further luggage coming, Sir?' enquired the footman. More congenial were the expeditions that the friends made together in the country. Dickinson loved England, he felt its scenery to be trembling on the verge of an exquisite mythology which only Shakespeare has evoked and he only incidentally. Despite our vile climate and the increasing vileness of our towns he kept a vision of sunlight, water, hedgerows, flowers, and the names of flowers. These last—though he frequently forgot them— were an earnest of our native poetry, he thought; speedwell and traveller's joy represent something which has scarcely found entrance into our literature, and not at all into our lives.

It is a lovely place [he writes of the Frys' Somersetshire home], We sat in the garden and walked about the country, I remember an early morning sunrise, the sun coming up a huge red globe. I remember a hot walk when Roger who was afraid of sunstroke plunged his head into a stagnant and filthy pool. I remember a wood full of foxgloves which prompted the little poem printed in my book. Another time we walked along the Dorsetshire coast from Corfe and Lulworth to Weymouth and back by the valley of the Stour. I remember after a long day's walk supping out of doors at Weymouth and realising what so often I have felt before and since, the perfection of happiness given by physical and emotional well-being, a happiness by which the young and even the older are apt to interpret, as I did then, as somehow revealing the nature of the universe. Alas, it is but a little moment, casually permitted to one of the little creatures meaninglessly produced in a world indifferent either to their happiness or misery.

Fry's influence naturally increased Dickinson's interest in pictures. He had not here the same sureness of instinct as in literature and music, he desired to educate himself, and to share his friend's enthusiasms. Difficulties arose, for Fry was constantly developing both his theories and his practices. The chariot of art, as driven by him, has never pursued a straight course in the literary sense of the phrase, and Dickinson often flew out of it at a sudden turn of the road. Fry, though never scornful, was often surprised, for he could not understand why a jolt should have been communicated. He would reason with his fallen companion, and would induce him to remount and admire objects which he disliked or endorse arguments which he mistrusted. Here are two letters recording an early mishap. The first is from All Souls Place (April 18th, 1891):

I went to the English Art Club the other day, and I now feel sure that if that's what pictures are I have no sense for them. I suppose colour and tone are really lost on me. . . . I can't do without form, and if it once gets recognised that pictures have nothing to do with form I shall be much relieved, for then I can make up my mind once for all that I don't care a damn for 'art', and go no more to exhibitions. But I still cherish a hope that you're going to do some pictures I can like, or else give me the necessary perception for such things. I went with Furness who agrees with all I say, and ten times more.

FROM MYSTICISM TO POLITICS

And he remarks of the work of Steer: 'One can only hold
one's tongue and pray about it'. But his next letter, dated
from Cambridge a week later, is humbler in its tone; something persuasive must have arrived from Roger in the interval.

> I gave you my real feelings about the N.E.A.C., but
> they're too negative to be worth much; just the kind of
> criticism in fact that I bar in literature. It's quite true that
> I don't understand the thing because I don't feel it; perhaps
> you'll make me some day. You know I've learnt most
> things that depend on the eyes from you, besides many
> more important things. I'm glad to be up here again (the
> letter goes on), it's cold still but there are daffodils and
> primroses and undergraduates and all the positive things
> which it is the one delight of the world to present to one
> and then add ironically 'that isn't the truth nevertheless'
> and so she negatives it all with winter and death and
> politics and 'social questions' and philosophy....

The New English Art Club was not the last of his troubles.
It is true that he learnt to require tone, and that he was
conceded form, but he was conceded it rather too insistently,
and was asked to sacrifice on its rigid altar the one thing for
which he did care: subject matter. He took the 'literary'
view of art, if by 'literary' we may understand poetic. What
he wanted in a picture, and what he discovered with mis-
chievous friendliness in Roger's own pictures, was romance:
hills, not of this world, where the spirit could walk, people,
recognisably human yet transformed—all the trailing gar-
ments of Shelley. Thus when the Post-Impressionists came
along he should have been sorely tried, but by then he had
grown content to pick his own way on foot, and to realise
there were tracts he should never explore.

At the beginning of 1892 Fry's work took him to Paris, and
they spent many weeks there—rather a dolorous visit. Italy
had already been visited with Ashbee, and brought overwhelming delight; there are long paeans, respectably pagan,
about its blue skies and its wine: 'No words can describe the
divine enchantment of this place' from Tivoli, and from

Rome 'I've been lying on my back with Rome below and
the stars above and murmuring waters all around'. Paris
proved uncongenial, though he praises it to May as 'a city,
whereas London is a congeries of houses', and compares
Haussmann's architecture to Wren's. He did not feel easy
there. He was to develop no special sympathy for France,
nor indeed for any foreign nation except China.

Roger and I took a room in the Rue de Tournon, close
to the Luxembourg. He was studying art and I visiting
museums and galleries, attending lectures at the College
de France, and writing a kind of drama on Mirabeau. This
I still have, though I have not the interest or patience to
read it through and I daresay it has no merit. Still, it
interested me at the time. I used to write at it in our
untidy attic, after we had had our roll and coffee and when
Roger had gone out to his work. I should think that few
young men ever got less out of Paris than I did. For to
get anything out of it, it seems to be essential to approach
it by the route of women and that was no route for me.
I am amused, as I look back, to remember a visit to one
of the dancing places—was it the Moulin Rouge?—and my
boredom for the short time I could stay. And also, how
a very ugly old prostitute came up to me once, in some
eating place, and began fondling me. I fairly ran away.
Paris, to me, at that time, was merely a place where one
continues one's own thought in more or less discomfort.
But of course I liked being with Roger.

The 'kind of drama on Mirabeau' is often mentioned in his
letters at this time. He writes to Fry: that 'behind all these
feverish actors I must get a divine ἀνάγκη, partly from lyrical
interludes, partly from giving the irresistible brute force of the
populace—which I find is rather difficult to treat'. He was
hopeful of himself as a poetic chronicler, and had already
published 'From King to King'. I must be the only person
for many years who has read 'Mirabeau'. It is partly in prose
and partly in verse, and it is less interesting as literature than
for its connection with 'Revolution and Reaction in Modern
France'.

This constant companionship was interrupted when Fry fell in love.

I still recall the conversation we had, late at night, in the house where he was then living in Beaufort Street, Chelsea. I was unhappy, yet not very, nor lastingly. For Roger did not cut me off from anything I had had. Later, he became engaged, then married, and I saw less of him, yet still a great deal. All our life we have been friends, and I have indeed a kind of married feeling towards him. Now, when age is coming on, we seem to have less in common in our interests, for he has become more and I less and less interested in art. Still, I think our affection will last as long as we do; it rests on so long an intercourse, so continuous, so varied. At Dorking, at Hampstead, in Italy, in Switzerland, I see myself with him, and always happy with him.

He got to know Jack McTaggart at the same time as Fry. He has himself written about McTaggart with respect and affection, so it will be sufficient to quote a passage from the 'Recollections'. It was written about 1926, before his friend's death, and it is more vivid than anything in the published memoir, and also more frank about the estrangement necessitated by the war. Since it is chiefly concerned with early memories it finds its proper place here. Note Dickinson's method of depicting character: he begins from within, and then proceeds to the oddities which make up the visible man. Method of the dialogue-writer rather than of the novelist, who hopes, by recording the surface, to indicate the forces beneath it.

McTaggart, if I may digress for a moment about my old friend, at one time the most intimate and most frequented of all, was, from the philosophic point of view, quite uninterested in the concrete, for he did not believe that philosophy could handle it, except in one important point—important enough. For he held then and I suppose does still that in the relation of love we come into the closest contact we can attain with Reality; for the Reality is an eternally perfect harmony of pure spirits united by Love. This then is the key to McTaggart's philosophy, and the real thing that drove him to pursue it. The rest has been a continuous and (I suppose) vain attempt to prove it by logic.

The concrete and phenomenal world being excluded from philosophy, he was able to submit frankly to his prejudices, as something so to speak too low to be taken seriously. But if he did not take them seriously, he took them very violently. When he first came to Cambridge he was an unkempt young man, thin, crooked, walking always with a twist of his body towards the wall because as was credibly affirmed he was always being kicked at school; and with amazing grey eyes, through which his soul shone. He was a follower of John Stuart Mill, a radical, and an empirical realist. But after a year or two, having discovered Hegel, he became an idealist, and also became, for most purposes, a conservative. He has been, ever since, an imperialist, a believer in public schools (of the older type), a lover of all ceremonies and traditions, of feasts, port wine, gorgeous robes, professorships, mayors and corporations, bishops, the House of Lords, and in fact everything English except the House of Commons. One of his suggestions for the reform of the Upper House was that those bishops should be added to it who were excluded under present rules. He became in fact, and is still, the most curious combination imaginable of Doctor Johnson, Hegel, and Robert Browning. He was at this time the most intimate friend of Schiller, Fry, and myself, the inspirer of our thoughts, witty, profound, sentimental, absurd, everything in turns, at once exasperating and delightful, and never more delighted than when he exasperated. When I see him now, with all that shut in under so thick a veil, when I consider what he was to us and compare what he now is for younger generations who hardly take him seriously, I could weep or I could laugh. Yet both attitudes are probably irrelevant. For the same man I believe is still there behind the mask. And occasionally the mask lifts and astonishes the young men with the vision of something they cannot understand or accept, yet cannot fail to be impressed by. The war broke off my intimacy with him, and I suppose it will never be renewed. But there have been few men to whom I owe so much, few who have been more part of my life, and I salute him here, in words that he perhaps will never read, but that spring from a depth below our estrangement, from that common fountain in which once the springs of our youth were mingled.

Happy in his friendships and his dislikes, McTaggart is said, by those who are qualified to judge him, to have been a great and a lovable man. But to a biographer of Dickinson it is rather the greatness of Dickinson which comes out in the foregoing passage. Few men can so have combined the powers of the head and the heart, and by the use of reason have so fortified the affections to withstand the inevitable shocks which await them. It is sometimes said 'What is the use of education?' Well, here is an instance of what education can do.

A recent letter to their contemporary, G. C. Moore Smith (Dec. 7th, 1931) says:

As to Jack's character and performance of course one's judgment depends upon what one thinks is the proper use of the mind. Desmond MacCarthy was insisting last night that its only proper use is to attempt to comprehend the whole universe and that Jack was the last of the great philosophers who pursued that purpose. My own view now is that that route is closed and that presumably the human mind and senses are so limited that men while they are men cannot expect to comprehend, though they ought never to abandon the aim, pursuing it however by other methods. What lies behind death I do not know but suspect it may be stranger than we are apt to suppose. We are both getting near it now, and it remains true anyhow that the 'readiness is all'.

The fourth of this group of friends who centred in the discussion society is Nathaniel Wedd. When I was at King's, Wedd taught me classics and it is to him rather than to Dickinson—indeed to him more than to anyone—that I owe such awakening as has befallen me. It is through him that I can best imagine the honesty and fervour of fifty years back. Wedd was then cynical, aggressive, Mephistophelian, wore a red tie, blasphemed, and taught Dickinson how to swear too—always a desirable accomplishment for a high-minded young don, though fewer steps need be taken about it now.

He is, I think, one of the ablest men I have ever known. He became a fellow and classical tutor at King's, and his teaching was universally admired by his pupils. But he was more than a teacher. He gave up all his time and energy to the undergraduates, was at home to them at all hours of the night, stimulated comforted amused, and generally maintained the best tradition of King's, that of friendship and intimacy between undergraduates and dons, but over-worked and oversmoked himself so that in the end he fell seriously ill and many years of his life have been frustrated. During all that time I never saw him cast down, nor did his mind or memory ever seem to weaken. He is now back at King's and in better health than it ever seemed likely he would achieve, though not able to do much teaching.

Some memories still survive of that far distant discussion society of theirs. The paper by Dickinson which made most impression was called 'Shall we elect God?' It imagines a meeting of a celestial branch of their group convened for that purpose. The members present are Goethe, Hegel, Turgenev, and Victor Hugo. They speak in turn, and each from his own standpoint is doubtful or hostile over the proposed election. They know too little about this God, or do not like what they have heard about him. Just as they are going to vote, there is a knock on the door and God comes in. He wears a hat and cloak, and his face cannot be seen. They must hear him speak before deciding, he says, and he tells them that how-ever little they think they know him, it is he whom they meet at every turn of their lives. If they go into the street, it is his eyes which peer out at them from the faces of every passer-by, he is all they struggle against, all they believe in, they cannot exclude him if they would, for he is himself the founder of their society. The four members are moved, but unconvinced. 'Let us see your face', they say. God agrees and throws off his hat and cloak. They all cry out at once—Goethe 'Das Schöne!' Turgenev 'La Vérité!' Hugo 'L'Idéal!' Hegel 'Das Absolut!' This paper of his and another by McTaggart entitled 'Violets or Orange Blossom?' were preserved for many years. The peculiar mixture of honesty and idealism which inspired them has now passed away.

One more friend of this period remains to be mentioned: Ferdinand Schiller. He stands apart from the rest and he was to occupy the supreme position in Dickinson's life. Although Schiller belonged to the same set and had strong intellectual powers, he had an even stronger vein of common sense, which led him to take a sardonic view both of philosophic speculations and of schemes to regenerate or improve the world. He was naturally drawn to the business career in which he has since become successful. In the summer of 1888 he had left Cambridge and was preparing to go to Calcutta, and though he and Dickinson had been previously acquainted it is from this moment that they begin to know one another well. Schiller's people were at Gersau, on the Lake of Lucerne. Dickinson, Fry, and McTaggart all went to stay there, and the visit seemed in retrospect an idyll of laughter, wit, and romance.

His mother was the kindest humanist most pagan woman I have ever known. Her husband being in India, she had brought up her sons at home in England. Her devotion to them and to all whom they cared for was her almost exclusive motive for living. I remember as though it were yesterday our first arrival at Gersau, Max (now a K.C.) on the tennis court, Canning (now the pragmatist and don at Oxford) and the dear lady overflowing with gaiety, kindness and shrewdness. There was a tennis court behind the house, a bathing shed in front. Close by was the church with its clanging pitiless bells. The house is now the Pension Fluhegg. How it lies bathed in sunshine and gaiety is in my memory! There was a largish party, and I shared a bedroom with Roger outside. We walked, played tennis, bathed, chaffed, for a happy month. Then the end came and Ferdinand, that autumn, left for India.

Five years later he returned on leave, and there was a second visit to Gersau, and the foundation of a relationship which was to be affectionate and permanent, yet disturbing. Devoted to Schiller, but constantly parted from him, and doubtful whether his devotion was returned, Dickinson suffered for many years from a sense of frustration which the sensitive will understand. They corresponded regularly, he writing every week and Schiller once a fortnight. Their letters are pessimistic in different ways. Schiller is despondent about the world, and amusingly bitter over the poor chances it offers to people who want to be decent, or even wealthy. Dickinson, equally despondent, dwells rather upon its hostility to perfect intercourse, and hopes for the 'company of pure spirits related to one another by perfect love', which constituted McTaggart's heaven. 'I cannot understand', he comments afterwards, 'how I thought that this personal passion in transitory individuals could be the key to the universe.' Schiller could not understand it at the time. He left India in 1899, for reason of health, and settled in England, and Dickinson looked forward to being with him constantly. This was not to be; the diversity of their occupations and interests kept them apart and it was not until later that affection and fidelity triumphed over circumstances, and bore fruit. Schiller is implicit in much that Dickinson wrote, particularly in the sonnets and in the character of Philip Audubon, of the dialogues.

Scenically this relationship was set against a background of mountains and mountaineering. In Schiller's company and on his account he climbed the Piz Palu in the Cima di Forno group as well as minor heights and also walked all one night to the top of the Gemmi Pass. On one occasion (August 19th, 1902) he did with J. J. Withers a climb which has been recorded in the 'Alpine Journal'—the ascent of the south-east face of the Piz Pisoe in the Ofen Pass district. One does not think of him as an athlete, but he had toughness and determination, and delighted in the life of the body provided it was unorganised; he could scramble, ride, boat, swim, and when he could combine any of these exercises with romance he was perfectly happy. Though he deplored the ugliness of Switzerland, its lumpiness, spikiness, and woolliness, and often contrasted it with Italian grace, he could not forget the deep emotions and the radiant health vouchsafed there, nor the visions—oh that they were true!—where precipices and avalanches seemed to promise an ecstacy unattainable on earth, and

> the valley waters found,
> Far gleaming to the dim horizon's bound,
> Among the cloudy islands of the Blest
> In that most ancient river Ocean, rest.

It has been necessary to dwell on these early relationships because though he made other friends they never sank so deeply into his life. His nature was not only loving, but tenacious, and it is impossible at any period of his life to conceive of him as apart from Fry, McTaggart, and Wedd, or, more particularly, as apart from Ferdinand Schiller. Similarly, though he made various women friends, there were none who could ever take the place of his sisters or of Mrs Webb, or of two who have not yet been mentioned— Mrs Moor and Miss Stawell. It is now, when his mind is developing, that his heart is most sensitive to joy and pain, and his surrender to intimacy most complete. It is now that he writes to Mrs Webb: 'I think the one immortal thing we are given in direct experience is love; I don't believe it goes when it seems to; it only gets hidden'.

4

Through his emotions we approach his poetry. In his own judgment, he was too much interested in ideas, and too little interested in form to be a great poet; his diction was facile rather than distinguished, his style was derivative and he had not the power of transforming little things. But as an expression for what would otherwise have remained unexpressed he valued his poetic craft highly. It is not only in early manhood, when emotional developments were agitating him, that he turned to verse; the impulse recurred—

for instance in 1913 when he was in China, and again in 1929.

The tribute to Shelley under the robes and cowl of Savona-rola has already been mentioned. His next printed work was 'Jacob's Ladder' (1887), a twenty-two page brochure, which he had multiplied in about twenty copies for private cir-culation. It is a curious experiment, consisting of a pro-logue and seven sections. The theme is the progress of man-kind through the ages, towards some lyrical consummation, 'and as usual it was the idea not the form which interested me'. A dying Viking (who exhibits the influence of William Morris), a Greek (M. Arnold), a Roman of the empire (in the style of Browning), an ecstatic Christian, and a tough optimistic evolutionist (Browning again) are followed by the twilight which is passing into dawn. Two ideas (he tells us) were in his mind at the time of writing: the idea of perfecti-bility in time and the idea of perfection in eternity, and he was not clear how the two were to be reconciled. If, as the nineteenth century thought, the universe is getting better and better, when will it become best? how does progress cul-minate in heaven? And heaven, the absolute, was necessary at that time to him, as at all times to McTaggart, because without it he could neither explain the strength of human love nor justify its shallowness. It is the experience of most of us that personal relationships are never perfect, but that when they are intense they hint at perfection. A modern young man is inclined to dismiss such hints as unimportant: Dickinson's temperament and upbringing inclined him to take them very seriously. The Rev. Page Roberts shrewdly remarked to his father that 'Jacob's Ladder ran up rather oddly into personal passion', and indeed it must, for without the personal the universal could not be attained.

> Where we oft had been
> We sauntered by familiar sweeps of lawn
> And silent places waiting for the dawn,
> Where chestnuts arched above, and, rarely heard,
> Sounded the note of night's enchanted bird.

These are the Cambridge Backs, and because of the emotion felt there the ladder can reach heaven. He wrote the poem mostly in the British Museum reading-room, but part of it on a backwater above Henley, lying in a sort of ecstasy throughout a golden summer morning.

Robert Bridges was encouraging, and said that the Greek section 'gives promise of poetry of a new and original character'. Dickinson now became less doubtful of his powers, and writes to Mrs Webb (January, 1891):

> Last Sunday I spent with Robert Bridges the poet. I like him. He was particularly kind to me, and we talked much on poetry, metres, &ct., and agreed a good deal, though he's not interested much in some things which are the most interesting to me. He was very encouraging about my poetry and I begin to be surer myself that my faculty is in that direction: certainly, by a negative exhaustive process, it appears demonstrately not to lie anywhere else.

The idea of progress was more successfully expressed in 'From King to King' (1891). This, his first book to be offered to the general public, is connected both with his historical studies and with his theory of history. Its theme is the puritan revolution, treated in a series of prose and verse scenes, and it illustrates his belief that history should be a form of art, and that it had never been better treated than by Shakespeare. He retained that belief in later years, but when he wrote 'From King to King' he held that history should also be a philosophy, and he had spent much time in reading the eighteenth-century and early nineteenth-century theorists. This did not spoil the freshness and charm of the book. The early summer meadows at Thames Ditton, a foal in the grass, Milton's 'Penseroso', a moonlight walk, friends absent and present, are entangled in its charming sequence. Writing to Fry, shortly before its publication, he says:

> It is a kind of satisfaction to me to have got something done at last; we used to defend 'being' as opposed to 'doing', but I can't now; one must create somehow or other in order to be. Creation's a sort of digestion, and there's

all the world to be digested before a single soul can be finished.

And thirty years later, in the 'Recollections':

> I still have a weakness for that little book; for I believe it was a good idea of handling history, that the moments were well chosen and the drama succinctly unrolled, from Eliot in the Tower to the execution of Vane. And the words of Mr Pepys introduced at the close still strike me as an admirable ironic commentary on the whole. I suppose however that the conception was inadequate. Anyhow the book excited no interest.

Those who have read 'From King to King' probably share his favourable opinion of it and wish it could be reprinted. He issued an American edition of it in 1907, containing a few alterations, chiefly in the prose scenes.

'Mirabeau' has already been mentioned, and he was evidently hoping at that time to develop the poetic chronicle as a form of art. But critics were discouraging. Robert Bridges was disappointed with some further work which was sent to him, and considered it inferior to 'Jacob's Ladder'. For one reason or another Dickinson experimented no more in this particular direction. His two acting-plays, which will be mentioned in their place, are of another type, as are the dramatic fantasies which he wrote during and after the war.

But it is in his lyrics and sonnets, rather than in longer poems, that he best expresses the spirit of these early years, their unrest, yearning, rapture, sensitiveness to nature and to man. He had begun to write verses as soon as he emerged from the nightmare of school, and he could dimly remember a poem evoked by the event of his mother's death, and the mood of pleasure, pain, romance, sentimentality, in which it was composed. One of his early efforts was sent by a friend of the family to Christina Rossetti for her opinion. She replies (May, 1883) with a long and unfavourable judgment; the poem submitted to her, she writes, 'shows talent rather than genius'. And he complains of his own work to Fry:

MS. Written about 1893

There's something terribly Tennysonian about it, however, and Tennyson *will not do*; he's only half alive, and
that half is diseased. But as Heine says, Modern Literature
is one vast hospital. What if Walt Whitman isn't a poet,
he's got the temper the next great poet will have.

The numerous MS. poems of this period confirm these discouraging opinions; they are sensitive, sincere, and elevated
and have a sort of generalised charm, but they lack vitality or
distinction or the magic of words.

He did, however, write some poems which satisfied him,
and he issued them in 1896 in a small privately printed
volume for circulation among his family and his friends.
Here are twenty-five 'Shakespearean' sonnets written in
1893-4, and some lyrics of the same or of an earlier date.
The sonnets are in his opinion 'my best poems and have
I think really some permanent value'. I hope that there may
be some opportunity of re-issuing this volume for the general
public. I quote from it now wherever I can. He does, here,
attain Parnassus. Personal passion, mountaineering, rowing
on the Thames, sunsets in Surrey, foxgloves in Somersetshire,
the music of Tristan—all the experiences he enjoyed or endured in those sensitive years—are secured by the accident
of art against the ravages of time.

> The thing that hath been, is. Those heavenly lights
> That made a marriage of the hills and sky,
> Those azure shining days and shadowy nights
> With all their golden candles set on high,
> Even in this wintry fit of rain and snow
> Fade not nor fail because the summer's dead....

The beauty and the accomplishment of the 1896 volume have
delighted and sustained his friends for many years; and it is
surprising that his desire to be a poet, his honesty, his intense
feeling, his musical ear, and his technical ability, did not
between them carry him further. But he had not the temperament which creates verses out of nothing and has produced

so much worthless yet authentic stuff. He could only write in a mood of high seriousness, and there are perils in such a mood which he did not avoid. Escaping the dust, he became involved in the clouds. It has, indeed, been objected against him that his poetry is too philosophic and his philosophy too poetical, and that this has endangered his supremacy in either sphere. Probably it has. But there are certain people who cannot be judged in terms of spheres. Their total achievement is greater than the sum of its parts. They triumph through a medium of which they are not consciously aware: through the capacity for visitation accorded in theology to certain angels.

It is convenient to mention at this point a later volume of poems, 'A Wild Rose'; ten short studies in unrhymed verse, a form in which he became interested. He wrote them about 1906, when he was stopping with Ashbee at Broadway (the title poem was published in the 'Albany Review', June, 1907), and he showed them to his friend, J. H. Mason, a scholar and a printer, who conducted a printing class under the London County Council. Mason grew to like the poems, and personally printed an edition on large paper as a tribute (1910). He also produced a small-paper edition, as an exercise for his students. One of these poems from 'A Wild Rose' ('If as I love my friend...') is included among the lyrics of 'The Magic Flute'. Another ('Do you name your hope?') was reprinted in the brochure which was issued on behalf of the college after Dickinson died.

Poems by him, signed and unsigned, have appeared in various periodicals. There is a fine one, for instance, in the 'Cambridge Magazine' for April 1912, called πάντα κόνις. It is about the wreck of the 'Titanic', and may be compared with Thomas Hardy's 'Convergence of the Twain', which the same catastrophe inspired.

If I had been a poet I should I suppose have had to be one. But I had, it would seem, some justification for my experiments in that direction. Anyone who reads this memoir [i.e. the 'Recollections'] will quickly perceive that I had no overmastering impulse at all, only a wide range of sensitiveness.

There was one direction in which he did have an over-mastering impulse, and here is the place to mention it. His feeling for music went far beyond the sensitiveness of the ordinary cultivated man, and had his specific gift been adequate he might here have achieved the ideal which he vainly pursued through poetry. Mozart and Wagner, the main pillars, show that the edifice was of catholic scope. Once inside it he felt sure of himself, and in a place more real than the other arts provided. Mozart received homage at the end of his life in 'The Magic Flute', Wagner near the beginning of it in the 1896 Poems. With them were Gluck and Bach, Beethoven and Schubert. To these six he probably owed even more than to Shelley, Plato, Goethe, because they were not an extension of his life, but a revelation which he would have missed if they had not existed. Music, returning via them to his philosophy, convinced him of transcendental truth, which existed as surely as the reunion of Tristan with Isolde when the final curtain falls, or as the union of passion with peace in the last movement of the Choral Symphony.

On the executive side he was becoming an attractive pianist with a charming touch and marked facility. He played duets not only with O. B. but with a much finer musician, his friend Adolf Behrens, down at Richmond. His range was increasing when it was checked by the loss in muscular con-trol which also affected his handwriting. He never com-plained of this, but it was a serious blow. Later on rheumatic trouble developed, and he gave up the piano before I knew him well. His sisters remember his Handel in childhood. Munro speaks of the Beethoven and Mozart at Charterhouse, Fry of the Cambridge period; all agree that, for an amateur, his performance was remarkable. There is no doubt that, though he lost the power to play, the fact that he had once had it allowed him to enter more deeply into music, both technically and passionately, and to pass beyond the antechamber of 'appreciation' where most of us have to stop.

5

While his emotions deepened and flowered into poetry and music, his intellect developed on practical lines: indeed this period in his life may be labelled 'from mysticism to politics', though such labels are rather misleading, for his mysticism always remained in his heart, folded up like a flower before the heat and brightness of a new day. He desired, as the sun rose, to help humanity, and realised that he could not do so without discovering what people are like and how they live. Some young men who have this desire rush about the world in search of what is termed 'actuality', but Dickinson, to his own regret, was ill-equiped for field work, and descended into the public arena by the slower route of academic history.

A few years before he would have been impatient of history, and invoked Mohini or Plotinus instead. But by 1887 he could no longer accept their assumptions that the universe is a veil to reality, for the reason that this view, though it may well be correct, offers no scope for action or thought, and ignores the existence of pain. Pain, to Dickinson, was indisputably real. There is no getting round the toothache. He dreaded pain both for himself and for others, he was impatient of any attempt to explain it away, and outraged by any theory which glorified it. His knowledge that people suffer pain, his belief that suffering can be cured, are the two foundation stones of his political life. And just as he had been attracted to medicine because it heals the individual body, so now he turned to the diseases of the state, and examined the remedies philosophy prescribes. The worst of these diseases—international war—had not yet expanded in his consciousness, it too lay folded up like a flower. He was rather occupied with such problems as forms of government, social distinctions, the distribution of wealth, the franchise, and war in the nineteenth-century sense of that activity. Behind every problem he sought for a solution.

This gradual movement towards practical affairs is coupled with the unexpected name of the German philosopher Hegel.

We have seen from the letter to Grant that his first struggle with Hegel dates back to 1884. Three years later he writes to Fry:

> I've really begun my tussel [sic] with Hegel; it's the hardest work I ever had, worse than Plotinus. I don't get in more than a couple of hours and then collapse into idiocy and physicality. You will wonder doubtless why I bother myself, but it's worth bothering about, for the thing that Hegel professes to do (I haven't the least notion whether he's done it) is the thing I've already wanted done as a preliminary to anything else in thought: i.e. to establish the relation of thought in general to the objective world and what it is thought everywhere is trying to do and what is its necessary movement.

He now began to read the monster systematically under the guidance of McTaggart, to whom Hegel meant 'a release from his empiric realism to the idealism he has since pursued'. They did so many pages a day, in an English translation, and got through the Great and the Small Logic. It was a curious situation, because though he followed McTaggart faithfully into the 'Hegel of Eternity' and was pleased at any road which seemed to lead into a mystic world, he was also peeping about for a path of his own in the 'Hegel of Time'.

> Our reading seems to me in retrospect to have been very unprofitable. We never really discussed the difficulties: and the whole notion (so preposterous as it now seems to me) that the world can be deduced from abstract logic, and that, being so deduced, it somehow changes its whole character by merely becoming what is called 'rational', we accepted as a kind of article of faith.

That was the aspect of Hegel which interested McTaggart.

I was however myself more interested in the applications
of the logic, though I was compelled to admit that they
were not logical. Nevertheless I believe that the real merit
of Hegel is in that extraordinary survey of the life of man,
his history, his art, his religion, which brought it all into
a seeming concord with postulated laws of thought. I remember sitting down with a sort of intoxication to a book
like the Aesthetics, and I know not how long it took me
to discover that this fascinating rhapsody omits altogether
the thing that is specifically art. But in that it resembles
most other treatises on aesthetics. And I did not then care
about art. I wanted to see Reason progressing magnificently
through the panorama of life; and so she did, in the crabbed
cunning imaginative works of that pedantic and poetical
enchanter.

What he gained from his 'Hegel of Time' was a belief in
the understandability of history, and a hope that by understanding the past he might influence the future. He had first
found this hope in the political writings of Plato; now it was
extended and confirmed. Since the accumulation of facts for
their own sake did not interest him, he neither became nor
wished to become a professional historian, and only one of
his works ('The International Anarchy') shows any high
degree of research. His aim was to interpret rather than to
record, and if he did not become viewy and careless, like his
admired O. B., the explanation lies in his scrupulous regard
for truth.

His political opinions at this time were illogical and harmonious. Was he conservative, liberal, or socialist? It would
be difficult to say, but it is easy to recognise his voice. By
temperament he loved tradition—old houses, old trees, all
the feudal charm with which he has surrounded the figure
of Lord Cantelupe. Nor was he even insensitive to the joys
of Jingoism; there are some letters to R. C. Trevelyan during
the Diamond Jubilee of 1897 which make painful reading for
his steadier admirers; he explains how wonderful it is to see

the Empire marching past, and he contemplates bicycling down to Spithead to see the Naval Review. He never reached Spithead. It was too far. And even oligarchy did not carry him over the edge. 'I unfortunately like anachronisms but do not believe in them' he writes to Grant, and he knew that old houses and old trees, exquisite as they are, breed old men. His conservatism was not mere sentiment, and he could find serious arguments for it. But he found that as a working proposition it would not do, and by the end of the century he had moved to the left, and had re-occupied with stronger forces the position marked out fifteen years before under the influence of Henry George.

For the working classes as then existing he had little enthusiasm, and it was not until much later in his life that he established personal contacts with them. He had been brought up in a Victorian household, he minded h's being dropped, he knew he ought not to mind, still he did mind. And—a more serious aversion—he could not see that the working class movement was proceeding in a direction which was either good or new. He writes to Fry after the Trades Union Congress at Liverpool: 'We're really in a revolution without knowing it, and how dull it is! And all things except "friendship wit and love". As soon as the working classes begin to *get* their bread and butter they show up as a new and equally dreary bourgeoisie'. He might have written 'an even drearier', for when Labour gets thoroughly respectable, and is stimulated neither by danger nor by art, it does seem to acquire a sausage-and-mashed quality unknown to Suburbia. Miss Stawell remembers him once denouncing 'a state of things where we have men enjoying their work, enjoying their play, enjoying their food, and wondering in the discussions of their well-regulated debating societies what in the world Shelley could have meant by "the desire of the moth for the star"'. He was lecturing at the moment on the Spencerian ideal of progress, but the stricture applies to modern democracy generally. He feared that there would be a levelling down, instead of a levering up, and that the Many, in the process of making themselves comfortable, would throw away the pearl of great price which has been handed down to them by the Few. Art, literature, music, culture are not external decorations, but age-long secretions in the soul of man, and one of the problems of our revolution is to prevent man from despising or forgetting his own past. Thus, although he came more and more to condemn our economic system and advocate drastic changes, he had no sympathy whatever with the Marxian who rejects Shakespeare and Tchekov on the ground that they wrote for Capitalists. Such a view seemed to him childish and self-conscious, and best corrected by an intelligent study of history.

As soon as one has got the general hang of his character— and I do not think it is a difficult one—his apparent political contradictions fall into line. From his main idea he never departed. He wanted a democracy where everyone will be an aristocrat. And all his work as a teacher is directed towards this Utopia.

6

His earliest historical work, 'From King to King', has already been mentioned under the heading of poetry. In his own opinion, there is no distinction between the two muses: 'dramatic treatment is the only one that really represents truth at all, and most history books are mere materials for books' he tells Mrs Webb. It was, however, followed next year (1892) by a work very different in form: 'Revolution and Reaction in Modern France'. This was the outcome of a set of University Extension lectures at Norwich, and it attempted 'to see what had become of the revolution, and to test (or ought I to say to impose upon history) my rather vague and tentative theory of progress, and to trace the ideas underlying events down to the establishment of the Third Republic'. It was his first attempt to write in prose at length, and 'the style I evolve, a series of very short sentences, grouped into paragraphs and unconnected except by the colon, which I misused for the purpose, is not good. But it was sincere, in the sense that I was determined to avoid all mere talk and meaningless empty sentences, such as fill so many text books of history'. Indeed it anticipates in its bareness, though not in its accomplishment, the prose of his latest period, when he frees himself from 'literary' apparatus and brings us into direct contact with his mind. It was well received, both in England and France, 'mais je crois que vous tirez trop les choses au tragique ou plutôt au romantique', writes the historian James Darmesteter, 'et que vous les considérez en poète plus qu'en historien, sans peut-être vous en rendre compte vous-même'. In 1927 the book was reprinted with slight modifications in the last chapter.

The next book, published in 1895, is remarkable for its conservative tendency. It is thus described in the 'Recollections':

> I sat down to study the Parliamentary history of England from the first Reform bill onwards, still with the idea that the history of the recent past would give guidance for the future. I ploughed through debates, pamphlets, histories, innumerable dry-as-dust stuff, which ultimately turned into the book 'The Development of Parliament in the Nineteenth Century', which was published in the year 1895, and has long been out of print and never reprinted. As may be seen from this book, I was then in my political opinions a kind of socialistic Tory. This was due I suppose on the one hand to a contempt for the House of Commons, as I imagined it to have become, a contempt really based on Carlyle; and an absurd belief in the House of Lords, based upon nothing but antagonism to the Commons.

The book argues that the House of Commons can only express the forces which excite the nation, whereas national wisdom is expressed in the House of Lords—which is furthermore necessary as a rallying point for the Empire.

> I was not then a socialist, but I saw at least that the question of labour and capital would overshadow all others

in the future. (Of foreign politics and war I was not then thinking.) This is expressed in a book which is at any rate genuine and sincere. Its weakness was that it was written from a place so remote from the actualities of politics; and from that point of view the annoyance or contempt of such practical radicals and socialists as attended to it is probably justified. Here I am only concerned with it as an indication of my attitude at the time. I had had since my early youth the double impulse both to deal with contemporary problems and to maintain detachment and impartiality. Perhaps this is impossible. But the impulse kept me all through my Cambridge life in a state of tension and unrest.

In 1906 'The Development of Parliament' was translated into French, and Dickinson wrote a new preface for it, which is interesting as showing the growth of his political opinions. He says that further study of democracy, particularly in the United States, has convinced him that it is a menace to the poor rather than to the rich, because the rich have the intelligence and the leisure to manipulate the political machine, whereas the poor are too inexperienced and too much occupied in the struggle for existence. He notes, furthermore, that it is the Cabinet rather than the House of Commons, which governs: also that the governing classes tend to experiment in the direction of socialism, and that a revolution may be obviated or mitigated thereby. On these points he disassociates himself from the opinions expressed in the English original published eleven years before.

Neither the original nor the French translation attracted much notice and the failure seems to have suggested to Dickinson that his life had become too secluded. 'Not wholly from the world withdrawn, Not wholly to its service sworn' was his motto for himself, 'bad verse but a good maxim', and he was always faced by the problem of using Cambridge without being used up by it, a problem which in the long run he surmounted triumphantly. His immediate move was in the direction of academic teaching, and though the progress of a don from his own rooms to his lecture-room is not spectacular it may have important developments. When he had lectured before it had been either in a missionary spirit or because he needed money. Now that his mind and his heart had developed teaching became a pleasure to him. This change, and its consequences, form the subject of the next chapter.

The chapter now ending has emphasised Cambridge, architecturally, emotionally, and intellectually, and has said little about his home life. He remained in very close touch with his sisters, and the marriage of Arthur in 1888 served if anything to emphasise this. Most of his vacations were spent at All Souls Place, where his father continued to work as a portrait painter, and where Hettie and Janet kept a little school. He met quantities of young people there of various types, was frivolous and domestic, took part in the musical evenings, was charming to the girls of all ages, and then would vanish to his room at the top of the house. This home life is not easy to convey in a memoir, it was so light and so quiet, but it belongs to his permanent background and must never be forgotten. Though its social ease never quite penetrated him to the core, it did act as a partial solvent and stop him from becoming eccentric. A friend of the Dickinson family, Miss Townsend, well remarks: 'No one could be so intellectually unselfish as Goldie quite without effort. He came from a home where an analogous and perfectly successful effort had become second nature'.

CHAPTER X

THE SOCRATIC METHOD
1893–1914

I

IN the autumn of 1892 the question of the renewal of his fellowship came up before the governing body of the college. A committee had been appointed to report, and expressed the opinion that his studies were 'likely to be of material service in the promotion of Historical and Political Science'. They quoted the favourable critique of Lord Acton on 'Revolution and Reaction', and they recommended that his fellowship, which ran out in the following spring, should be renewed for five years. However, when the motion to renew was proposed in the college meeting it was defeated by one vote. The news was brought to him by his friend Laurie. He was playing the piano at the time, was 'more excited than distressed' and began to wonder what he should do now that he was thrown on his own resources and obliged to make his way in London. He did not speculate for long, for that same afternoon the college held a second meeting and made him librarian, a sinecure post to which a fellowship was attached. He held the librarianship till 1896, and was then appointed college lecturer in Political Science, also with a fellowship. This he held till 1920, when he was given a pension fellowship, tenable for life.

This chapter covers events between the renewal of his fellowship and the outbreak of the war, with the exception of his visits to America and the East and their implications, which will be considered separately. The outstanding event is his emergence as a teacher. He becomes more and more anxious to stimulate, and less interested in learning and artistic expression for their own sakes. His studies, his political

opinions, his lecturing, his published works, his capacity for
friendship, his interest in the young—all flow into a single
channel, which might be called educational if the word were
not so misused, and 'maieutic' if the word were not a little
pedantic. Though he does not remind one of Socrates personally, though he had neither the nagging qualities which
wore down the sophists, nor the physical high spirits, nor the
toughness to fight at Potidaea, nor the desire to fight there,
yet Socrates is his master. It is as a teacher who was constantly being taught that he must be regarded during these
twenty-one years.

A letter to May, dating from the threshold of this period,
will serve as an informal preface to it, as did the letter to
Grant in the case of the period preceding. While quoting in
full I have missed out most of the underlinings, because like
the stresses in his talk they are faint, the pen travelling lightly
beneath the word, and only emphasising half of it.

King's College, Cambridge,
March 10th, 1889.

Writing the date reminds me of your birthday, for which
I send all possible good wishes and greetings—and would
send a present if I had one! Isn't this spring weather
delicious? At least it is here—snowdrops and crocuses and
aconite everywhere, and that delicious sense of beginning,
which is so much better than fruition.
'And then, and then came spring and rose in hand
My threadbare garment of repentance tore',
which is a sentiment of Omar Khayyam I quite understand. Fred was here last Sunday, that perhaps was partly
why I didn't write, and also I was busy with papers. I'm
not pleased with my lectures, but I don't quite know how
they ought to be; they're certainly not interesting enough,
and I should be very angry with myself if I were in the
audience.
I'm growing magnificent ideas of what a university *ought*
to be; it ought to lead thought, as it did in the Reformation,
and not skulk behind and talk of vested rights. And there

never were places with such chances as Oxford and Cambridge. I don't want them popularised, I want them to educate leaders, and let there be other universities to educate the rest. So we ought to teach politics somehow through history, which has always been O. B.'s idea, and like all his ideas is good. We do teach people how to live, how to make friendships, &ct, but I don't think we teach them, as a rule, how to think, i.e. how to apply their knowledge to here and now. All this is 'ideal', and one gets ashamed of what's ideal, but it may become practical. I shall probably come to London next Thursday week, or thereabouts. The Choral Symphony must have been fine. We had Mozart's Requiem on Thursday in chapel; music, different to anything else of his. Great as Beethoven, I think. Best love. I heard of you from Miss Johnson. Isn't she nice? A. Berry was up yesterday, and Lennie —— (?) gets nicer and nicer.

Lennie's surname is indecipherable, but that he got nicer and nicer there is little doubt: most of the people who constantly saw Goldie did that, though he did not realise why.

2

He ceased to be a bad lecturer and became a good one as soon as he ceased to 'lecture' and began to speculate aloud. In his University Extension days he had tried to convey facts, to impose opinions and to arouse emotions, but he modified considerably on all these three points. As for facts, he soon realised that they are best learned from text-books and that the lecturer who ladles them out to an audience who gobbles them down is only carrying on the educational traditions of the Misses Woodman's morning classes for the sons of gentlemen. As for opinions: the formation of these was indeed his chief aim, but his method became more tentative as his grasp on reality tightened. He believed that his own opinions were right or he would not have held them, but he never dictated them or desired that they should be accepted; instead, he

encouraged clear thinking and decent feeling and hoped that
on such a soil right opinions would flourish. And as for
arousing emotion: he neither aimed at this nor did he achieve
it in any crude sense. The seriousness of the theme provided
its own emotion. Knowledge of the past will help us to
control the future, and unless we can control the future our
happiness, private and public, is at the mercy of chance.
Thus a subject like the History of Political Theory which is
on the face of it academic, became arresting and disquieting
under his treatment, because he made his audience feel they
might influence Fate. For instance the dilemma of Jeremy
Bentham—how can a selfish statesman provide an unselfish
policy?—appeared as real to his audience as it had been
when Bentham formulated it.

Dickinson had the external framework necessary for a
lecturer; he was accurate, well informed, polite, dignified,
clear, punctual. But it was the light within which impressed
his audiences—no will-of-the-wisp of the Coleridge variety,
but a light which for all its spontaneity shone steadily and
guided to a goal. His voice and his expression are not easily
conveyed, because they were not dramatic; it was no mission
of his to vibrate with emotion, or to point out the choice
before us with his forefinger, or to stamp upon international
anarchy with his foot. He left such achievements to orators.
What did come across was a modulation in the tones and a
light upon the face, which showed that the whole man
was alive and was working at a distance to bring help.
This helpfulness was present at all times, but it was unusually
moving when it shone through the formality of a lecture-
framework.

His official subject at King's was Political Science, then
locally known by the title of Analytical and Deductive Politics,
and he continued in it two terms a year from his appoint-
ment in 1896 to 1920, when he resigned the lectureship. He
was, during precisely the same period, lecturing at the London
School of Economics, and some reference must now be made

to his activity there. It has not the glamour of the Cambridge connection, and it is not so generally known, but it was important to his audiences and to himself.

The London School of Economics and Political Science was founded in 1895, chiefly owing to the efforts of the Sidney Webbs. Dickinson's early socialism had brought him into contact with Fabianism, and he had already arranged for visits to Cambridge from Webb, Hubert Bland, Olivier, Bernard Shaw, and others then belonging to the group. The visits had caused some excitement. Webb had argued with McTaggart, neither side scoring a victory. Bland had talked football to the young men. Shaw had lectured brilliantly, also telling a story about an Irish uncle who thought he was in heaven and hung from the ceiling in a basket dressed in gauze. Asked on behalf of Dr Westcott what his moral basis was, Shaw had replied to Dickinson on a postcard, 'Ask the old boy what his is, and tell him mine's the same'. So, though Dickinson's temperament was far from Fabian and his methods anything but statistical, it was natural that he should be invited to teach at the newly established School. His connection began in 1896. In 1911 he was put on the permanent staff as lecturer in Political Science; in 1920 he resigned. His lectures at the School were, so far as their subjects and general outlook went, a repetition of the courses delivered at Cambridge. Here is a complete list. He began with 'The Machinery of Administration in England'. He followed this by courses on 'The Use of Political Terms', 'The Bases of Political Obligation', 'The Structure of the Modern State', 'Popular Government', 'The British Empire and other Composite States', 'Some Theories of the basis of Political Obligation', 'The Government of the British Empire', 'The Structure of the Modern State', 'The Functions of the Modern State', 'The Central Government of England comparatively treated'. This brings us to the year 1902, when he began to deliver the most noteworthy of his courses, on 'The History of Political Ideas', and repeated it with constant changes

until 1920. In 1924 he returned to the School to give one
short course on 'The Causes of the War of 1914'—one of the
pieces of work preliminary to 'The International Anarchy'.

Since the London School of Economics is non-residential,
there was little opportunity for social intercourse. He travelled
up, gave his lecture in the afternoon or evening, held an
informal class in connection with it, and then went back.
But even such an arrangement as this leaves a mark when it
continues for twenty-four years. Besides doing good there,
he enlarged his experience, for he met students who were not
as well off as their Cambridge contemporaries, and were less
exclusively the products of Public Schools, and he also became
acquainted with Indians and Chinese.

The titles of some of his Cambridge courses were: 'Modern
France' (1892), 'The Transition to Democracy in Modern
England' (1894–96), 'The Machinery of Administration
under Democracy' (1897), 'The Theory of Law and Government' (1897–99), 'Analytical and Deductive Politics' (1900
onwards). When he looks back at his lecturing both there
and at London his summary is as follows:

My business was to enlarge and concretise my subject,
which became, in fact, a general discussion of modern
political problems. I came in time, I believe, to lecture
well in the academic way. I spoke always from notes,
added continually year after year to my matter, as was
natural in a subject so continually developing, not to say
bulging and obtruding outside all skins of general theory.
I was interested myself, and I think I interested my pupils,
most of them. At any rate my audience always continued
to the end without any defalcations to speak of, and varied
round about a hundred in the latter years. I had a quite
definite idea of what I wanted to do in lectures—to stimulate the students' interest so that they should feel they were
dealing with a live subject which was going to be of interest
and practical importance to them all their life. I used not
to conceal my own opinions, but also not to preach them
unfairly, having in fact, in many important questions, a
very open mind. I lectured in this way for some twenty-

five years, never losing my own freshness and interest. Whether I produced any result, or what, who can say? The parable of the sower applies to all such work, and a single teacher is rather a light makeweight against family and social interests and preoccupations. Still I expect I helped to wake up some minds. What more can a teacher do, or what better?

Most people would say that he was a really great lecturer of his type. That type, as he is careful to point out, was the academic. Neither his matter nor his manner could move masses of people, and he believed indeed that it is impossible to touch men to any fineness when they are gathered into anything so clumsy as a mass. Towards the end he was a triumphantly successful broadcaster; he had the opportunity of addressing numbers of individuals who remained individuals, an opportunity which no speaker has yet had since the beginning of the world; and he was extending his audience in this sense when he died. But except at an election (for instance, at Scarborough in 1909), he never addressed a crowd. His hatred of crowd-psychology was so great that he could scarcely bear to discuss it, much less to utilise it; in fact it was too great, and limited his utility; when two or three hundred were gathered together, he felt too sure it was in the name of the devil. And it must be remembered that he believed in the devil—that is to say in the existence of evil; it was one of the points on which he differed from his more youthful audiences.

After his death one of his former London students contributed this impression of him to the 'Journal of Education':

We were an odd job lot at those evening classes! Clerks and students and teachers, young and old, men and women of all sorts and conditions: but he interested us all and aroused us in a truly wonderful way.... He had no physical advantages except a charming smile and a very sensitive mouth. His voice was always husky though very pleasant to listen to, and he had none of the arts of the orator. But there was a distinction about his whole individuality that arrested attention and in some curious way kept his large class of not highly intellectual students, such as he lectured to in Cambridge, spellbound. I think perhaps we never knew what to expect and we never quite grasped his point of view....He seemed now to be an aristocrat, now a thorough going democrat, so that often his class was left gasping. You went away to *think*—and that was, I suppose, what he wanted.

A sympathetic impression of his lecturing at Cambridge is to be found in Osbert Burdett's 'The Art of Life'.

Lecturing, as he conceived it, was a thoughtful conversation. No reply was anticipated, but the speaker had to keep the naturalness and good manners of talk. So that the transition from the lecture hall to the class, in which his pupils did talk, was easy and welcome, and the transition from the class to luncheon or to a ride, where his pupils could both talk to him and lecture him, was easier still. He broke up the illiberal distinction between lessons and leisure which has done so much to cramp human development; hard work lay at one end of the scale, amusement at the other, but both required intelligence and sensitiveness, and were aspects of education. So continuously did he believe in education that he seldom used the word; it was the air breathed by the spirit of man, and if the air a man is breathing is resolved into its components, the result may be stimulating to experts, but the man himself dies.

Besides the classes held in connection with the lectures, he took the third and fourth year History men at King's in Essays. The sort of subjects he set were: Church and State, Machiavelli, Toleration, Malthus, Wells' 'Utopia'. When the essays came to be corrected it became apparent that, like all genuine educationists, he did not teach for teaching's sake. He roped people in to get ideas on some problem which puzzled him and so would talk more about the problem itself than about their treatment of it. This disconcerted his weaker pupils, who wanted to be shown where they went wrong, but his indifference to their heresies was counterbalanced by his severity over their style. 'It hasn't come yet', he would say. He knew very well when sentences went wrong, had no patience with the 'mot injuste', which often seems so marvellous to the young, and came down, perhaps rather too heavily, on the side of limpidity and logic. How good is his own prose style? He was at that time disciplining it and paring away 'beauties', so that it might respond better to the movements of his thought.

From his classes and essay-talks we slide onwards into social intercourse and hospitality, and this is the moment when I want to introduce myself.

I first met him in 1898. A friend of his father's and of my aunt's had asked him to be kind, so he invited me to lunch. We had Winchester cutlets, a sort of elongated rissole to which he was then addicted, but I can remember nothing about the conversation, and probably there was none. Impressions get so mixed; but I recall him as sadder and older than he appeared to be fifteen years later. He knew nothing about me—there was nothing to know—and I had never heard of him. His rooms were on staircase H of Gibbs, ground-floor—the staircase nearest the chapel (see illustration p. 122)—and we sat alone in the large front room silently eating the cutlets and drinking the reddish-brown sauce in which they lay. The food was less good than it became in later years, the host shyer, the guest shyer still, and I departed unprepossessing and unprepossessed. A few weeks later I asked him to lend me a play which had a great vogue among my fellow freshmen. I forget its name. He handed it to me gloomily, and asked when I brought it back what I thought of it. I replied nervously that I was afraid I didn't think it so very good. His face lit up. 'No, of course it's no good', he said. This lighting up of the face was a thing to watch for. It meant that he had seen something which must vaguely be called 'life', and it brought life to anyone who saw it. It was part of what—vaguely again—must be called his charm. Charm, in most men and nearly all women, is a decoration. It genuinely belongs to them, as a good complexion may, but it lies on the surface and can vanish. Charm in Dickinson was structural. It penetrated and upheld everything he did, it remained into old age, and I saw it first that afternoon at the end of last century, when he was only thirty-five, and when I kindled him by managing to be honest over a trifle. The 'lighting up' really belonged to a greater occasion than this—to the entrance into the room of a friend. Then he would emerge from his inner life with a smile, which made him for the moment indescribably beautiful.

He photographed well, so that I need not try to describe his features. The complexion was not good, the head bowed a little forward from the shoulders when he walked, though the shoulders themselves, like the body generally, were shapely and strong. The hands were large. The clothes, except during the American visits, erred on the dowdy side—dark blue serges, shirts of indistinction, podgy ties. I dress like that myself, except for illogical flashinesses, and once when I invited him to accompany me into one of these he replied that it is hopeless to dress well unless one's personal appearance corresponds. This made me realise that he was at all events not contented with his own appearance. I did not understand why. There was a beauty about him which cannot be given that patronising label 'spiritual', a beauty which, though it had nothing to do with handsomeness, did belong to the physical, so that his presence was appropriate amid gorgeous scenery or exquisite flowers. The portrait of him on the frontispiece by Roger Fry features a sumptuous costume, which is not typical, but it is satisfactory that he should have been obliged to wear it once.

I did not see much of him while I was an undergraduate, and when in my fourth year I turned from classics to history and planned to go to him for essays I was dished by Oscar Browning, who said: 'You're not coming to me at all, you must come to me'. So once a fortnight I read aloud about Wallenstein or Louis XIV to the handkerchief which covered

O. B.'s face, and Dickinson's power to teach remained unknown to me, except as far as I have heard of it from others. I belonged to his 'Discussion Society', however. He had founded it in 1904 as the result of some popular lectures on philosophy which had been delivered by McTaggart. It was a blend between the type of society described on p. 65 and the tuitional type presided over by a don. Dickinson presided, but there was freedom for the rank and file. The papers I forget, with the exception of one on Sex, read by George Barger (now Professor of Chemistry at Edinburgh). Sex was not mentioned at Cambridge in those days—that is to say, not in the small circle I knew—and there were some high anticipations about Barger's paper, and some care on Dickinson's part to ensure that only seriously minded youths should attend. The paper was statistical, the discussion stilted, the evening interminable, yet I recall it as an example of his sensitiveness and tact; he knew just how large a stone it is wise to drop into the pond.

The above trifles may show how consistent his influence was, and how it could penetrate unpromising material. 'I think of him', writes Dominick Spring-Rice, 'at the queer society he ran in which you drew lots as to your turn for speaking and had to tell what you believed was the truth; standing, at the end, in front of the fireplace, rubbing himself and saying clearly for each of us what in our muddled way we could not say clearly for ourselves.' Teaching, to him, was a process which transcended any formula and went on at all times, and it could not be distinguished, in the final analysis, from being taught. By the end of his life he had become so wise that he was able to learn from the young. His affection for them and his desire to help them were joined with a much rarer quality: respect. 'Maxima debetur pueris reverentia'? No, certainly not. It was not that type of respect. It was a recognition that the young may instruct the old.

Financially his lectureships enabled him to live and to write books, and since the college considerately let him confine his teaching to the two winter terms, he was left with the Summer Term and the Long Vacation for creative work, 'an arrangement which no commission would ever approve; it slipped through under the freedom of the old Cambridge'. Before coming to the books themselves we must glance at his general attitude towards the university, the university for which he entertained such high and unusual hopes, as the letter quoted at the beginning of this chapter testifies.

3

His love of Cambridge was touched with fear. He only trusted her in so far as she is the city of youth. For him the undergraduate is the true owner of the University, and the dons exist for the purpose of inducting him into his kingdom. Having taken his degree there, he passes out into life, bringing with him standards of conduct and memories of affection and beauty which cannot be elsewhere obtained. Cambridge did this much for Dickinson, and she did it through him for dozens, perhaps hundreds, of young men who now mourn his memory. 'An unspoilt youth of twenty with his mind just waking up and his feelings all fresh and open to good is the most beautiful thing this world produces', he writes to Mrs Webb, and Cambridge shared with Ancient Athens the maieutic power which brings such minds into the light. The Cephissus flows with the Cam through this city, by the great lawn of King's under the bridge of Clare, towards plane trees which have turned into the chestnuts of Jesus. Ancient and modern unite through the magic of youth.

But there was another Cambridge which filled him with dismay and which he connected less with the scenery than with the weather: the Cambridge of the organising and the researching don. Stuffy yet raw, parochial yet colourless—what a city was this! What a hole! Schoolmasters paraded its streets, specialists riddled its walls, governesses, married to either, held their lugubrious courts in its suburbs. Here the east wind blows for ever and the mist never lifts off the mud. Yes, he dreaded the increasing fuss and rush of university business, not for selfish reasons but because it tended to neglect the needs of the individual undergraduate and to keep him in the position of a child, children being more easily managed. And he mistrusted research even more, although it is in itself so admirable and so necessary, because research atrophies the mind and renders it incapable of human intercourse: 'the spectacle of learning gets more depressing to me every year', he tells Mrs Webb, 'I care only for fruitful and vital handling of the eternal commonplaces or else for a new insight that will really help some one to internal freedom'. If the schoolmaster teaches wrongly, the specialist cannot teach at all, and between the two of them what room is left for Socrates?

There is something to be said against his views, as he realised, and there is a third Cambridge whose existence he forgot—the agglomeration conveniently known as 'the varsity' which takes pass-degrees, roars round football fields, sits down in the middle of Hammersmith Broadway after the boat race, and covers actresses with soot. Silly and idle young men did not come his way, no more did hearties and toughs unless they had intellectual leanings. This was due partly to his own constitution and partly to that of King's, which only admits men who are reading for honours and does not duck an intellectual in the fountain oftener than once in twenty years, apologising elaborately to him afterwards. In its exquisite enclosure a false idea can be gained of enclosures outside though not of the infinite verities. Dickinson, pacing up and down with his arms behind him, kept in touch in his own fashion with the world, but he could never slap it on the back or stand it a drink. And he loathed its brutality and bullying—with them there could be no compromise; his objection to rowdiness was not its noise but its inability to flourish without a victim.

Essentially a college man, he did not take much part in

University affairs. The chief occasion was in 1903, when at the invitation of Professor Marshall he helped to form the new Economics Tripos. Economics had hitherto been inadequately included in the History course. Realising its importance in modern life, he sought separate recognition. What interested him though was not economics proper, not the laws of supply and demand, not the mathematics of wealth, but the reaction of men to material surroundings and their attempts to improve them. He held that the study of recent history and of political institutions could help them here, and it was as an advocate of his special subject, Political Science, that he joined forces with Professor Marshall. He became a member of the 'Economics and Political Science Syndicate' which was appointed to report to the Senate. In the ensuing debate he made a short and effective speech, in reply to the pure historians. He regretted that everyone could not know everything, and especially that historians could not know the whole of history, but pointed out that there is a profitable alternative in the analytical method, which studies causes and effects among coexistent phenomena. When the new tripos was established, he became the first Secretary of the Economics Board.

His other university activities are not important. When it came to a vote at the Senate House he was on the side of freedom, but freedom is a word variously applied. We find him for instance in 1898 voting against recognising a Roman Catholic lodging house as a hostel, on the ground that any institution recognised by the University ought to be free to all creeds. Henry Sidgwick and others of his friends voted for recognition, on the ground that Roman Catholics ought to be free to have a hostel. In 1902 he voted for the abolition of compulsory Greek ('disliking the word "compulsory"', comments one of his classical friends, 'and not seeing "Greek" came after it'). And he assisted in the unchaining of women, but without enthusiasm. His suicidal sense of fairness left him no alternative here. If women wanted a degree or a vote or anything else which men monopolised, it was his duty to help them to get it, even if they over- whelmed him afterwards. There were a few women to whom he was devoted and a few to whom he would have confidently entrusted the destiny of mankind, but he was not a really creditable feminist. He did think that men on the whole are superior. 'Oh dear, what is to happen to them?' he once murmured sadly as a stream of aspiring and uninspiring spinsters flowed round the front court of King's; 'I don't know and they don't know.' And then in still lower tones as if his bookshelves might overhear him 'Oh dear! What they want is a husband!' These were his unregenerate thoughts. At other times he remembered the cruelty and parsimony of the Victorian girl's upbringing, and felt that no restitution could be too generous, and there exist among his manuscripts a few pages of a fantasy about Héloïse and a Chorus of Cats which is conceived in this spirit of atonement.

One other academic activity must be recorded, and it is a surprising one: on March 14th, 1900, he rejoined the Cam- bridge University Officers' Training Corps. He did this not because he wanted to crush Kruger, but because he hoped to avert conscription. He is said to have been no more efficient as a soldier than he had been twenty years before, and on January 22nd, 1902, he resigned. The episode is significant: at no time was he a thoroughgoing pacifist.

4

The first of his maieutic books is 'The Greek View of Life' (1896). He had been brought up on Latin and Greek, in a stupid and wasteful way, and it was not until he had got away from the classics that he saw what they meant. Now that he had studied modern conditions and begun to teach politics intelligently, he realised that the Ancients are modern, and that Athens in particular had expressed our problems with a lucidity beyond our power. Nor was this all. Greek literature combined beauty and depth, wisdom and wit, gaiety and insight; it was the greatest literature the world had yet produced, its drawback being that it could only be read by people who had sweated at it for years, and by most of them imperfectly. Translations are the only hope, and while he admitted that most readable translations—e.g. Butcher and Lang's 'Odyssey' and Gilbert Murray's 'Euripides'—get the colouring all wrong, he preferred them to nothing at all. 'The Greek View of Life' might be called an introduction to translations. It is an attempt to show the non-expert the character and environment of hidden treasures and to leave him among them. The idea came to Dickinson 'in our dining room at All Souls Place, in the old arm chair now long vanished from my life—who bought it, I wonder? Does it still exist?' and he began to carry it out at Kandersteg, 'where it consoled me through some bad times'. He looked back on the book as the most useful he had written, and its large circulation in England (it is now in its seventeenth edition) and in the States was a satisfaction to him; 'I still think I have got hold of the central thing, the thing that makes Greek of permanent value to civilisation'. Some of us feel that he got hold of it more satisfactorily in the book of his old age, 'After Two Thousand Years'; he had by then wider experience and greater mastery of style. But 'The Greek View of Life' is the more ordered survey and has found favour with educationists.

Three years after publishing it he went to Greece itself. It was a happy visit with perfect companions: Wedd, Robin Mayor (afterwards a high official in the Education Office); A. M. Daniel (afterwards Director of the National Gallery); and C. P. Sanger.

I had been depressed and worried. But from the moment of landing at the Piraeus life renewed itself in perpetual interest and delight. The Acropolis at Athens revealed to me the meaning of the architectural mouldings I had seen parodied all over Europe. It was like hearing music at last played in tune after a long perversion by slight discords.

Then he remembers 'far too faintly' the line of the sea against Marathon, the Sunium column rising from a sea of red poppies over the sea of blue waves, the plain of Eleusis, the Delphi charioteer. And then comes a passage which carries us on from Greece to another stage in his Socratic activity.

Above all I recall the evening spent at Mistra, above Sparta. We rode through the little village, for such it now is, hidden among orange groves, and then up the slope of Taygetus to that deserted mediaeval town of whose very existence I was unaware. There we stayed the night in a monastery inhabited by a single monk, strolled under the full moon round the deserted streets and churches, and heard from below the chant of the frogs, the 'brekekekex koax koax' of Aristophanes. It was here on this night that there occurred to me the idea of writing a dialogue on Good, which I carried out in the following year or so.

Mistra might symbolise the synthesis at which Dickinson, like Goethe, aimed, and it is appropriate that it should have inspired him to write the first of his dialogues. He often spoke of that moonlit scene where, as in the pine woods above Heidelberg, Classic and Mediaeval seemed to unite and herald the modern, where Faust reigned with Helen and Euphorion was born. He visited Mistra again, thirty years later; the hour was the afternoon, the hills seemed lower, the wild romance had gone, yet how beautiful the place still was, and how solitary. And how exquisite did Greece as a whole remain! How the Mediterranean stimulated his feelings and perceptions as it stimulated Goethe's when he first saw Italy and tore himself away under a sense of duty to return to work in the unfriendly north!

The dialogue form, to which he turned after this visit to Greece, exactly suited his genius. It allowed him to assemble opinions and, so to speak, to tint them. The personages through whom he converses are never coloured vividly; whether they are taken from public figures, like Cantilupe and Remenham, or from his friends, like Audubon and Coryat, or made up entirely, as Wilson appears to be, they are quieter and paler than their equivalents in the world of fiction. He had not the novelist's eccentricity, which permits a sudden swerve from the main course. Whether such eccentricity makes a book more 'like life', is arguable: he, with his generous admiration for method differing from his own, often praised it. His own method, working from within, allowed no vagaries, not even the development of a character under the stress of talk. His business was the argument, human and humanly held, but not allowing irresponsive interludes. Plato and Berkeley were his models, and, like them, he would sacrifice dramatic excitement for consistency and dignity. It is significant that none of his disputants is a female, unless we may include the Queen of the Night, and she is the despair rather than the life of the argument. The instincts and passions could be discussed, and they were discussed with insight and frankness; but they could not be illustrated, any more than the interlocutors could walk away from their chairs. Thus from the opening of 'The Meaning of Good' down to the sombre conversation in the Hermitage of Jesus in 'The Magic Flute', and the Elysian encounter of 'After Two Thousand Years', his people are always sedentary, and the appeal to reason, however much they may ignore it, hangs like a sword over their heads. An essay on 'Dialogue as a Literary Form', which he wrote at the end of his life for the Royal Society of Literature, may be consulted in this connection.

'The Meaning of Good' was written partly at Thursley, where he was stopping with Roger Fry, and partly in lodgings at Westcott. By now he had established his life-long friendship with Miss Melian Stawell, formerly a student of Newnham, and he corresponds frequently with her about his work. They discuss alternative titles, such as 'A Dialogue concerning Good', or 'Many that Say', and she persuades him to print a sonnet from the 1896 Poems as a preface. The dialogue did not displease him in retrospect, though he felt that there were too many characters, and that much of it was frigid. From the philosophical point of view:

What I believe to be true in my own book, is the tension

of experience, the quest of Good, the perpetual dissatisfaction, and the knowledge therefrom derived. When I say that this is 'true' I mean that it is true of those who count in such matters, of Goethe, let us say. What is more questionable, is the mysticism which still haunted me, as it haunted Plato and which appears in the concluding myth. ...It is perhaps worth noticing that while I was still influenced by McTaggart's idea of an eternal perfection of spirits related to one another by love, I also suspected that this might be an illusion, or perhaps I should say an imperfect parable. For my myth, though it does not go beyond that conception yet suggests that there is a beyond.

Just at this time another philosopher had risen to power in Cambridge, in the person of his friend, G. E. Moore. It would be too much to say that Moore dethroned McTaggart, who was essentially undethronable, but he did carry the younger men by storm, and cause Lytton Strachey to exclaim, 'The age of reason has come!' Dickinson, while not going so far as that, felt uneasy. Moore's steady questioning as to What *is* good? What *is* true? had already torn some large holes in the McTaggartian heaven. More care—I speak as a complete outsider here—more care had evidently to be taken as to what one said and how one said it, and intuition seemed less than ever enough. Two years before, in a letter to R. C. Trevelyan (August 8th, 1898), Dickinson is already complaining of the strain:

I'm fagged to death—result of a metaphysical talk with Moore. What a brain that fellow has! It desiccates mine! Dries up my lakes and seas and leaves me an arid tract of sand. Not that *he* is arid—anything but: he's merely the sun. One ought to put up a parasol—I do try to, one of humour, but it has so many rents in it. Oh dear! Surely I once had some rivers? I wish you were here to water me. All poets water. They are the rain. Metaphysics are the sun: between them they fertilise the soil.

Yours so far as there is anything of me,

G. L. D.

Moore's 'Principia Ethica' came out while 'The Meaning of Good' was in proof, and Dickinson, on reading it, discovered that he had been guilty in his dialogue of a new philosophic error which Moore had discovered and had named 'the Naturalistic Fallacy', 'a phrase which always amuses me, for it suggests some kind of unnatural vice. I tried to dodge this error at the last moment, but expect it is there, and also that it doesn't much matter as Moore has probably long ago altered his position on this, as on many other points'. On which note of gay defiance the Naturalistic Fallacy may be left. The dialogue came out in 1901. I remember the enthusiasm, the attractive blue cloth of the binding, the lightness of the volume, the solidity of the contents and my great friend and fellow undergraduate, H. O. Meredith (now Professor of Economics at Belfast), reading as he stalked along King's Parade and chanting, 'You shall never take away from me my Meaning of Good...'. This must be the moment when Dickinson won a name in his own university.

Four years later he published a second dialogue, which won him a name in the outside world. This was 'A Modern Symposium'. It is dedicated to a Cambridge discussion society, and it represents in a glorified form the sort of evening he loved—an evening of contrasted opinions, stated fairly, sincerely and good temperedly. The personages are supposed to be members of 'The Seekers', a club which he had actually tried to found, and they build together, before the morning breaks, a dome of many coloured glass through which eternity shines. It is again the harmony of Plato and Shelley—Goethe perhaps harmonising. Plato contributes most. Dickinson always needs a form which will allow him to express the views of others without judging them by his own, and having experienced in 'The Meaning of Good' the difficulty of the dialogue proper he turns here to the particular form of it used by Plato in the 'Symposium'. Set speeches take the place of conversation and argument. The thirteen speakers

of his choice can state their positions without fear of inter-
ruption all through the calm of an English summer night,
and their rhetoric can pass into poetry when they wish. When
the dawn comes and they vanish into mist or sunlight they
leave a strong impression of actuality behind, and it is no
wonder that the book has been admired not only by Utopians
but by men of affairs.

But still it does not solve the problem, which is perhaps
insoluble, of making the bridge between speculation and
art and that side of life, and what is called practical
politics. For practical politics involves fighting, and the
object of such a book as mine, as it was Plato's object long
ago, is to raise the mind above the fighting attitude. There
lies here obscurely the great problem of the relation of
ideals to passion and interests which I do not seem able
clearly to formulate. It seems impossible to go into active
life of any kind without being ready to kill to lie or to cheat.

And following this line of thought he considers the case of
the man who will think his 'Modern Symposium' and all his
books either pernicious or futile.

I am conscious, in all I have written. and thought, of
complete disinterestedness in the pursuit of truth. But it
does not seem to follow that the other kind of man therefore regards me with particular respect. 'What have you
done?' he will say with Kipling. And if I reply, 'No particular harm', he will say 'No, and no particular good'.
'Neither have you', I might reply, 'I see nothing but
harm.' And somewhere about there the imaginary debate
would end. We have not in fact either the knowledge or
the standards to deal with the subject.

He had to write 'A Modern Symposium' twice before it
satisfied him. It was finished at Baslow in Derbyshire. His
father, now very old, was deeply moved by it, and, in a
conversation reported by Miss Stawell, told her that it was
like 'a re-statement of the incarnation, a vision of the divine
that is growing in men and more than we can comprehend'.
Goldie was impressed by this unexpected sympathy, and said

to Miss Stawell a few days afterwards, 'Isn't it curious that
of all my friends it is my old father who has understood best
what I wanted most to say?' He added, 'Of course in old age
the body fails and the mind is hampered, but it seems to me
the soul goes on and goes further'. His father was perhaps
thinking of the final speech, where Geoffry Vivian (who is
George Meredith) pours new wine into the nineteenth-century
bottles of evolution, yet not more than they can hold. The
episode is interesting as suggesting that Dickinson never
broke from his family tradition, only remodelled it and re-
expressed it.

Following as it did on 'The Letters from John Chinaman'
and his first American tour, 'A Modern Symposium' brought
him some notoriety, and there is no doubt that he could have
become a prominent figure if he cared to improve his position.
But he was bad at improving positions. Each time he wrote
or spoke he went straight back into the inner world, and had
no sense of those subtle movements of the surface which
indicate the drift of popularity. Some writers, and they are
not necessarily worldly or corrupt, have a natural instinct
for self-advertisement. Dickinson lacked this. He had not
the little touch of swagger which draws a crowd, nor the
counter attraction of faroucheness. When he was taken up for
a little by 'society' he found the people he met agreeable,
easy, amusing, sympathetic, quick. But he had nothing in
common with them. He sat in their flickering aviary like a
little dusky bird on a perch, and, being wise, like a bird of
passage. So with the greater public. Although he never did
anything to affront it, he never kept his hand on its pulse,
and by the time the war came it had already begun to move
away. He began to recover it at the very end, through
broadcasting, and many then heard of him for the first time
whom one would have expected to know him well. To a
biographer, the movements of fashion's barometer are interesting, so let me emphasise the very high level touched
by the mercury about 1905. It looked then as if Mr G. L.

Dickinson would easily beat Pater and Gobineau, and even creep up towards Voltaire and Mr Bernard Shaw. Such competition was not to be.

In 1907 appeared 'Justice and Liberty', the last of the trilogy of dialogues. It is more closely connected with his teaching work than the others, and tries to set out the fundamental political truths in which he believed, and upon which he was lecturing in Cambridge and London. He wrote it with difficulty, and felt that it must be difficult to read and repellent, in spite of his effort to introduce Platonic charm. Perhaps he was disappointed with it. It was his last experiment in the Socratic method for twenty-two years.

'The Greek View of Life' and the three dialogues are all closely connected with his main activity during this period: an educational activity. He was always giving out, and chiefly nourishing himself in order that he might give out. He had become aware of other people, and realised that whether we like it or not we are members one with another, and this had led him to concentrate upon politics. He was at one time a sort of Tory-Socialist, during the period covered by this chapter he was a Liberal, and in consequence of the War he became Labour, and remained so till the end of his life. But politics, as he understood them, are not based upon party. They represent the attempt of Man to adapt himself to his environment and to control his future. Knowledge of the past may help him here, and both as a writer and a lecturer Dickinson had this in view. Art and philosophy were subordinated, and the problems of personal salvation and survival after death, which obsess so many introspective people, now occupied less of his time. We must first get the house straight then fill it with beautiful things—such was on the whole his attitude in these years, though he was sensible enough to know that unless we have a certain amount of beautiful things lying about we shall not think it worth while to get the house straight. Which is what distinguished him from the Fabians.

At the beginning of the century he was concerned in founding a monthly magazine, 'The Independent Review'. The first number appeared in October, 1903. Edward Jenks was the editor; Dickinson, F. W. Hirst, C. F. G. Masterman, G. M. Trevelyan and Wedd were the members of the editorial council; Roger Fry designed the cover. The main aim of the review was political. It was founded to combat the aggressive Imperialism and the Protection campaign of Joe Chamberlain; and to advocate sanity in foreign affairs and a constructive policy at home. It was not so much a Liberal review as an appeal to Liberalism from the Left to be its better self—one of those appeals which have continued until the extinction of the Liberal party. Dickinson thus defends the opening number of his review against the free-lancing of Ashbee (Letter of November 11th, 1903):

> If Liberals as you say are not 'constructive' that perhaps is due to the fact that they believe in Liberty which means that they think all legislation can do is to give the utmost scope to individuals to develop the best in them. That I confess is my own point of view. But I believe that to do that will mean gradual revolution of all the fundamentals of society, law of property, law of contract, law of marriage. Yet all that revolution would be abortive unless people have ideals for which they individually care and which are of the spirit and not mere megalomania. I find in Joe and his followers no trace of such ideals. And I shall be very much astonished, I confess, to find them in colonials.

He did not contribute much to 'The Independent' on politics. His article in the first number was on Ecclesiasticism, and directed against the argument that, though religion may not be true, it is necessary to society. Other articles are: 'Religion and Revelation', 'Euthanasia', 'Faith and Knowledge', 'How long halt Ye?' Another article entitled 'Motoring', is a desperate outcry against speed and materialism, and has a magnificent descriptive passage about Hampton Court—one of the finest bits of 'writing' he ever did. The religious and philosophic articles were afterwards included in two little volumes—'Religion: a Criticism and a Forecast' (1905) and 'Religion and Immortality' (1911).

'The Independent Review' did not make much difference to the councils of the nation, but it struck a note which was new at that time, and had a great influence on a number of individuals—young people for the most part. We were being offered something which we wanted. Those who were Liberals felt that the heavy, stocky, body of their party was about to grow wings and leave the ground. Those who were not Liberals were equally filled with hope: they saw avenues opening into literature, philosophy, human relationships, and the road of the future passing through not insurmountable dangers to a possible Utopia. Can you imagine decency touched with poetry? It was thus that the 'Independent' appeared to us—a light rather than a fire, but a light that penetrated the emotions. Credit must be given to Jenks, an able and a pernickety editor, and to his colleagues, but the inspiration was Dickinson's. The first number lies on the table as I write: as fresh and attractive to hold as when I bought it on a bookstall at St Pancras thirty years back, and thought the new age had begun.

5

There is another side of him which finds expression during this period. It is what he calls the religious side, though I am inclined to use the words more cautiously than he himself uses them. When a man is modest, gentle, unselfish, and generally decent, and confesses, as he did, to possessing and valuing certain instincts, there is a disposition among people who have formalised such instincts to annex him as one of themselves. They want him—and no wonder. Christians often said he was a Christian, and when he went to India he was hailed as a devotee of Krishna. If these tributes are regarded as foreign decorations, conferred on a distinguished alien, they

will pass, but they are not issued by his spiritual country.
'All the creeds', he writes, 'are guesses and bad ones.' And
he not only rejected authority and mistrusted ritual. He
condemned the specifically religious virtue of humility. He
effaced himself—never abased himself. He was also suspicious
of martyrdom, believing it to be a method of casting out the
devil by Beelzebub. Only Socrates (he writes in 'After Two
Thousand Years') has managed to remain human and
humorous through martyrdom, and has escaped 'not only
from hypocrisy and hatred but also from the righteous indignation which clouds even the noblest souls'. His opinions
on sex ran contrary to Christian ethics. He also believed
that we have the right to take our own lives, and the duty
of taking the lives of those whom we love if they desire us
to do so, and if by doing so we can save them unbearable
pain. He was a great heretic though a quiet one. And if his
religious feelings are to be incarnated in one figure, Socrates
and no one else is that figure.

'For my own part I've always had a curious feeling that
I should be at my best in old age. I believe it depends on
whether one gets religion', he writes to May. The letter is
dated 1903 (when his actual age was forty), and six years
later he is writing to her again and defining more clearly
what 'getting religion' is. The occasion is their father's death,
and the breaking up of the home which the three sisters had
made for the family at All Souls Place.

> There is no remedy that I know for any trouble centering
> about oneself except a complete and disinterested absorp-
> tion in interests outside oneself. And that sometimes seems
> beyond one's power. My notion of religion is the attitude
> which can say 'Well, what does it matter what I am or
> what happens to me in this extraordinary interesting
> world'. But it is not an easy attitude to get or keep hold of.

This was not his whole notion of religion; and what definition of religion does cover all that we attach to the word in
our varying moods? He was not only concerned with 'this

interesting world' but with whatever may be outside its walls
and he suspected that there is a key to our prison, though we
shall never hold it in hands of flesh and blood. Though the
intellect is our best friend, there are regions whither it cannot
guide us. He touches on this in a letter to Mrs Moor.
Mrs Moor was a friend of his family, who though many years
his senior had become a close personal friend of his own. He
is writing to her (July 27, 1904) about the launching of her
children on the world, and by the characteristic avenue of
sympathy he approaches the unseen.

> I can only dimly conjecture what goes on inside you.
> You have your reserves. And, du reste, how little one
> knows of anyone. 'Quel [sic] solitude que l'âme humaine.'
> But to penetrate that solitude seems the thing most worth
> while, if one could. In any future world in which we might
> meet I think it will be you who will have to look out for
> me, rather than vice versa. I'm sure the 'brainy' people
> will be at a discount there compared to the religious ones!

Three days earlier he had written a 'brainy' letter to Miss
Stawell in which the relations between the intellect and
religious intuition are more carefully analysed. Miss Stawell
had sent him her paper on Christianity and Hellenism.
After discussing it, and agreeing with her that 'Huxley's idea
of nature being "just" (of all things!) makes one foam at
the mouth', he tackles the question as to whether it is possible
to have an 'experience of God', and he concludes that if such
an experience were established, after the requisite critical
tests, it would be a part of knowledge, and not something
unique.

> I mean as much a part of knowledge as the perception
> of beauty, which you instance. People may lack that per-
> ception. And they may lack a perception of God (if there
> is such a perception). But the things would appear to be
> strictly on a level. Only unfortunately, God is a word full
> of the most diverse and confused associations, and therefore
> a very difficult one to use without great danger of sophistica-
> tion. E.g. people have edifying feelings under the stars,

and call it a perception of God. And that carries with it a whole illegitimate theology, as that he is at once omnipotent and good, and other such things, which may be shown to be contradicted by all experience. I mean, that the clarifying process would have to insist rigidly on the exact character of the alleged perception, or apprehension, and on the relating it to all others. Much as we do when a man says he saw a ghost. I daresay you agree. But then the result of such a process I should call a result of knowledge. And that's why I say religion doesn't give us knowledge. What gives us knowledge is knowledge.

He wanted knowledge to extend as far as it can. He had the religious temperament, but he hated all the religious weapons, and thought that much evil can be traced to their use. In the above letter, his caution over the word 'God' is significant. 'God' and 'Jesus' and 'Krishna' trail so many associations and are coloured by so many earthly passions that it is difficult not to be carried away by them, and he was more reluctant than his women friends to be carried away. He saw at the end of those famous short words, which boom like a gong out of darkest night—he saw not light, but more darkness, mass-psychology, crowd-cruelty. To be carried away? Yes, but in which direction? Away from the truth or towards it? We cannot know, because the tests of knowledge do not apply. Towards kindness or towards unkindness? That we can know, and the sinister record of religious idealism in the past made him scrutinise his intuitions carefully, and stick to the intellect, which anyhow sheds less blood.

One may almost say of him that he held nineteenth-century opinions in a twentieth-century way. For him, as for the Victorians, life was a pilgrimage not an adventure, but he journeyed without donning their palmer's weeds. It is significant that though he felt the questions of personal immortality and the existence of God to be so important he never got fussed over them. The struggles and shames of the previous generation with its 'Do I believe?' 'Couldn't I

believe for my family's sake?' 'What will the servants say
when they find out I'm an agnostic?' did not trouble him
after he was mature. One can contrast him, here, with
another academic speculator, Henry Sidgwick. Sidgwick
wanted to believe in God, and his inability to do so caused
him a constant strain. Dickinson, equally conscientious,
was somehow freer and less glum. It would never have
occurred to him as it did to Sidgwick to compose his own
funeral service. As soon as it came to the question of his own
death, his own fate, he turned easy and modern, and one
of the reasons that attracted the young to him was that he
never gave them the sense of nursing a private destiny. He was
not only selfless here, he believed in the imagination—believed
in the sense that he was interpenetrated by it, and so was
not personally mortified either by the victories or by the
defeats of reason. 'Sidgwick was the Cambridge spirit at its
best, and therefore with its limitations most clearly and
tragically apparent', he writes to Mrs Moor. 'He felt, as
he said, that he was put like a soldier to hold just that
position. I have the same intellectual position. Only I feel
increasingly that *all* intellectual positions "hang in a void of
nescience". And in the void and the dark strange wonderful
things brush me. Well ——'

It is difficult for most of us to realise both the importance
and the unimportance of reason. But it is a difficulty which
the profounder humanists have managed to solve.

His most considered pronouncement on religious subjects
was made in America. During his second visit there (1909)
he delivered the Ingersoll Lectures at Harvard. According
to the terms of the lectureship he had to deal with immortality
and he chose as his theme, 'Is Immortality desirable?'
He came to the conclusion that it is—if we can have
a continuity of experience after death and an opportunity
for developing those impulses towards good which seem
so significant on earth. In that sense, not in any other,
Dickinson wished to be immortal, and whether immortality

is possible in any sense he did not know. He hoped. He had no faith. But he was concerned to point out that no conclusive argument against immortality has been brought forward so far. The lecture is reprinted in 'Religion and Immortality'. The dryness of the reasoning and the heat of the emotion are held together by the simplicity and honesty of the style. Only a man who was at once imaginative and devoid of self-consciousness could have delivered it. It is his classic utterance on this particular problem.

As a footnote to these more academic studies comes his interest in psychical research. This had begun when he was an undergraduate, and Colonel Olcott handed round the turban. Now it links up with his general attitude. He valued all evidence about the unseen, and seances, planchette and the rest had to be tested in case they revealed anything of value. Consequently he formally joined the Society of Psychical Research in 1890, and was a member of its Council from 1904 to 1920, also attending its Jubilee celebration. In later life his interest declined. His attitude was of course always sceptical, but he did believe that there was an unexplained residuum in the phenomena which must be carefully examined, whatever religious orthodoxy may feel or scientific orthodoxy think. He did not expect to discover the supernatural because whatever is discovered becomes natural; no, he hoped to increase the sum of ordinary knowledge.

An example of his method shall be given. In 1906 he came across the case of a lady whom he calls 'Miss C.' and investigated it with other observers. Miss C., when she was in the hypnotic state, professed that she had previously lived in the reign of Richard II. This was mixed up with a good deal of tosh about planes and going up into the blue, and would not have interested Dickinson but for its wealth of historical detail. As far as he tested them by the documents all the details were correct. Miss C. alleged that her chief friend at the court was a certain Blanche Poynings, and

Blanche proved to be a historical personage, and—what was so intriguing—a personage of no importance. All the events of the reign were described from the standpoint of this obscure woman, whose character came out vividly as a fussy self-important matron. Miss C., who was truthful and reliable, declared in her waking state that she had never studied history and had read no historical novel of the period. Dickinson began to wonder whether she really had not lived in the reign of Richard II and might not still be visiting Blanche Poynings there. The explanation was distasteful but it had to be contemplated until a better turned up, it could not just be labelled 'unscientific'. Fortunately he solved the mystery. He was at tea with the C.'s, and Miss C. began to use a planchette. Nothing occurred until she was questioned about Blanche Poynings, when the planchette wrote out the words, 'Countess Maud'. 'Countess Maud' proved to be a book which she had read when she was twelve and had forgotten. Blanche Poynings occurred then in passing— a pious, dull person, who owed all her liveliness to the workings of Miss C.'s subconsciousness. Dickinson published this piece of research in the 'Proceedings' of the Society for August, 1911, under the title of 'A Case of Emergence of a Latent Memory under Hypnosis'. It illustrates his seriousness and the high value he places on the creative imagination. Some of the meetings of the Cambridge branch of the S.P.R. were held in his rooms. I attended one of them and remember a funny scene before a mixed audience when a young man who had been hypnotised was told that the room was a flowery glade with a stream down the middle of the carpet. 'How beautiful', he said in mincing tones, as he gathered a nosegay of books. 'I think I'll have a bathe', and he began to take off all his clothes. He had to be restored to the waking state as quickly as possible, and conceivably he had never left it.

With psychical research, that dustbin of the spirit, this imperfect survey of Dickinson's religious outfit must close.

Gibbs's Building

Like all sensitive people, he behaved differently with his different friends, and owing to my limitations we kept to personal matters, literature, and gossip, when we talked. But I could see that everything linked up, that friendship had to do with politics and philosophy with both, and that if he too had his limitations he was, within those limitations, complete. Of most of us this cannot be said. We do not link up within us such gifts as we have. With him, one had the experience of contact with a person who had allowed no internal barriers to survive, so that on whatever side one touched him there was the same impression of unity—an impression which he himself received from his master Goethe.

6

The chief event in his home life during these years was the death of his father, which occurred in the winter of 1908. It came as a terrible blow to his sisters, and particularly to Janet, who had been a devoted nurse. He himself lay crippled with sciatica in the next room, and went to and fro with difficulty during the last hours. 'Janet somehow typifies for me everything best in women: the things they have and men haven't', he writes to Mrs Webb. The letter continues:

Looking back and seeing my father a little in focus I see what a really remarkable man he was—so many sided and so human and in spite of much worldly success so unworldly. I feel I never knew him properly—that is so often the case with near relations. He had a very complete and happy life, gathered the best of all earth had to give, and always kept his horizon open too. To see him dying was like seeing a machine run down. He wasn't there. Is he anywhere or anything? I somehow think he is: but our thoughts are mere inarticulateness, after all, in face of the fact of death.

The absence of intimacy between himself and his father was always a regret to him, especially since he could assign no definite reason for it. It was an inhibition, perhaps dating back to the tuck shop catastrophe at Beomonds. He always spoke of him with affection and admiration, and he was, in every external sense, a devoted son. He now became more and more the support of his sisters, and the actual though not the titular head of the family. All business arrangements devolved on him, and he developed an aptitude for practical affairs and for the handling of money, which is not uncommon among unpractical men. The house at All Souls Place was vacated and finally sold. Hettie had married a Mr Lowes, a distant connection, and had gone to live in Northumberland. May and Janet took a charming little house in Edwardes Square. They often came to Cambridge and there were pleasant travels abroad—for instance in 1910, when they ascended Etna while it was in eruption, and in 1911, when they went to the Italian Lakes; I joined them there and I remember a long walk with him, westward from Iseo, and his remark that it was only in upland çountry such as this that humanity would survive in the event of a great war.

His personal interest continued to centre in Cambridge, though his two greatest friends seldom came there, Fry being often abroad and Schiller usually at Esher. About the time of his father's death he got to know O. P. Eckhard, who was then up at King's. With Eckhard, with his mother, and with others of his family, he remained in touch until the end of his life—indeed there can seldom have been a life where so little was lost. Much had to be sublimated, but that was a process which he expected, and which he furthered as well as he could. When he looked back, he could say with truth that his personal relationships had been enduring, though he was sometimes appalled by their austerity. They were rooted in his idealistic philosophy. And philosophy for him was not only a subject of study, it was the source of all conduct, as it was for his ideal man, the Platonic Socrates.

CHAPTER XI

AMERICA, INDIA, CHINA

I

HE had spent the summer of 1901 in lodgings at Betchworth. There was a long garden sloping down to the river Mole, where he sat and worked through the exquisite English weather. Far away raged the Boer war, disturbing him but slightly. Nearer at hand, also unseen, someone kept singing out of the solitude and the greenery, singing the words of a popular song:

> There is not any other
> To take the place of mother.

The peace, the gentleness, the sentimentality, made his heart ache, for he was about to venture on his first American tour.

He was ostensibly going to visit his brother Arthur, who had been transferred to New York in the course of his accountancy business, as senior partner in the firm of Price Waterhouse. He intended to cover expenses by lecturing at Universities and elsewhere. 'The White Man's Burden' was the title of one of the courses he was preparing; it dealt with India, with the problem of native races generally, with the South African crisis. In 1901 there was no escaping from Kipling, and 'The White Man's Burden' was the obvious title for all coloured problems and implied no cynicism. The alternative course, 'Self Government with British Empire', followed the lines of his academic teaching; it dealt with the English in America, with the British Commonwealth and with Imperial Federation. But neither the visit to his brother nor the lecturing was the real motive of his expedition. He went because he feared that he was falling into a rut at Cambridge, and acquiring the oddities of the unmarried don— those oddities which purport to enrich the personality yet often suck all the juices out of it. America was a drastic pro-

phylactic. She worked, and on his return Mrs Schiller com-
plimented him on his improved appearance and manner.
He became more self-confident, lost his shyness, and could
talk to all sorts of people without displaying or causing discomfort. More than that America did not do and was not
asked to do.

'My enterprise looked a gigantic one for a small skinless
creature to embark on. However once in it it went easily
enough.' He sailed (August 25th) on a transport from Tilbury
with about two hundred fellow passengers and ninety stallions.
The voyage was steady and dull, the Atlantic unattractive,
and for the first time since school he was thrown into continuous contact with 'ordinary' people. They proved to be
alien rather than alarming.

> I have three others in my state room [he writes to May],
> of whom one is the most amusing inconceivable little cad
> I have ever seen. England had the honour of producing
> him, but he has early changed his nationality to America.
> He looks about 17 but professes a rich experience of men
> and things, having run away from school at 14 and taken
> up his abode with a music hall actress. His language is the
> choicest I've ever heard and I've had a great deal of ex-
> perience in that particular respect. His insufferable cheek
> is only equalled by his incapacity. He got up to perform
> at an entertainment we had, and half recited half sung a
> music hall song fortunately inaudible to most of the com-
> pany. I heard only 'D'ye follow me? You do?', and the
> word damn. The funny thing is I rather like the little
> beast.

At his table he was the only male, and successfully coped
with six American ladies at once. He also experienced the
organised merriment which forms so large a part of ocean life:

> At the 'entertainment' [the letter continues] a certain
> 'Colonel' recited a poem composed by himself. The moral
> was that if you don't say your prayers your child will get
> run over by a dray.

But the interesting point was not the moral but the

'style'. It was a sort of newspaper-paragraph telegram English hitched into rhyme, but ignorant of the fact that verse also involves rhythm. We were all much affected and I had the cheek to ask him to send me a copy. I do want one for reasons. He's a dear good 'Colonel', owner of the stallions, and the 'poem' represents a genuine feeling—or would do if it were a poem.... In conclusion I may say very honestly I have not met one single person on this boat who has intellect. They may have every other virtue. But I suppose most people don't have or require intellect. Intelligence no doubt they have.

He was only in America for three months and the detailed diary which he kept is a collection of reminders rather than an account of his impressions. After visiting his brother and founding a durable friendship with his two little nieces, he went straight across to San Francisco. He felt romantic as the train drew out of New York and reminded himself that the country he saw had been recently inhabited by Red Indians. But he was unable to sustain such feelings for more than a few miles, and after a week he arrived something of a wreck. His lectures at Berkeley were on the British Empire, and were very well received. Thrown upon his own resources, he found he could get on with people well, met administrators, business men, missionaries in Chinatown, Chinese: 'but I experienced then what is a common phenomenon with me, the sense that all the time I was acting a part, and that the essential in me was looking on with some detachment and disapproval at the performing animal'.

When this course of lectures was over he went to the Yosemite Valley and wandered about there alone. One day (September 26th), high up above the Yosemite Falls, he had one of the experiences which befell him about half a dozen times in his life. 'Mystic' is too specialised and pretentious a word for the experience. The language of every day can adequately describe it. It represents a heightening of normal consciousness rather than a revelation. In the Yosemite, as at Heidelberg, Frensham Ponds, Snowdon, Mistra, his inner life showed itself more clearly. Writing in his diary that same evening, he only says: 'Saw no one all day. Had idea of a book on America and things in general—sort of a "free Rhapsody", analytic—synthetic—critical—dithyrambic—above all clean cut and intellectual'. Twenty-five years later, the 'Recollections', describe the experience again, and the 'book on America' now appears as part of a larger scheme, and as a symbol of the expansion of his mind.

> I felt convinced at that moment that my business was to discover and illuminate the fundamental notions that should guide modern civilisation. That sounds pretentious enough and I suppose it was, but not consciously to me. Only I did not realise the magnitude of the task nor the pitiably little I could achieve. But the aim was, and is, mine and I cling to it still for what is left of my life.

Of course this aim was not a new one: what is remarkable is its reinforcement by the means of grand scenery, and American scenery. America had already become an inspiration as well as an irritant.

On his way back from California, he stopped at Strong City, Kansas, to see his old friend 'Plump' Hughes, who was ranching there; Pip and Plump had both been with him at the Misses Woodman's school and Tom Hughes their father had tried to protect him at Chester. Then more lecturing at Boston and elsewhere; invitations from Goldwin Smith, Cabot Lodge, and other celebrities; Niagara—which obsessed him as an epitome of the continent. He found the Falls neither attractive nor beautiful. They gave him the sense of tremendous power and bulk, but these were the very things he was learning to hate. For the question always arose, 'Is this power good?' and nature gave him no answer or not a hopeful one.

Sometimes America was the Yosemite and elevated him. At other times she was Niagara and repelled him. It is as Niagara that she usually appears in the 1901 tour:

To C. R. ASHBEE

Pittsburg,
October 20th, 1901.

The two things rubbed into me in this country are
(1) that the future of the world lies with America, (2) that
radically and essentially America is a barbarous country.
...The life of the spirit—the one and only thing which
justifies and dignifies the life of men on earth—is, not acci-
dentally or temporarily, but inevitably and eternally killed
in this country. All that man has achieved in this region,
from Buddha to Goethe, is non existent for Americans.
They have, in their own phrase, 'no use for it'. (I don't
count the adventitious fringe of cultured people who cling
to the skirts of Europe and are despised and hated by true
Americans.) And this American spirit, alias the Chicago
spirit, is to dominate the world. Don't reply with the usual
excuse that the country is 'young'. It was much better
when it was younger still. This is its adult age, its deliberate
choice now it has broken loose from Eastern tradition. It
is a country without leisure, manners, morals, beauty or
religion—a country whose ideal is mere activity without
any reference to the quality of it, a country which holds
competition and strife to be the only life worth living.

This diatribe—which suggests the speech of Ellis in 'A
Modern Symposium'—would have been modified by him in
later years. Perhaps even at the time he writes more violently than he feels, in order to get a rise out of Ashbee.
Perhaps he was feeling tired. Fatigue, in his own opinion,
explains a good deal of his sourness against America. He was
thankful to get away. He escaped to his own country on New
Year's Eve. Never had he felt more British,

> There is not any other
> To take the place of mother.

At Niagara he had received the first copies of 'John
Chinaman'. We shall see that this book, under the title of
'Letters from a Chinese Official', was soon to make a great
stir in the States, partly owing to the naïvety of William Jennings Bryan, who mistook its author for Chinese, and wrote

'Letters to a Chinese Official' (1906) as a reply to it. 'A Modern Symposium' was also to succeed. So that by the time Dickinson paid his second visit to America in 1909 he had become a celebrity, and he was inundated with lecturing engagements, and entertained on an enormous and exhausting scale.

The diary of this second tour (April–August) is a whirlpool of little entries—speeches to the Twentieth-Century Club at Brooklyn on New Evidences of Survival, to the University of Wisconsin on the Aesthetic, the Intellectual, the Religious Ideal, to a public dinner on the Tariff, to schoolgirls on Democracy and Art; delivering the Ingersoll Lecture on Immortality at Harvard. This alternates with meeting Coolidge and Eliot Norton, seeing Niagara again and Mrs Gardiner's house, picnicking on a golf course, sampling Colorado Springs. Long Island: 'See Jolly Trixy the world's fattest girl she weighs 685 pounds, Holy Smoke, she's fat she's awful fat'. He has stuck Jolly Trixy's lilac coloured advert at the end of his diary with the comment 'Inter alia!'

The letters written on the second tour repeat inter alia the previous note of irritability, but they are more sympathetic. Here is an example of the change:

To O. P. ECKHARD

University Club, Madison, Wis.
May 6th, 1909.

I find I can always rise (or fall) to these occasions. My lectures seem to me always to go well, that is I always feel I've 'got' the audience in the first two minutes, and I believe one can't be mistaken over that. I talk quite simply, always in my head, and am sometimes surprised to hear my subconscious self turning out epigrams and exhortations which weren't in the programme at all....

This is rather an interesting place, about the antithesis of Cambridge. It's a 'state' university, and the university helps the state to assess its taxes and value its property, and even has a bureau of classified information for legislators. Whether, in the midst of this, anything like culture survives

I can't judge. I'm inclined to think, after all I've now seen here, that Oxford and Cambridge really now are the last refuges of that. And that perhaps we ought to realise that, and concentrate on that aspect of things. Three Canadians the other night besought me almost with tears to resist all reforms in our ancient universities. They said, in their picturesque language, that they had 'got us skinned alive' in all applications of science, but they knew in their hearts that we have the one thing they won't get by all their efforts: disinterested intellectual culture. Certainly America is only drawing interest (hundred per cent.) on the capital of European ideas. And if we cease to generate the ideas...?
I feel that all I have said about America is true; but I omitted a good deal—perhaps all—that is most important. Their candour, good temper, immediate and fearless experimentation, sense for fact &ct. is the positive pole of their incapacity for discussions and ideas. They *bore* me as it is impossible to be bored in Europe, but that is because *any* fact interests them, and *no* idea except as it can be shown to be in direct relation to fact. That makes a type of conversation particularly assommant. But I don't think it implies a bad type of character. Of course I confess myself terribly flattered by the way they read my books, though that seems incompatible with what I have just said. All the economists here take my Justice and Liberty quite seriously.

So, half charmed, half critical, and wholly fatigued he flounders through an experience which was familiar to other foreign lecturers but which is particularly humorous in his case, for one contrasts it with the calm of Cambridge, the slipping into the train for the London School of Economics, All Souls Place, slipping back, rowing down the Thames, bicycling with Fry, going to Greece with Mayor and Wedd. 'Good Lord, what a life!' he exclaims to May, and though he is pleased at being appreciated more effusively than in England he wonders how much lies behind the uniform cordiality of Americans. In one way he merited their praise, for he never talked nonsense to them in the dishonouring and dishonourable way which was quite common at the time, and he never talked down to them. He gave them his best. In particular the Ingersoll Lecture ranks with his finest and most careful work.

His real objection to the country was the absence of personal relationships as conceived in Cambridge discussion societies and indeed in England generally. So much cordiality, so little intimacy, such gleaming teeth, so little tenderness, such mixing, so little fusion! Co-education, as exhibited at the Madison University at Wisconsin, fairly made him shudder. The young men there went 'girling' or 'fussing' and the young women said 'our fussers are coming to-night' and the indecent game didn't even culminate in sexual acts. He sympathised with the Scotchman who wanted less chastity and more delicacy. Human intercourse, whatever its type, seemed sterile, all faces (except the negroes') seemed devoid of emotion and thought. This—not the absence of culture— intimidated him. Culture can wait, but how can any civilisation grow out of people who can't or daren't be intimate with one another? There just isn't the soil.

Fortunately he made one great American friend who, if he didn't solve the problem, complicated it, which was a relief. Just as he had found Mrs Webb when Extension lecturing as a youth, so in this later and more triumphant scramble he managed to discover Russell Loines. His friendship with Russell Loines—whom he had first met when returning from the 1901 tour—made all the difference in 1909. He had here an American with whom he felt at home and who gave him a home. He stopped with Loines on Staten Island, where Rupert Brooke was afterwards to be entertained at his introduction, and went with him for a short tour in the Adirondacks. Loines was more than a host; he helped to make the continent less like Niagara. His death in 1922 was a great loss to Dickinson, and incidentally impoverishes his biography, for he would have given some inside information which I lack. I should like to have known what general impression Goldie made upon the Americans he met. Did he seem to them better or worse than the other cultured lecturers from the old world who were in circulation at the time? Did his candour strike them as offensive, his fairmindedness as feeble? Or, like Mrs Webb and Loines, did they see through to the light within and realise its kinship with earth and heaven? These questions cannot now be answered. The moment of his American notoriety has passed. Niagara continues. But, sharing his optimism about America, I would like to think that his influence still persists there, though the newspapers have ceased to quote his name and the friends who treasured it most are dead.

On getting back to England he contributed some articles to the 'English Review', and republished them, rather reluctantly, as the first section of 'Appearances' (1914). His feelings about America had changed after the election of Wilson and were to become still more favourable, and he regretted his earlier note of exasperation. However, the articles made a good pendant to the letters about the East, which form the bulk of the book, so he admitted them and he emphasises that however critical he is of the West, it is there rather than on the East that he fixes his hopes.

Another result of the American tours was a four-act play, 'Business'. I will give a short résumé of it since it has not been printed. He got the idea partly from I. M. Tarbell's 'History of the Standard Oil Company' and partly from his personal impressions of Chicago, Pittsburg, etc. 'Business' deals with the efforts of William Rackham, a petroleum king, to crush his rivals and establish a monopoly. Circumstances bring him up against the owner of a petroleum refinery, his old love, Mrs Bond. He ruins her, firstly by corrupting one of her employés, and secondly by taking advantage of her private difficulties, for her son has forged a note to pay his gambling debts, and it has to be redeemed. Here is the world of Rockefeller; only money counts, human relations are eviscerated, religion is distorted into something false and insipid. Into it drifts an inhabitant from another world—a picture by Giorgione and the contest between the two makes the spiritual plot of the play. Money can buy a Giorgione, but cannot measure it: that has to be done on a different pair of scales. When Rackham is murdered by the employé, to whom he refused a job on the ground that he could not be trusted, he leaves Mrs Bond an enormous legacy, on condition that she enters his combine. She refuses, and her son will be arrested, but the situation is saved by the connoisseur from Europe who owns the Giorgione. Realising that cash will now be of practical use, he sells the picture to Rackham's widow, who fancies that the nude figure with a star on its forehead symbolises petroleum. 'What's money for except to be used?' he remarks; 'I might be a rich man if I liked. I shall be, perhaps, when I'm degraded enough. Art's a very profitable thing if you make a business of it.' And he redeems the forged note, and presumably marries Mrs Bond. 'Business' was produced by the Stage Society, on March 19th and 20th, 1911, the author's name being given as John Goldie. The part of Mrs Bond was taken by Kate Rorke. Before Rackham is murdered, he reads out to his wife his forthcoming address to 'Christian young men of business'—a document for which Dickinson had historical evidence.

He heard conflicting opinions about the play and cherished a casual printed remark of Shaw's referring to him, among others, as a playwright of promise. 'I had the personal experience (only too common I suppose!) of finding my own play very interesting and moving on the stage. But I am pretty sure that was not the general opinion. However, I was satisfied and thought of writing other plays.' He did, as a matter of fact, finish two just before the war. One of them was on the subject of Lassalle and Helene von Racovitza. The Stage Society rejected it, but the Manager of the Little Theatre professed enthusiasm and was to produce it in the autumn of 1914. Then came the war, the Manager lost both the typescript copies, and Dickinson was left with only two acts of the final version and 'felt no impulse to reconstruct the rest from memory'. The manuscript of 'Lassalle' exists in composite form, but I have not succeeded in getting a clear estimate of it in this condition. His own view of it was favourable. His third play, a fantasy called 'Peace and War', has fortunately survived intact, and will be considered later.

Neither 'Business' nor the chapters of 'Appearances' offer that imaginative pronouncement on America of which he had a vision in the Yosemite Valley. Other activities claimed him. America survived as a distant prospect, which at the time of the Peace Conference included a rising sun, and which never excluded the stars.

2

On October 11th, 1912, I hung over the edge of a ship at Port Said—my first glimpse of the East or of Dickinson in a sun-helmet. He bobbed far below me in a little boat, looking dishevelled and tired. He had been stopping at Cairo, and he was joining R. C. Trevelyan and myself to visit India. G. H. Luce was also with us on his way to a job in Burma.

Dickinson was the holder, and the first holder, of an Albert Kahn Travelling Fellowship. Kahn, a French Jew of imagination and disinterested genius, believed that acquaintance with other countries may help international peace and had founded fellowships to the value of £660 each for this purpose. He was a Bergsonian, and his fellows were the extreme forward point of the 'élan vital', and bore a grave philosophic responsibility. Dickinson, no Bergsonian, was an excellent choice. He was both open-minded and well-grounded—an unusual combination. His Report, which he presented to the Kahn Trustees in 1913, is within its limits a masterpiece. (Reprinted in 1914 as an 'Essay on the Civilisation of India, China, and Japan'.) The normal itinerary of a Kahn Fellow included America; but since he had already been there twice it was arranged that he should confine himself to the East.

We hated the boat, but the voyage to Bombay was fascinating. I have been that way since, but have never again seen such colours in the sea, so many flying fish, dolphins and sharks, such sunsets, such flights of birds and of butterflies (the last named meeting us when we were still two days from the Indian coast). On board were many Anglo-Indians, as they were then called. These I have often seen again. The contrast between their clan and our clique was amusing. We were dubbed 'The Professors' or 'The Salon', and there was the same little nip of frost in these jests as in the title of 'The Three Graces' which had been fastened on Dickinson and his school friends at Charterhouse. They recognised that we were gentlemen, sahibs even, yet there was a barrier. No doubt we did look queer, and once when we were all four in a row at our tea a young officer opposite could not keep grave. We played chess on Sundays, compared Dostoievsky with Tolstoy publicly, argued over the shape of the earth at the breakfast table, balanced on bollards instead of playing deck games, and discovered another young officer, a very different one, Kenneth Searight, who pursued romance and poetry in a solitary deck chair. We kept diaries. 'The extent of the heat may be judged from the fact that, on descending to my cabin, a tube of Kolynos was found in a semi-liquid condition' is a sentence which Dickinson gave me to put in mine. He said it was the ideal Diarist style. I transcribe it here not for that reason but because nonsense is too seldom recorded. Wit and humour get put into a biography, foolery is missed out. It is so evanescent, it needs a gesture or a smile to fix it, and these cannot be transcribed. Dickinson could be ever so gay and ridiculous, laughing and talking at once, making everyone laugh, shooting out little glints of nonsense like flying fish. If one could convey the little glints, the sea and the sky would take care of themselves. The last time I saw him (outside a hospital) was in my garden which was overdone with pink sweet-williams. He murmured: 'I don't like pink. I did speak to God about it; however some people do, and anyhow it can't be helped'. Here again it is futile to transcribe nonsense. One needs the gentle voice, the innocent and unsuccessful flowers.....

We went on shore at Bombay in a native boat, rowed by ugly men with beautiful skins, who reminded us of the stupider apostles. Then we parted for a time, Dickinson and Bob Trevelyan going off with a deplorable servant called Samuel, whom they shared, and who wailed 'this is no proper arrangement' as soon as he had to do any work. They took turns at controlling Samuel. From the moment he landed, Dickinson's tour became strenuous. In three months he not only saw the most important sights of India, but presented many introductions, official and non-official, English, Hindu, and Mohammedan, and also did some speaking. His anxiety to learn, his great conversational powers, his intelligence and gentleness, his interest in religion, his readiness to enter into every point of view, made him popular with Indians of various types. But as a rule he was not very happy with them, and though he was stronger socially than he had been on his American tours he still longed, vainly, to be alone. For the English he felt either strong sympathy or strong aversion and in either case he pitied them for having such an uncongenial job.

For the hardworking and conscientious Anglo-Indians I met I felt a sympathy tinged with a kind of despair. For it seemed almost that the more conscientiously they did their work the further they were from the native sympathy and mind. But that too may be an illusion. I am however pretty sure that the irony that brought the English into contact with the Indians is only equalled by that which brought them into contact with the Irish. The barrier on both sides of incomprehension is almost impassable. I feel this incomprehension very strongly myself. Indian art, Indian religion, Indian society, is alien and unsympathetic to me. I have no sense of superiority about it, but one of estrangement. What indeed is there or can there be in common between the tradition of Greece and that of India?

Our paths in India crossed several times, and I will add a few personal memories, mostly of a light character. I can see him cowering under the great sandstone portal of a temple, repelled by the monstrosity of its forms. I can hear him apologising for keeping an elephant waiting under the Fort at Gwalior and receiving the monumental reply 'Elephants sometimes wait four hours'. I attend an address which he gives to orthodox Hindus at Lahore, under the misconception that they belong to the Brahmo Somaj; the audience is polite and sad. I watch him receive the good news of the election of President Wilson, also at Lahore. And there are two memories which dominate. The first is Peshawar, where we went to stop with Kenneth Searight. We were escorted up the Khyber as far as Ali Masjid, and there Dickinson sat by the edge of the track, watching the caravans pour past him out of central Asia, and registering this new proof of the restlessness of the world. We dined at the mess that evening—the Royal West Kents. He was instantly beloved. The young officers were charming to him, and looked so fine in their gay jackets that militarism became permissible. They called him 'The Don', and said 'I say, will he put you in a book', to one another. They made him swallow prairie oysters. They got rather drunk, in exquisite style, while Bob Trevelyan sported with them, and Dickinson and the C.O. sat apart, a couple of benign but contrasted uncles. Looking back to that jolly evening, I see him then for the first time as a solid figure, who has won his own place in the world, and holds it firmly. This is the time when I begin to use him as a touchstone, and to condemn those who fail to appreciate him.

My second memory is of Chhattarpur, a remote native state in the Bundelkhand Agency which has since figured in J. R. Ackerley's 'Hindu Holiday'. We lived for nearly a fortnight at Chhattarpur in the Guest House on the top of a little hill. Monkeys played with their children on the slopes, the city lay below, lovely at all times, but loveliest in the early morning, when the spires of the Jain temples pierced up through the grey and white mists and the trees looked like cushions of clouds. Down in the city, struggling to meet us, dwelt our host, the Maharajah, and a constant stream of notes, counter-notes, landaus, motor cars, and horsemen passed up and down the hill. The Maharajah was a tiny and fantastic figure, incompetent, rusé, exasperating, endearing. He lived for philosophy and love, and he hoped that the two were one. He is dead now. 'Tell me, Mr Dickinson, where is God? Can Herbert Spencer lead me to him, or should I prefer George Henry Lewes? Oh when will Krishna come and be my friend? Oh Mr Dickinson!' I found these questions grotesque, but Dickinson attuned them to his own Platonism, and there was instant sympathy. When he was well enough (for Chhattarpur disarranged his digestion) he sat with the Maharajah in the palace courtyard, under an umbrella as big as a tent, and spoke with him as one seeker with another. Sometimes the Chaplain from the military cantonment joined them, a friendly bounder who shouted 'Come Maharajah, why don't you eat beef? do you good', and we winced with horror and the Maharajah smiled into his sleeve, and the Private Secretary said afterwards 'The padre sahib is a very nice man indeed, he has no interest whatever in religion, and that is suitable for a clergyman'. Or the Political Agent would come, a more sinister figure, and try to interfere with the Maharajah's private affairs. Or there would be religious plays—the Birth of Krishna, etc.—enacted in the evening. Or Dickinson and his host drove out to another palace, Mau, a lovely ruin on a lake, and arrived there when their car did not break down ('See, Mr Dickinson, that balcony—did Hamlet climb up there to visit Juliet?'), and they meditated over the lotuses, upon which a nymph, the daughter of the lotus who fed upon lotuses, had once walked, and they saw the myriads of water-fowl cloud the setting sun, and the Maharajah offered Dickinson his palace of Mau for ever, forgetting that he had given it to me only two days before. For we were all philosophers. But Dickinson was philosopher in chief, and here the Maharajah showed his sense. If India ever came near winning, it was at Chhattarpur.

China, not India, won, and on Tuesday, December 12th

our paths divided finally, and my friends set off in the direction of the Far East. The stars were cantankerous, and no day could be found by the court astrologers which favoured both them and myself, who was stepping westward. The Maharajah was distressed, but he could scarcely hesitate where the safety of Mr Dickinson was concerned. 'Mr Forster, I am very sorry, but. . . .' So I lost my train connections, my servant got no food, and when I arrived at Bhopal armed with a distinguished introduction to its Begum, she omitted to receive me. The other two proceeded safely, as did Samuel.

He came to feel that the main cleavage in civilisation lies not between East and West but between India and the rest of the world. His further course was to Benares (where Trevelyan had to read 'The Oxford Book of English Verse' to exorcise Hinduism), to Calcutta (where they enjoyed the hospitality of the Tagores), to Madras, Southern India, Ceylon. Here are extracts from letters both written on January 20th, 1913 from camp near Madras, to illustrate his later impressions.

To MRS MOOR

We're in the real jungle, forest around us for miles, and I'm so happy! I sit alone in a dry river bed and watch things and listen. Monkeys are jumping by in the trees. And though I don't see tigers I hear they do pass at nights and leave trails. The butterflies are exquisitely beautiful. Unfortunately there are other flies, at this moment tormenting me. But you can't have everything; or, rather, you must have everything! A wasp has been depositing paralysed spiders in a hole in one of the tables, laid her eggs, and carefully sealed it up with wax. What a thing nature is! How do the spiders feel? Let's hope they're unconscious! In the face of these things, most religious talk seems 'tosh'. If there's a God, or gods, they're beyond my ken. I think perhaps, after all, the Hindus took in more of the facts in their religion than most people have done. But they too are children, like the rest of us.

To H. O. MEREDITH

Anglo-Indian society is the devil—it's worse than America. We eschew it all we can. It's the women more than the men that are at fault. There they are, without their children, with no duties, no charities, with empty minds and hearts, trying to fill them by playing tennis and despising the natives....

There is no solution of the problem of governing India. Our presence is a curse both to them and to us. Our going will be worse. I believe that is the last word. And *why* can't the races meet? Simply because the Indians *bore* the English. *That* is the simple adamantine fact.

I disagree with the last paragraph. Perhaps he was overtired, perhaps temperamentally averse, but he never found in Indian society either the happiness or the peacefulness which have made my own visits to the country so wonderful. He has recorded some of his impressions in the Kahn Report, in 'Appearances', and in articles written at the time for the 'Manchester Guardian' over the signature of 'Don'. At the end of his life, he wrote a significant letter to an Indian correspondent (p. 228). As to his main conclusion, it is that India is the home of religion; a conventional conclusion, but he reached it by his own route. It was a revelation to him that men could take such constant and passionate interest in the unseen, and less of a revelation that neither their conduct nor their art seemed to benefit thereby.

3

If Dickinson visited America in the hope of self-development and India from reasons of curiosity, it was in a very different spirit that he approached China. He came to her as a lover, who had worshipped from afar for years. In a life which contained much disillusionment, China never failed him. She stood firm as the one decent civilisation, and when he mourned over her it was not because she had disappointed him but because he had lived to see her destroyed by the violence and vulgarity of Europe. In his last years, her fate seemed to epitomise mankind's. If China could have been saved, he would have been persuaded that humanism is indestructible. His was an impersonal love; no private relationship coloured it, although he became friendly with many individual Chinese. It rested upon natural sympathy and intellectual affinity. He once amused the students at a Summer School by saying: 'I am speaking to you about China, not because I know anything about the subject nor because I once visited the country, but because, in a previous existence, I actually was a Chinaman!' And when one looks at the portrait of him in his Chinese cap (p. 234), or indeed as a boy (p. 14), one realises a physical as well as a spiritual kinship. The Hellenist, the disciple of Shelley and of Goethe, is precipitated, with a slight alteration of focus, into a Confucian plane.

The first link in the connection was fortuitous. At the beginning of the century, previous to his first American visit, he was in a restless state of mind 'such as usually, in my case as in those of greater men, precedes composition'. He wanted to make some fundamental criticism of western civilisation, which should be read by the general public, and should have some kind of artistic form. He experimented in various ways, and tried to utilise one of Swift's myths in the form of 'Letters from a Houyhnhnm'. The gulf between his temperament and Swift's was too wide, and the medium proved unsuitable. Roger Fry then suggested that he should try a Chinese setting; China was in the foreground politically, owing to the Boxer riots and the European expeditions to suppress them, and he had read Giles' 'Gems of Chinese Literature', and 'La cité chinoise' by Eugène Simon. The suggestion bore fruit, the painful period of incubation ended, and at the same time as he was writing 'The Meaning of Good' he produced the first four 'Letters from John Chinaman' and sent them to the 'Saturday Review' where they appeared anonymously.

A comedy then developed. He intended no deception, knowing that there was good precedent for that kind of form in literature, and not supposing anyone would be taken in. A correspondent of the 'Saturday Review' pointed out that the letters could not really be by a Chinese and there the matter seemed to end. He added some more letters, and after he had sailed for America the little volume, soon to be famous, was published by his friend R. Brimley Johnson, with a grotesque picture of a Chinaman on the cover. 'I didn't think much about the book for I was well accustomed to being ignored.'

The presentation copies of this edition followed him over the Atlantic to Niagara of all places, and when he was lying in bed in the hotel there his brother Arthur entered in a state of great animation.

My brother said that he had been reading the book, and that it was 'wonderful'. He did not know it was mine, and felt a natural disappointment when I revealed the fact. For who can think as much of the opinions of a friend or relative as they do of an unknown author? They know too much about him! I remember being much pleased and excited at the moment. But the book would I suppose have fallen as dead as my others, if George Trevelyan had not quoted it in an article in the 'Nineteenth Century', which excited some attention. People then began to speculate as to whether it was really by a Chinaman, and a good many copies were sold. It then penetrated to America, and there everybody seems to have accepted naively its Chinese origin. It was attributed to the then Chinese ambassador; and Mr Bryan, the famous politician, thought it worth while to write a special reply to it, in which he observed, among other things, that clearly the writer had never seen the inside of a Christian home. Before publishing his book, he ascertained that the author was really an Englishman, and he said as much in his preface. But he thought his book none the less worth publishing, and it is not for me to dispute that it may have been.

Unlike much that he wrote, the 'Letters from John China-man' appeared at the right psychological moment. The re-action from the Boer War and from economic Imperialism was just gathering force, and Englishmen were sensitive about aggression and exploitation to a greater degree than they would have been a few years before, and to a degree which became impossible for them after the Great War. For a short time his words travelled far beyond his usual liberal and academic surroundings, and, by their power and beauty, moved people to think of the flaw in European civilisation. For that, and not the wrongs of China, is his theme. 'I still think this book well written and its contents true and important.' There is said to be a translation of it into Gujarati by Gandhi. When this was reported to him he displayed no pleasure but characteristically remarked that he had written for the West, not for the East.

Besides being topical, 'John Chinaman' is famous for the beauty of its prose, and particularly for the sumptuous yet delicate passage beginning 'A rose in a moonlit garden...', a passage which has been quoted by Logan Pearsall Smith in his anthology. Here is oratory—so winged with poetry that the words nearly leave the earth, but they just remain on it, and rightly, for their purpose is persuasion. All that is delicate and noble challenges all that is brutal and vulgar, and he employs for the contest neither appeals to the empyrean nor arguments of force, but the subtlest of all weapons, good taste. To Mrs Moor he writes (February 9th, 1902):

My little J.C. book is approved by many people whose approval I value, and that gives me satisfaction. I am just beginning to realise that I have a certain faculty of appealing to what I call the 'life of the spirit', and that I have no other faculty. So I may as well do what I can in that line for the future, and let others, more competent, run the affairs of the nation. Only I can't illuminate the spirit—my own or anyone else's—without bringing an immense amount of the fuel of contemporary issues, worries, and controversies. G. Trevelyan sent J.C. to Meredith—and he says it is 'excellent' and 'might be thought timely, were the ears of England open'. A most Meredithian phrase.

Though he never affected scholarship, and learnt no Chinese, he now began to attract educated Orientals who were visiting England, particularly students. An Anglo-Chinese society was formed at Cambridge—largely recruited, it is said, by Chinese from Singapore who knew less about China than he did, but the interchange of ideas flourished under his auspices. The Chinese amused and charmed him in a way in which Indians did not. 'Clearly I'm Chinese and not Indian, though I believe I was Indian from the age of twenty to twenty-five and would have become an ascetic with the smallest encouragement', he tells R. C. Trevelyan. And as the time of his Kahn Fellowship tour approached, it was chiefly for China that he prepared himself.

To o. p. eckhard

King's College,
June 12th, 1912.

We had an Anglo-Chinese dinner on Monday. The secretary of the Chinese legation, Mr Kwei, was there. He sat next me and talked the whole time, and I hardly understood a single word. It was like a nightmare. One thing however I grasped after half an hour's explanation. He applied to my 'Letters of John Chinaman' what I understood is a Chinese proverb: In another's wine cup I make my own complaint. This I think explains itself, and is quite true in its application. Mr Kwei got drunk before the end; he began to embrace me, and I thought he would never have finished shaking hands. The net result is that I hope I shall get much assistance in my travels to China.

When we parted at Chhattarpur as already described, he went via Ceylon to Singapore, made a trip to Java and Sumatra, and then proceeded from Singapore to Hong Kong and Canton. As soon as he was among people whose features and physique were Mongolian, he felt happy. At Canton, Bob Trevelyan left him, and hurried back to Cumberland, in order to be in time for the Trinity Lake Hunt, an annual event to which he was romantically addicted. Dickinson found Trevelyan a delightful companion, yet he probably gained by being left alone on the threshold of China. He was thrown on his own resources, and was obliged to look at a country about which he had hitherto only read, written and dreamed. Canton he loved. Then came Shanghai and politics and an interview with Sun Yat Sen; he was too sensitive to be a good interviewer, and 'didn't get much out of him!' Then a solitary voyage of ten days on the Yangtse, in pouring rain, which kept him in his cabin and obliged him to play many games of patience. Then a long railway journey to Peking.

At Peking he stopped several weeks, seeing much both of English and Chinese, and it would be possible, from his diary and letters home, to construct a complete account of his movements. But the movements of a tourist's body are not worth recording unless they generate movements inside his mind. Here are two typical reactions. The first is a rhapsody in free verse, such as often occurred to him while in the Far East. As soon as he got clear of heavy India little poems began to flit and glint as though winged by some new spirit in the depths of him. This particular poem records a visit to the Temple of Agriculture at Peking.

A Temple

What do they hide?
The cypress Avenue and the coral wall,
The green and amber roof, what do they hide?

A wooden plough and an altar consecrate to earth.

An emperor once held the plough,
An émperor made sácrifice.

The coral wall is falling now, falling the amber roof,
The cypresses decay, the altar crumbles;
Crumbles the altar consecrate to Earth;
But Earth abides.

On the day previous, he had been taken to visit a very different type of temple. He writes of it to a friend:

Oh, but the most amusing thing I want to tell you, I went to a Chinese banquet, at which 'sing-song-girls' were introduced. They are in fact superior accomplished and expensive tarts, rather pretty, and I shall suppose attractive to the normal man. But imagine me behaving as is expected on such occasions, with one of them on my knee at one time, and smoking the same cigarette; really it was rather funny, though very embarrassing. And though the girls are to be had, I gather it is only if they like you, and for large money. Some of them were wearing pearls and diamonds. We adjourned to their house—I suppose really a superior brothel—and had a second feast of Chinese dishes, very trying to a weak stomach. Most people seemed to leave without anything happening. They were all very 'respectable' commercial Chinese.

One compares this banquet with the restaurant in Paris many years back, where in even greater discomfort he had met a French lady. And one contrasts it with the 'girling' and 'fussing' which had so revolted him in the mixed university at Wisconsin. What seemed important to him in sexual as in other relationships was the quality of the emotion aroused. He disliked vulgarity more than frivolity, more indeed than anything, and at all events these Chinese were never vulgar; they showed a well-bred combination of reticence and frankness in their levity as in the more serious intercourse of life. They understood personal relationships in the sense in which he and Cambridge understood them and America has failed to understand them, and that is why Chinese civilisation did not disappoint him, nor vary greatly from his preliminary vision.

Dear Forster,
Peking,
June 8th, 1913.

(Hand this on to Bob, if he enquires for me. I can *not* write to everyone, at least not in an interesting way. I get bored with repeating myself. But I was glad of Bob's letter by yours of the 22 May and will probably write later from Japan.)

Yours of 22 May. (That, I think, is the business method.)

China is a land of human beings. India, as it glimmers in a remote past, is supernatural, uncanny, terrifying, sublime, horrible, monotonous, full of mountains and abysses, all heights and depths, and for ever incomprehensible. But China! So gay, friendly, beautiful, sane, hellenic, choice, human. Dirty? Yes. Peking, the last day or two, is all but impossible even in a rickshaw—pools, lakes, of liquid mud. One understands the importance of the sedan chair, and the wall side 150 years ago in Europe. Poor? Yes. But never were poor people so happy (I speak with all the superficiality you care to credit me with). A Chinese house in Peking is beyond description exquisite: its court yard, with trees and flowering shrubs, its little rooms and hall, paper-windowed, perfect in proportion and design, its gaily painted wooden cloisters. And you approach them by a slum. A level, rational people—a kind of English with sensitiveness and imagination. An immense background, I admit, of ghosts and devils—just to add spice to life—one prays to them, when things go a bit wrong, otherwise one laughs at them. No reaches into the infinite, but a clear, non-restricted perception of the beautiful and the exquisite in the Real. But the hand of the Powers, or rather the foot, is on her throat, I don't know whether she can pull through. Said one of them to me; 'The Powers put their foot on China and say "Get up, you brute!" "I'll get up", says China, "when you take away your foot!" "No! you get up, and I'll take away my foot!"' The same gentleman remarked: 'British rule in India is excellent—at water closets'.—This, of course, is technically incorrect.—He was mad, but a madman of genius. He called at 3, and talked till 7.30, when I had to dismiss him —remarking, at intervals, 'but I came to hear you talk'— whereupon he was swept away even more on the flood. Yes, China is much as I imagined it. I thought I was idealising, but I now doubt it. Of course, Lama priests are sturdy beggars and buddhist priests aren't much better. Then the country! Round Peking, it's Italy. You go out to the hills, and wander from monastery to monastery, each more exquisitely placed than the last. Happy people who have travelled in the interior tell even more wonderful tales. One province, Rose tells me, is a land of beautiful mountains, fields of flowers, and farmers tilling their own land who are also scholars and gentlemen. He told one of them about intensive methods of cultivating rice. And when they parted, the Chinaman said: 'You, a stranger, have come to us and honoured and delighted us with your talk. I shall consecrate to you a corner of my farm, and try the experiment you suggest'. Then they are the *only* democratic people—in their manners as well as their institutions—perfectly self-respecting, perfectly courteous and friendly, and altogether declining to be hustled into doing anything they think unreasonable. If such a people could be lifted on to a higher economic level, without losing these qualities, we should have the best society this planet admits of. Whereas I believe *everything* in India will have to be and ought to be swept away—except their beautiful dress and their beautiful brown bodies—there they *do* score off the ugly, but fascinating Chinese. But their caste! And their whole quality of mind. No, it's all wrong. C'est magnifique, mais ce n'est pas la vie, any more than the Middle Ages were. I am rather surprised at all this that has tumbled out of my pen. I suppose the 'Subconscious' has been working it up, unbeknown to me. Take it for what it is worth, and not too solemnly. It has truth in it—a little scintilla of that dry flint. Well, you did well in India. Does it seem like a dream, now you're home? I must get on to Japan before long, but plans are difficult to make. If you write, best address at 11, Edwardes Square. *Shall* you write a book on India? *I* shall *not*. I shall write a book of essays called 'East and West', gracefully alluding, in a remote way, to facts. G.L.D.

He does not mention in this letter that he had lately had a serious accident. He had gone out one morning riding on a pony, been thrown, and fractured the base of his skull. He was carried back in a dazed state to his hotel, bleeding from nose and ears, and the consequences would have been serious but for the promptness and skill of his friend Yetts, who was at that time Acting Physician to the British legation; he is now Professor of Chinese Art and Archaeology in the University of London. Yetts received him into his own house, performed a slight operation, and he made a rapid recovery. In a week he was writing again, and before a month elapsed he was strong enough to make an expedition which may be regarded as the soul of his visit to China.

This was a pilgrimage to the home of Confucius. Leaving Peking with Dr Yetts on June 17th, he climbed, two days later, the sacred mountain of T'ai Shan. It was dusk when they reached the top. They slept in a temple, saw the full moonrise and the sunrise, and spent the next day wandering about. Moved by the beauty, freshness, and antiquity of the mountain he experienced once more the enhanced sensibility that came to him through scenery. Mistra had turned him to dialogue, the Yosemite had inspired him with the idea of interpreting America. On T'ai Shan his feelings were definitely religious. He desired to worship, like the thousands of pilgrims who had preceded him. To worship whom or what? He discusses this in 'Appearances'. Writing to Mrs Webb at the time he says:

> Two cuckoos calling to one another across ranges and ranges of hills, bare and grey-green with sun. And me lying on the top of the most sacred mountain in China, where for four thousand years God has been worshipped, according to Chinese legend; where certainly Confucius came, and emperor after emperor, and streams of pilgrims year after year. A path lined with cypresses and flight after flight of rock stairs brings you to the top. And there we slept in the temple with images of Taoist gods watching us and saw the full moon over the plain at the sunrise. And I have had one of the great days that come now and again. I wish I could communicate it to you. But it evaporates in words, so I got this down to show I was thinking of you.

The same day he writes another verse rhapsody; the most touching of the series.

On T'ai Shan

Not for the young alone
Cuckoo, voice of the spring,
Not for the young alone that liquid note:
But for all whom the years have freed
From the prison of youth and age,
To the one Life freed that is not old nor young,
The Life that on this spot
Thousands of years have adored
Thousands of years and millions of men, as I now
    stand and adore,
While you, cuckoo, sing.

He descended from this altitude into rain and realism.
They went on to Ch'ü-fu, where Confucius had been born,
and where his descendant, the 76th Duke, still lived on a
domain secured to him by the Chinese government. Their
visit to the Duke had been officially arranged through the
British Legation, but he slept, as so often happens in the East.
His secretary asked them very politely to do their sight-seeing
first, and Dickinson in his naivety would have consented, but
Dr Yetts saw they would 'lose face' and he sent a message
that they regretted missing the Duke and would retire. A
friend of mine, only a year ago, found himself in an analogous
position with an English Duke who had invited him to tea,
and he sent a similar message, but his Duke sat tight. The
Confucian Duke was more trammelled by etiquette. He
knew that if the visitors went away in this fashion he himself
would 'lose face', and he immediately appeared fully dressed
with his entourage—a handsomish rip of a man. An interview
ensued, carried on amid much linguistic difficulty. How old
was Mr Dickinson, why was he not married, why had he no
beard, etc. Then followed a symbolic incident: the offering
of a copy of 'John Chinaman'. What did the representative
of Confucius make of the austere little volume? Not much.
An attempt was made to explain to him that the writer was
a distinguished western sage, and he was understood to enquire what present he might give the sage in return. Asked
for a set of rubbings of the Confucian portraits and inscriptions, he agreed graciously, and after an interminable interval
produced some raspberryade. The visitors then took their
leave and Dickinson had his first and last experience of a
Chinese inn. It was not too terrible, there were no vermin,
and he felt happy. A great deal of time was spent in calling
on and being called on by 'a mandarin whose attentions and
courtesy were rather overwhelming in our humble shed', and
who showed them over the temples and the great cemetery
of the K'ung clan. The Duke's present has not yet arrived.

Homage paid to Confucius, he went on to Japan, going via

Kobe to Kyoto. Japan was more of a treat than China and
he writes long happy letters home about its cleanliness and
charm, and the gaiety and beauty of its people: 'I really
begin to look with horror on our civilisation, I suppose I shall
recant and settle down into it again. Anyhow I'm fit for no
other'. But it is China which dominates his memories. A
collision had of course occurred between the ideals which he
had been fostering for the last twelve years, and the actualities, which included decay and mud. But the collision was
not at all a severe one, and the picture given in 'John Chinaman' continued, in its essentials, to satisfy him. Politeness,
gaiety, imagination, good taste—these he found or thought
he found. Dishonesty, dirt, immorality—these were discon-
certing, but they did not strike at the root of civilisation, like
the commercialism of the west. As he climbed T'ai Shan
and passed 'the pavilion of the phoenixes', 'the fountain of
the white cranes', 'the tower of the quickening spirit', and
reached on the summit a gate called 'the portal of the clouds',
he must have seen the full flowering of that fancy in names
which budded so shyly in England: speedwell, travellers' joy.
And as he looked at the exquisite caligraphy on the mountain
rocks and at the pavilions set up where the views are loveliest,
he reflected what the west will do to T'ai Shan when it gets
hold of it: funiculars and advertisements. If vulgarity brought
peace to China it might perhaps be bearable, might not be
too high a price to pay for the destruction of good manners
and beauty. But no: with vulgarity comes organised violence,
commercialism is followed by aggressive imperialism, the
body as well as the spirit must be destroyed wholesale. With
these melancholy thoughts, which the events of the following
year were to intensify, he returned to England by the trans-
Siberian in the autumn of 1913. India had been impressive,
Japan delightful, but China retained his heart.

During the war his interests became mainly European.
After the Armistice and the establishment of the League of
Nations he began to think of the beloved country again, and

it is in connection with her, and with her alone, that his name has ever been the subject of discussion in the British Parliament. When the first Labour Government was in power it appointed a committee to decide how the Boxer indemnity should be spent, and Dickinson, among others, consented to serve. The money was to be spent in the interests of the Chinese; and the phrase can be interpreted in various ways: it has in fact been interpreted as meaning that we ought to build military railways. He had other views; he had read much about the country, he had visited it, he had many Chinese friends, his qualifications seemed obvious. However, when the Conservatives came in they turned him and Bertrand Russell out and made two new appointments in their places. Since the Bill had not yet been passed, they were technically within their rights, still, it is, I believe, without precedent that one Government should thus alter the composition of a committee established by its predecessor. On December 18th, 1924, Mr (now Lord) Ponsonby asked in the House of Commons 'what was the reason of cancelling the invitations to serve on the Committee to be set up under the China Indemnity Bill?' The debate continued as follows:

Mr Austen Chamberlain. The reason is that on reconsideration it was found that the composition of the Committee—the numbers of which it is important to keep small—was not sufficiently representative, and, in particular, that it included no member of practical experience of educational organisation in China.

Mr Ponsonby. Considering that these gentlemen were both very well qualified for the post which had been offered them, was this decision really only because of their connection with the Labour party?

Mr Chamberlain. I am not anxious to discuss the qualifications of these gentlemen unless the Hon. Gentleman forces me to do so. I have given a sufficient reason, in my opinion, for altering the composition of the Committee.

Mr Riley. Have any other persons who were appointed to serve on the Committee been excluded?

Mr Chamberlain. No.

Mr Stephen. Is this an instance of the Class War?

Mr Buchanan. I beg to give notice that I intend to ask leave to move the adjournment of the House on this question.

The Speaker ruled this out of order, and nothing was done. The Government was evidently determined to exclude Russell and Dickinson because they would have spent the money in the Chinese rather than in the British interest, but it is surprising that it could not effect its purpose less clumsily. Dickinson's friends felt some indignation at the way in which he was treated, but he himself remained unaffectedly serene. Incapable of snubbing others, he was incapable of resenting a snub. He had offered his help and been rejected, and he passed on to other work.

In his later years when he was feeling the draught, which was often, he wore a little Chinese cap. The first of this series of caps was given him by his friend Hsu. Foreign trimmings do not as a rule suit the Britisher, but the little cap seemed natural and harmonious in his case even when it broke the line of tufted heads which compose the High Table at King's. The black silk of which it was made, the tiny red button crowning it, were a familiar and delightful sight in Hall, the best talk was in its neighbourhood and the talk never a monologue, it bobbed about Cambridge and reached London, it would be lost, found, trodden under foot, renewed. Never was a man less suitable than Goldie to become the subject of a legend: his whole career was a protest against that particularly silly form of fame. But if the legend-mongers ever do work him up it is on his mandarin's cap that they will concentrate, and perhaps they will relate how Confucius placed it on his brows in return for a copy of 'John Chinaman'.

CHAPTER XII

THE WAR AND THE LEAGUE
1914–1926

For lo, what comes!
This blessed isle with all its congregation
Of friendships made and making, this Elysium,
Whose willow glassing streams and flowered fields
Invite to love and contemplation, this,
Which like a spirit sings in the cuckoo's voice,
Breaks into war, whose issue, win who may,
Is but defeat.   'From King to King' (1891).

I

DICKINSON'S feelings when the war broke out are best conveyed by an analogy: they resembled the feelings which arise when a promise has been broken by a person whom one loves. One knows all the time that the promise will not be kept, perhaps cannot be kept, yet the shock is none the less mortal. Though all his observations had convinced him that men do not live by reason, he hoped that they would be converted in the hour of trial, that conciliation would take the place of arrogance and trustfulness of fear, that the lion would lie down with the leopard from motives of self-interest if not at the dictates of religion, and that a youth would lead them. He had studied the English Civil War and the French Revolution and the contemporary Boer War and the disintegration of China, and in the case of China there had been the first shudderings of personal horror. But that modern Europe, including his own country, should fall into the Devil's trap—that he never believed, however much he may have maintained its possibility in argument. The shock broke something in him which was never mended, and when at the close of his life he again functioned he had evolved a new apparatus, not repaired the old.

How difficult it is to write about the sufferings of any one person under the war! One of the evil things about war is that it provokes a sort of competition in grief, and perhaps some readers will say with a sneer that Dickinson was only a sheltered don who went through no physical hardships and lost no dear friends. This is true, and he realised it, but it is also true that he was, in Shelley's words,

> a nerve o'er which do creep
> The else unfelt oppressions of the earth,

and that if his suffering is rejected as meaningless we can ignore the accounts of Jesus Christ weeping over the fate of mankind. There are two sorts of grief. There is a resentful querulous grief which throws the sufferer in on himself and makes him petty and tedious. There is a grief which expands towards the universal and generates action. Dickinson, like most of us, expressed both sorts of grief during the war, and did not avoid personal irritability and melancholy. But his desire to help others dominated.

He was at Cambridge during the final days of peace. On the evening of the Sunday he bicycled alone by Barton and Haslingfield, looking from a railway bridge at the sunlit meadows and the stream and trying to realise the unrealisable. Then he went by Hereford to Chipping Campden where the Ashbees were still happily installed, and there he contributed to the 'Nation' the first of his many war writings. It is called 'The Holy War'; it is about the sacredness of reason, and it asks those who have loved reason in the past to defend her in her hour of need.

The perfect weather continued, and the dumb impotent feeling of the gulf between nature, the past, all beautiful true and gracious things and beliefs, and this black horror of inconceivability that nevertheless was true. I had felt nothing like it since my mother's death, but this was infinitely worse. I was fifty-two; there was for me no question of enlisting though I think I should have enlisted if I had been younger, for I was not 'a conscientious objector', though I had no illusion about the war nor anything but

despair in my heart. I did in fact for a time oscillate as
to whether I should enter the Friends Ambulance Corps
under my friend P. H. Baker, but I decided finally, and
probably rightly, that so far as there was anything I could
do it must be of a different kind. I devoted myself, so far as
there was any opportunity for such work, to propaganda
for a League of Nations.

The work which he achieved in this direction will be
discussed later. As to his personal equipment for it, he
was at a disadvantage, for the reason that, though he sympathised with pacifism he did not think that the taking of life
is, per se, wrong. He could not take up a religious attitude
about bloodshed. He was condemned to the agonising task
of convincing the world by argument—agonising, because he
was fully aware of facts. He knew that he was unimportant,
that he would be ignored by statesmen and soldiers, that he
would be accused of weakening the national effort, that
the young men whom he wanted to save did not for the
moment want to be saved, but, war mad, rushed to mutual
immolation with the young men of Germany. All this he
knew, and yet he could not put on the armour of 'peace at
any price' which protects its wearers not indeed from physical
martyrdom but from many shafts which assail the spirit. He
could only have come through if he was a strong man. And
the more I consider his character the more I am impressed
by its strength. He was morally wiry. To regard him as a
wistful sufferer is to see only half of him, less than half....

No doubt he needed sympathy and agreement. We all did.
The difference of a hair could cause irritation in those nerve-
racked years, and it was not only the sedentary who suc-
cumbed, but right up in the trenches the same poison seems
to have been at work, dividing man from man in the so-called
hour of national union. And since he could not keep his
views to himself, for by their nature they had to be imparted,
he often found himself severed from his friends. People who
romanticised the allied cause, people who romanticised the
Germans, people who took the war lightly, all became alien

to him, so of course did orthodox Christians, nor, though he admired the Sermon on the Mount, could he feel that that way was his. Here are some examples of his isolation.

To MRS ASHBEE   King's,
                                              Nov. 11, 1914.

I don't think however that I ought to write to you about the war. If you feel that there is a cause for it, other than mere folly and crime, you are more fortunate than I am, and I don't want to interfere. And again if you can get some mystic consolation out of it, as some do, you are more fortunate. It would be easier to bear, and probably one would get the perspective better, if one were a young man who could serve or had trained oneself for some function that might be useful now. But if one's whole life had been given up to trying to establish reason and suddenly the gulf opens and one finds that world's ruled by force and wishes to be so, one feels forlorn indeed and more than forlorn....

I don't think I could stomach Cramb. I have read enough elsewhere of that revolting view of life. It cannot be answered. Those things lie too deep for argument. One is one kind of man or the other.

The name of Professor Cramb has long since returned to its original obscurity. At that uncritical moment it was on everyone's lips. Dickinson elsewhere identifies it with the view that 'peace is only a lamentable interval before the next war' as opposed to the view that 'war is an evil and a crime, to be got rid of'.

A few days later he writes again to Mrs Ashbee:

No my dear Janet I did not mean to accuse you of being of the Cramb school. It requires a male to be led into such preposterous idealism. Nor have I any quarrel with your view of the cause other than to note that we are here to resist not to acquiese in these cosmic horrors. I don't mind what people think about the war so long as they are going to come down on the side of working to put an end to war. Do you prefer Oscar strenuous and dead to Oscar charming and alive? But I don't want to enter into controversy with you. I am glad to know how you feel and I have too much respect for your judgment and experience not to think there must be truth in anything you feel.

He encountered another example of war idealism in Rupert Brooke. He had known Brooke at King's not as an isolated god-like figure but as one in a group of brilliant young men; Ferencz Békássy was another of them, who died on the Hungarian side. The following note, dated October 28th, 1914, was written to him by Brooke from the Royal Naval Barracks, Chatham.

I looked in at Edwardes Square one morning two or three days after I got back from the Antwerp affair. But you'd just gone to Cambridge. I was sorry to miss you. I hope you don't think me very reactionary and callous for taking up this function of England. There shouldn't be war—but what's to be done but fight Prussia? I've seen the half million refugees in the night outside Antwerp; and I want, more than before, to go on, till Prussia's destroyed. I wish everyone I knew were fighting.

A friendly manly note, but Dickinson must have found it difficult to answer. Apart from its implied invitation to himself, it emphasised the notion of the anthropomorphic State, the very notion which his own Holy War had to combat. Many of his friends, both young and old, felt as Brooke did, indeed most of them went that way. And in the opposite direction went the 'pro-Germans', the little group who from gallantry, perversity, or exasperation reversed the patriotic engine and made it function backwards. Here too he felt isolated. For instance in the summer of 1915 he stopped with the Ponsonbys, who were extreme pacifists from his point of view, and who also differed from him in thinking that the war might have been avoided. They argued that Germany was not wholly responsible, with which he agreed, but they emphasised this so much that he showed up as pro-French in comparison. His fellow guest, Vernon Lee, became exasperated by his fair-mindedness and complained to her hostess that he was 'wrinkled with scruples', and he for his part sat silent when she poured forth fantastic diatribes against the allies. Here too he must have recognised the anthropomorphic fallacy. Rupert Brooke and Vernon Lee had both abandoned the pursuit of reason, and the fact that they could respectively act nobly and were prepared to suffer for their faiths did not make his own course the less clear. He was condemned to follow the intellect in a world which had become emotional.

The line taken by orthodox Christianity in the war ought not to have surprised him, but did. He lets himself go on the subject in some letters to Leonard Elmhirst. Elmhirst, who had recently been at Cambridge, was at that time an earnest Christian, working with the Y.M.C.A. in France; he is now director of an important experimental community in Devonshire. Writing to him under the date of May 6th, 1916, Dickinson says:

I can well believe that your work with the troops is uphill. You will find, perhaps have found, that the fact of being officially connected with any religious organisation cuts you off from all the decent English. They will not take their religion that way, and personally I think they are right. The Christian Churches will not I believe ever recover any influence nor do they deserve to. The greatest crisis in history has found them without counsel or policy or guidance, merely re-echoing the passions of the worst crowd. Civilisation is perishing, and they look on passive and helpless. Not from such comes the inspiration men are waiting for. If there is to be a religion in the future it will grow up outside the churches and persecuted by them— as indeed is now the case at home. I write all this hastily and crudely, and perhaps unwisely.

In a previous letter to Elmhirst he says that the essential teaching of Christ now seems to him 'sheer common sense and sanity, not the paradox I used to think it', but that he is still a follower of Socrates. He adds, 'I don't think Socrates and Jesus Christ are enemies. Perhaps they are merely supplementary'; compare his remark to another friend: 'I think Jesus acted quite rightly before Pilate, though not prudently, just as Socrates did when he refused to escape from prison. Remarkable men in their great moments are like that.

The rest of us do what we can and wriggle out if we can'. He felt, like many actual Christians, that Christ had been betrayed by the spirit of nationalism and when he saw religion becoming frankly tribal, and the army chaplain taking no nonsense from the saint, he believed that it would never recover its spiritual kingdom.

One more of these specimen extracts shall be quoted. He could not take the war lightly and quietly, even for a week end. His moral earnestness forbade him, just as his intellect forbade him to seek the solace either of patriotism, or anti-patriotism, or religion. This way and that, he was excluded from comfort.

To H. O. MEREDITH

My dear Hugh,
King's College, Cambridge.
Feb. 13th, 1918.

It is of course true that I have shirked seeing you of late. That's because my nerves are all to pieces, and I find it hard to speak and behave with the necessary self-control. And anything is better, between friends, than constrained silences about what one's mind is full of, or futile talks. Of course if you *want* to talk, I will. But I put it to you that since we feel so differently it is not likely to lead to much. I am not referring of course to mere differences of opinion about political measures, but you take the war lightly and I take it as an unendurable tragic horror. We are neither of us to blame for this. But it makes it difficult to enter into sympathy pro tem. I'm not 'drifting apart' at all for my own part, only lying low—wisely I think.

Except for two visits, to Holland, and to America, he remained in England during the war, and as much as possible in London. There he had the sympathy of his sisters, and could sometimes see the friend from whom he was never alienated—Roger Fry. Cambridge only increased his sadness. All that he had cared for and worked for had vanished, and a grim obscene power took its place. I saw that obscenity for a moment myself, during a passing visit in 1915.

It took the harmless form of some young Welsh soldiers. A solitary undergraduate in a cap and gown came round the corner upon them, and the soldiers naturally burst out laughing. They had never seen anything so absurd, so outlandish. What could the creature be? To me the creature was the tradition I had been educated in, and that it should be laughed at in its own home appalled me. My trivial experience symbolises Dickinson's feelings. He saw the tradition he had loved derided by militarism, and by the hangers-on of militarism. No one defended it or even seemed to regret it, it had become a wraith which the next puff of gas would drive away.

To me the worse kind of disillusionment was that connected with universities and historians. Hardly a voice was raised from those places and persons to maintain the light of truth. Like the rest, moved by passion, by fear, by the need to be in the swim, those who should have been the leaders followed the crowd down a steep place. In a moment, as it were, I found myself isolated among my own people. When I say isolated, I do not mean in any sense persecuted. I suffered nothing in Cambridge except a complete want of sympathy. But I learned once for all that students, those whose business it would seem to be to keep the light of truth burning in a storm, are like other men, blindly patriotic, savagely vigilant, cowardly or false when public opinion once begins to run strong. The younger dons and even the older ones disappeared into war work. All discussion, all pursuit of truth ceased as in a moment. To win the war or to hide safely among the winners became the only preoccupation. Abroad was heard only the sound of guns, at home only the ceaseless patter of a propaganda utterly indifferent to truth.

In 1916 Bertrand Russell was dismissed from his lectureship at Trinity because he had engaged in peace propaganda and been convicted under the Defence of the Realm Act. Dickinson felt this acutely, as a letter in the 'Nation' shows, and the breach between him and McTaggart and others of his friends grew wider. He was disinclined to speak of such matters and I have never gathered a precise account of them, but his general drift towards loneliness is only too plain. It happened everywhere. It happened most obviously in the city which had once seemed the impregnable stronghold of friendship and truth. The 'Recollections' continue:

> I was still carrying on my work at Cambridge, lecturing twice a week in term. But my class was naturally composed almost entirely of women. Cambridge had become a hospital and a camp. In my college there was almost nobody left except a few dons and the nurses who were quartered in the building by the river. My sense of alienation from common opinion, my melancholy, and my clear sense of fact (for so I must call it) caused me to retire altogether from such life as there was in the place. I lived and ate alone when I was in Cambridge and saw almost nobody. The long winter evenings still linger with me. Shut into my room, I seemed for a time to have shut out the world. My dim reading lamp, the rich red wall paper, the flickering fire, were my background. It was then that I used to think about...

Roger Fry remarks of him: 'He had been far too optimistic and naïve in his conception of human nature before the war —he had no notion of how much a primitive and pre-logical mentality still survived in civilised man'. I think that he had the notion, but refused to face its consequences. He had shirked the horrors of crowd-psychology, and Cambridge was now compelling him to view them in surroundings where he thought they could not occur. But he never abandoned his fundamental hope for humanity. He fought, all through the war, for the spirit of reason in human affairs.

2

It is possible that Dickinson invented the phrase 'League of Nations'; it is certain that he was the first person in this country to formulate the idea. In the opening fortnight of the war, while he was at Hereford, he jotted down on a piece of paper two schemes for such a league, and when he returned to London he went round to a few people who might be interested, and formed a group. He claimed no credit for this priority and effaced himself as soon as the idea became fashionable. At the time it was suspect, and the general opinion was voiced by his brother Arthur, who writes to him that 'the only organisation now called for is an anti-German league'. The secretary of Dickinson's group was Richard Cross, an able Yorkshire lawyer, who drafted the scheme, and 'without whom we should never have come to a point, so to speak'. Other prominent members were his namesake W. H. Dickinson (now Lord Dickinson), and J. A. Hobson. Arthur Ponsonby also attended, but was opposed to the proposed sanction of force, which figured among the group's recommendations. Graham Wallas, though in general sympathy, was more concerned to press international co-operation in general than their particular scheme for preventing war. Two of the meetings of the committee were attended by Lord Bryce, and since he was the first person of public eminence to countenance the organisation, it is known as the 'Bryce Group'. It ought to be called the 'Lowes Dickinson Group'.

The 'Bryce Group' is only one of the tiny streams which finally fell into the Lake of Geneva, but its course is interesting, both to a biographer of Dickinson and to the League historian. It did much to shape the Covenant of the League, one clause of which (that defining the disputes generally suitable to arbitration) was directly taken from its proposals. And it did still more to shape public opinion. In 1915 news of it reached the original members of the American 'League to Enforce Peace' and encouraged them to persevere at a critical moment. The two societies kept in touch during the war, to their mutual benefit. Their respective proposals, together with the proposals of other groups, will be found in 'The Framework of a Lasting Peace', edited by L. S. Woolf.

Dickinson's activities soon took him abroad. Foreign travel

into neutral countries had not yet been blocked, and in the spring of 1915 he attended on behalf of the 'Bryce Group' a small international meeting of pacifists at the Hague. Writing to Ponsonby, just before sailing, he says:

11 Edwardes Square,
Kensington.
April 2nd, 1915.

Dear Ponsonby,

Thanks for your letter and enclosure. I'm sorry your constituents are so intransigeant. I never realised before how war makes men mad. During the Boer war I took no part in political controversy and hardly realised the atmosphere. One could easily despair; but that is always a silly and feeble thing to do. In fact one's voice, I think, has value beyond the intrinsic, so comforting it is to find in print any expression of decent feeling and sound judgment. What disappoints me most is the collapse of Labour as a force for good. With the exception of the I.L.P., which I gather is numerically weak, the working men lie down and let the Times have it all its own way. I'm afraid our working class is the most ignorant and stupid in Europe, at any rate where foreign affairs are concerned. Ilbert's letter is interesting. What he says about Prussia and Russia is more than probable, granting a continuance of the old diplomatic game.

Nearly everyone who has replied about our proposals is in general and platonic agreement, but there aren't many useful suggestions. Our worst enemies are really men like Brailsford and Hobson, who go for a federation. They won't get that: but they may easily help to prevent our getting what we ask for. Always 'le mieux est l'ennemi du bien', and so men fall back frankly on the simply bad.

My kind remembrance to Mrs Ponsonby. I go to Holland on Sunday night. I fear I shall be the only Englishman there.

G. L. DICKINSON.

He was right in thinking he would be the only Englishman, though a member of Parliament, J. A. Baker, turned up at the end. Germans and Austrians attended, also several neutrals. At this meeting 'The Society for a Durable Peace' was founded, in whose 'minimum program' was a resolution in favour of a League of Nations, which he drafted. He brought the Society into general accord with the Bryce Group. No further international meetings were possible, for the belligerent powers began to tighten their regulations, and prevented a meeting at Berne, but a number of papers were published, three volumes of which have been collected.

On my return I was confronted by a statement in the press that Mr Baker and myself had gone to the Hague with the approval and under the commission of Sir Edward Grey. This of course was quite untrue. But on my return I had an interview with Sir Edward, and explained what we had done and showed him our resolutions. He expressed no objection to these, but of course I saw that the kind of peace we wanted would become impossible by the mere fact that there had been a war. For that matter I myself always knew that I was engaged on a forlorn hope, but saw nothing else on which I could engage with conviction.

The main object of the Bryce Group was research and study. Meanwhile another group came into existence for the purposes of propaganda, and Dickinson joined this also. Presently the two groups were co-ordinated, and on May 3rd, 1915, the 'League of Nations Society' was formally constituted. Various alternative titles for the Society were discussed, such as 'World Union of States', 'Union of Nations', but it adopted the phrase which was soon to be so familiar. W. H. Dickinson was the chairman of the committee, a membership of several thousand was built up, Lord Shaw was finally secured as President. In connection with its propaganda Dickinson went to America on a lecturing tour.

He had thought of this tour as early as February 12th, when he had gone with Ashbee and Laurence Housman to talk to Sir Edward Grey about it. As in the case of the Hague expedition, Grey expressed no disapproval, and seemed content that the idea of the League should spread, though the time had not yet come for official protection. He did not sail until January, 1916. It was his third and last visit.

He was coming now not to spread culture or study conditions, but to plead for civilisation, and the knowledge that the Old World had failed made him more tolerant of the New. He travelled out with Ashbee, also an enthusiast for a League. They carried on board with them the wreckage of a still more Utopian scheme in the shape of the members of the Henry Ford Peace Expedition, who had just been over to Europe to ask the war to stop. The war had made no reply, and they were returning to their native shores, minus Henry Ford and not greatly abashed. Their conceit, crudity, and superficiality were typical of the America Dickinson knew, but so was their idealism; they were children with the hope of children.

The diary of this tour consists of a few pages of scribble, recording his journeys and lecture engagements. From the beginning of February to the end of April he seldom slept twice in the same place. Keeping in touch with the American League to Enforce Peace he made a tour of universities and other institutions in the east and the middle west as far as Kansas and Minneapolis. He found the upper classes sympathetic to England and anxious to enter the war, especially in the east. In the middle west there was no idea of taking part and a general sense that it was another of the fool enterprises of Europe.

To H. O. MEREDITH

Minneapolis,
March 31, 1916.

I expect to leave this country on April 15, and be 'home' (!) some ten days later, barring a merciful target. You wouldn't be interested in what I have been doing here. But touring the colleges and universities has at any rate kept me from over much brooding. I like the Americans much better than I ever did before. They are, at any rate, human and kindly, and if they're uncultured and crude, at least they haven't got a false culture. However, it looks as if they will be in the bloody business directly, and then of course they will be as violent as Europe is. The college professors are much more tolerant and freeminded than the similar herd in England. And they are human beings, which most of ours aren't. Of course they have no influence to speak of. Colleges are an investment to Americans, and educate only as a means of getting on. And in this country if you're going to get on you must have a college education, and almost anybody can get it. They work their way through, at incredibly little cost. Perhaps after all I shall end my life in this country. No place in Europe will be endurable after the war. However, I may as well keep off all that.

From the 'Recollections':

The comparative sanity of America at that time, the mere contact with people who were not war mad, was a refreshment to me. But how superficial and transitory that feeling was, was shown a year later, when America came into the war, and, according to all accounts, precisely the middle west was the most intolerant and savage part of the country. This intolerance and cruelty of England was bad enough during the war. But anything that happened here pales into insignificance before what happened there. A modern democracy is a mere cloud of dust and blows any way the wind blows.

On returning to England he continued to work with the League of Nations Society, which made steady progress among humble and unimportant folk, and brought together the very few men and women in England who thought of anything beyond winning the war. He lectured in little schoolrooms, generally to small audiences—meetings too obscure to excite opposition or attract notice. He was in touch with another body, definitely suspect by the authorities, the Union of Democratic Control, which, under his friend E. D. Morel, became involved in an attack on allied propaganda. Dickinson and the Society he represented held that such an attack, though justifiable, was unwise, and that though the allies, as well as Germany, were to blame for the origin of the war, it was quite useless to say so at the present juncture. He writes to Morel (February 25th, 1918) 'My deliberate policy is to say all I can without provoking a reasonable reader. This may be bad propaganda. But it is me, and I can no other'.

Caution is relative, and in 1917 a new body came into existence which regarded the League of Nations Society with much the same wariness as the 'Society' itself regarded the Union of Democratic Control. This was the 'League of Free Nations Association'. Its members were for the most part good haters of Germany and people of importance and influence, who had plenty of money behind them and knew how to run a campaign. The idea of a League was becoming reputable chiefly owing to President Wilson, and it was possible to support it without loss of public credit. And Wilson's advocacy—so intricate are the threads—was due to that American League to Enforce Peace which the Bryce Group had encouraged two years before. This way and that, Dickinson saw his deeds coming back to him.

He and his fellow workers of the League of Nations Society had now to decide a most puzzling question: should they or should they not join forces with the League of Free Nations Association? The 'Association' was willing to have them on conditions, but did not wish to be compromised by their pacificism. It desired to form a provisional league of nations amongst the allies at once before the war was concluded. Dickinson was strongly opposed to this, since it would make the ultimate inclusion of Germany more difficult, and might even alienate neutrals. There was a good deal of 'to and fro' as he calls it, and some mutual suspicion. The problem was finally solved in a truly English fashion—over food. The executives of either organisation appointed representatives to dine at the National Liberal Club. The 'Society' sent its Chairman W. H. Dickinson, G. L. D., J. A. Hobson, and L. S. Woolf. The 'Association' sent C. A. McCurdy, Gilbert Murray, Wickham Steed, H. G. Wells. The dinner was a success, the representatives liked one another, and discovered no real obstacles to fusion. Rules were drafted and the present 'League of Nations Union' was formed under the presidency of Sir Edward Grey. It represents the union of two smaller streams—the 'Society' and the 'Association'; the 'Society' derives in its turn from the 'Bryce Group', and the 'Bryce Group' starts right back in the uplands of 1914, on the half sheet of paper which Dickinson drafted in the first fortnight of the war.

It is unnecessary to describe the negotiations for the union in detail. Here are two letters which give the general atmosphere. The first is to Mrs R. C. Trevelyan, who feared that the 'Society' was selling its soul, a fear shared by other supporters, notably by J. A. Hobson and Lord Parmoor.

Dear Bessie,   October 12, 1918.

This business of amalgamation has been and is a great worry, but I think suspicion on both sides has played an undue part in it. It is quite clear that either the L.N.S. must amalgamate, or it can play no effective part at all. For the other association knows how to carry on propaganda, and we do not. After seeing and discussing at length with the representatives of the other society, I think that really they want what we want; certainly some of them do, especially Murray and Wells; and I think even McCurdy. Their literature is bad, from my point of view, and they have committed themselves to the policy of the 'league now', which has been turned down by Wilson, and yesterday by Grey, who is to be our president. I think, as things are now, that policy, though they may continue to run it (partly out of obstinacy), is damned and done. On practically every point, Grey said the right thing, and I think we must trust to him and to 'our' element in the new society to keep things fairly straight. I hope therefore you will not look with too jealous an eye on the amalgamation, though of course I understand your fears. It was a splendid manifesto yesterday. Even the overflow meeting over-flowed. I am still playing the game [i.e. chess on postcards] with Bob. He seems very happy at present. What about you? Are you? Are you staying on at Shiffolds? So glad Julian is happy. What a relief for you. But I fear you must be feeling very lonely. I almost dare hope for the end now, but we have so often been cheated of it.   G.L.D.

The second letter is to H. G. Wells, with whom he became very friendly as a result of these negotiations. He had a warm admiration for the 'Outline of History' and Wells' work generally, and considered him one of the most important educational influences of our time. He is here commenting on a draft agreement which Wells has forwarded:

King's College, Cambridge.
October 25th, 1918.

Dear Wells,

I am here at present, and shall not have an opportunity, until next week, of consulting those of my colleagues who take exception to the paragraph in question, in its present form. If we are to arrive at an agreed draft, in this way, I must reserve a final opinion until I have talked to them. Meantime, as far as I am concerned, there is only one sentence in your draft to which I should take serious exception. It is the sentence 'and make reparation and amends for the crime of the great war'. I have two objections to this, which I do not think obstructive or unreasonable. First, it does not seem to me a matter for a league of nations society to prescribe punishment for the past. We are concerned with guarantees for the future, such as are sufficiently indicated in the rest of the draft. Secondly, the sentence is too vague and comprehensive. I should approve, if it were practicable (as it may be), the setting up of an impartial court of international justice, to try those accused of definite offences against the laws of war. Such a court, of course, would have to receive charges from *any* belligerent government against nationals of *any* other. But I strongly object to even the appearance of countenancing the kind of indiscriminate revenge against German towns and women and children which I have heard advocated by individuals, and which appear to be contemplated by many organs of our press. I expect you agree with me about this, and I should be glad if you could secure the deletion of that clause.

Mr Keen has also drafted an alternative paragraph, and he will perhaps wish to submit his draft after consultation with others to your committee or to whatever subcommittee you may have appointed.

I think it should be noted (though you may think this

criticism rather academic) that the phrase 'peoples whose collective will is embodied in the decisions of their government' quite obviously and definitely excludes Japan (whose constitution, in letter and in practice, is as autocratic and militarist as the constitution of Germany was until the recent changes). It would, I suppose, also exclude China, and I am strongly of opinion that China should be a member of the League. These difficulties however are inherent in any limitation such as Wilson himself has put forward, and we must hope that consistency will not be pushed too far. It is, of course, the fact that at present no one is thinking of anything except Germany, and that public opinion will exact the kind of statement embodied in the draft.

You see then that I have only one strong objection to your draft, but that I wish to be free, after consultation, to submit for your consideration an alternative draft, if that should be desired by other of my colleagues. No delay, beyond a day or two, will be involved. I find myself, so far as I can judge from our meetings, in very close agreement with you, personally, on what I regard as the fundamental points, and I am very glad that this should be so.

Yours very truly,

G. LOWES DICKINSON.

I suppose I am right in understanding that the passage at the beginning of the original paragraph about forming the league now is definitely dropped out? That was the point of my opposition, and I understand that policy to be definitely repudiated by Wilson and also by Grey.

There are of course awkwardnesses of expression in the draft which you yourself could amend better than anyone.

When the League of Nations Union was formed, he became a member of its executive council, but presently resigned. The idea was now well launched, he disliked committee work, and his taint of 'pacifism' kept him in the background of an organisation which was and indeed had to be respectable. He lectured when asked to do so. He received no recognition for his work and did not desire any. But those who had worked with him knew what he had achieved. At the time of his death his namesake Lord Dickinson wrote to his representatives:

He and I worked in very close co-operation during the period when he was laying the foundation stone of the League of Nations. I well remember his coming to my chambers in September or October 1914 to take counsel how the war might be made to serve the purposes of peace, and a little later he set up his committee for studying the question of a League to which Lord Bryce gave his name as President. Lowes Dickinson did the main part of the work of that Committee and it was due to his industry and courage that the scheme took shape which ultimately became the Covenant of the League. Too little was known of this, for he was modesty personified and when others took the work over he quietly dropped out of sight. But, nevertheless, the League of Nations owes its birth very largely to his idealism.

3

Dickinson's war writings date and were intended to date. He was never much tempted to address posterity, and on subjects such as war and peace his sole aim was to form contemporary opinion. With the possible exception of 'The Choice before Us' all that he wrote between 1914 and 1918 is likely to be forgotten.

Two pamphlets, 'The War and the Way Out' (1914) and 'After the War' (March 1915) come first on the list of publications. The first named attacks the 'governmental' theory of Bernhardi and his school; that states are the only realities and that they are natural enemies of one another. The second exposes the futility of crushing Germany, and discusses the formation of an international league to establish and maintain peace. Disassociating himself with regret from the extreme pacifists, he admits that such a league will require the sanction of force. The two pamphlets appeared (substantially) in 'The Atlantic Monthly' in America, and they were re-issued there as a single pamphlet.

'The European Anarchy' (1916) heralds both in its title

and its scheme his great work 'The International Anarchy' which was published ten years later. 'The European Anarchy' is a short historical survey of the events which immediately led to the war; like all his writings of this period, it ends with practical suggestions and advocacy of an international league.

'The Choice before Us' (1917) is a more considerable work than its three forerunners. The longer Dickinson thought on the problems of the war and the league, the more copious and persuasive became his writings. His range of illustration increased; so did his power of re-statement. He will put the same argument again and again in a slightly different light, which, in the world of propaganda, is the only method which drives an argument home. Statement is useless, repetition useless. Even to-day 'The Choice before Us' impresses the reader by its subtle variations. A man, not an automaton, is speaking of militarism and of internationalism, its two contrasted themes; of a league of nations; of the necessary sanction of force; of the necessity of democratic control of foreign policy. It was written at a moment of tension, just before the occurrence of two events which cheered him up for a little: the Russian Revolution and the entry into the war of the United States. The title suggests that mankind has come to the parting of the ways, and a sort of religious solemnity is achieved. A friend of mind read this book at an impressionable moment (he was just leaving school) and he was converted by it to opinions which he has never lost.

An Introduction to 'Problems of the International Settlement' (1918), an Introduction to 'Documents etc. relating to Peace Proposals' (1919), and 'War: its nature, causes and cure' (1923) may be mentioned here. And he became a prolific journalist, as the bibliography at the end of this book will show. 'The Manchester Guardian', under C. P. Scott, was his most influential mouthpiece. He contributed constantly to 'The Nation', then under H. W. Massingham's brave and brilliant editorship, and attended its weekly lunches.

He was on the editorial board of 'The Cambridge Magazine', where he could express himself more freely than elsewhere, if to smaller audiences, and he often wrote for 'War and Peace', afterwards the 'International Review'. In America the 'Atlantic Monthly', the 'New Republic' and the (New York) 'Nation' welcomed him.

It would be interesting to know how bad a bad mark stood against his name at the War Office as a result of all this activity, but censorship in England, then as now, worked as much as possible by suppression and as little as possible through open prohibition. He had reason to believe that 'The European Anarchy' and other writings were prevented from reaching the troops, but he could not be sure. He did know that his name was on a list (March 31st, 1917) of people whose works were forbidden to be exported to Norway, where they would have come before the Nobel Committee of the Norwegian Parliament. This suggests that the censorship flung its net wide. A net with a characteristic rent in it, for the list humorously assigns him the initials of his patriotic brother Arthur instead of his own.

Attacks in the press were not infrequent. 'The Daily Mail' did its duty and on one occasion the 'Morning Post' consecrated a leading article to him. He had been speaking at an Educational Conference on the educational basis of internationalism, and had roused the newspaper's wrath; the article notes with satisfaction that animals fight with one another, deduces from this the necessity for modern scientific warfare, calls for a 'national school of English history' and concludes: 'The writing of history has been left too much to gentlemen like Mr Dickinson who have been so carefully screened from the present that they do not understand the past'.

Dickinson replied in the following letter (Jan. 15th, 1918):

My attention has been called to an article in which you comment at length upon your reporter's account of an address delivered by me at the Educational Conference. It would serve no useful purpose, even if space allowed, for me to enter into controversy with you upon the fundamental issues which divide me from you. But perhaps you will give me the opportunity of stating to those of your readers who may have any interest in my views that your comments are a mere travesty of anything I have ever felt or thought or said.

As a rule he never replied to personal attacks. If they were on trivial points he felt them to be negligible, and if they were connected with important public issues he was anxious not to complicate the argument.

4

As soon as the war ended, Dickinson's spirits improved. The people whom he most loved were back, and the League of Nations seemed making a good start at Geneva. I stopped with him at Lyme Regis in the spring of 1919. We had not met for three years, so there was much to say. He was looking older and worn, but he was gay and chirpy, we took long walks, bowed to Jane Austen, played chess at the same level of badness and piquet under conflicting rules. He is said to have been the world's worst bridge player. May one allude to improper jokes in a memoir? Several were made. The world seemed settling down into its lost armchair for a moment's rest. My memories of Lyme Regis are rather vague and one is apt to drill one's memories into a consistency facts do not justify. Still the impression is happiness, hopefulness, clouds lifting. The re-appearance of 'The Athenaeum' under Middleton Murry's editorship was one of the things which cheered us up. Here at last was a paper which it was a pleasure to read and an honour to write for, and which linked up literature and life.

Perhaps this is the year when I went to a dinner of old Kingsmen and the Dean of St Paul's proposed his health and rallied him with somewhat bilish gaiety on being a prig. Anyhow this is the place to record his reply. The Dean said

Age 58

that he admired Mr Dickinson's English style but was dismayed to find at the end of one of his dialogues that a character, whose priggishness had sorely tried him, was intended to voice the author's own opinions. The sally was not quite a happy one, but Dickinson put everything right when he rose to give thanks; he recorded the days he and the Dean had spent together at Cambridge, and particularly their games of tennis 'when words, sir, would fall from your lips which did not lead me to suppose you would reach your present position'. There was laughter which the Dean did not endorse. Here, too, is the place in which I would like to insert another scrap—though it is a scrap behind his back. The scene is Cambridge itself, the period early post-war. 'Why don't you fellows chuck Lowes Dickinson into the Cam?' growls an adjacent schoolmaster to a friend of mine who had had a distinguished military career. They are bicycling together peacefully, and my friend shouts, 'More likely to chuck in you' with such violence that the adjacent schoolmaster almost falls off. I am glad that he did not quite fall—it would have been subtly unsuitable—just as I am glad that the words which did fall from the Dean of St Paul's will never be known.

While we were at Lyme Regis he was working on 'The Magic Flute', the most original of all his books if not the most perfect. It came out in 1920. It repays a debt. He tries to express in it all he owes to Mozart—'Marsyas to Apollo' the dedication says—and he mingled in his gratitude problems of which Mozart never dreamed. The slight pantomime of Tamino and Pamina is exalted into a mythology of Wagnerian scope. Can Mozart bear so much? Can the Fire be our war and the Water the doubts of the twentieth century spirit? Can the castle of Sarastro symbolise the modern mind? It seemed to me that Marsyas had bitten off more than Apollo could chew, but Dickinson would never admit that. Anyhow, what a lovely book! May one make a direct appeal in a memoir? I intend to. I urge anyone who has not yet read 'The Magic Flute' to read it. It is the writer's chief incursion into the kingdom of Ariel which had been shown to him when he was an unhappy child at school. Forty years in the world of matter had weighed him down but had neither broken nor tarnished his wings. These remained: and if an image in the style of Blake were permissible here, it would picture the 'soul of Dickinson' as unable to fly because it had laboured too long in the service of humanity, yet knowing more about flight than those happier beings who rise easily upwards until they are lost to us and to one another in the blue. 'The Magic Flute' has its faults. Read it and forget your own.

This seems the best place to introduce an account of an excellent verse play, called 'War and Peace: a dramatic fantasia'. It is earlier in date than 'The Magic Flute', for it was written before the war started, but the two works are emotionally related. 'War and Peace' was never published, and it is too topical to interest an audience of to-day, but it has invention, wit, action, colour, and it displays very movingly the feelings which Dickinson was soon to express in more permanent form. It opens with a prologue before the Gate of Heaven, and with the arrival of Violence and Futurist in an aeroplane. They wake up Peter, and learning from him that the Family is away induce him to let out War, a mighty monster with a dirty loafer inside it. Scarcely have they gone, when Reason and Cynic arrive on a second aeroplane, and demand Peace. Hitherto the Father has refused to release Peace and the Son has restrained War, and since the Holy Ghost does not vote there has been an impasse in heaven and neither war nor peace upon earth. Peter lets out Peace to equalise matters, and the first act of the drama then opens in the Fair of the World, with the nations of the twentieth century trafficking. Violence has arranged War in a box at the back, and provided him with placards such as 'Yellow Peril', 'French Menace', 'Entente Cordiale', 'Indian Unrest', 'Ulster will Fight', which are exhibited as the action

proceeds, and accelerate it. Violence takes various forms—
Salisbury, Carson, Larkin, a Militant Suffragette—but just
as the dance of death is at its height and War bursts out of his
box, the second aeroplane arrives, and Reason enters.

The next act is a brilliant debate, with the nations as
audience. Reason and Violence summon their respective
witnesses. Reason's first witness is Economist, who pops up in
cap and gown with a barometer. He can only register, he
never concludes. Violence summons Tariff Reform, habited
as an Archdeacon, and the two argue. They are not convincing, and the bewilderment of the audience is increased
when both Shakespeares are called up. For there is a Shakespeare on either side, one for war, one against, and each
quoting from 'Henry V'. Then Reason evokes Shelley, but
no one can hear what he says; India and Hibernia catch
murmurs, and Italy and France dream of their past, Ulster
hears nothing, John Bull nothing. Reason then soliloquises:

> What shall I do? I speak in my own tongue,
> The mathematical, and they laugh at me!
> I speak in verse, they say they cannot hear!
> Most that's in Man's below me. Yes. But something
> Must be above me! Something! What, and where?

He unwisely seeks the support of science, whereupon a pair
of sociologists jump up. The first, who is on the side of Violence, is dressed as a priest, and urges the human race to
procreate, lest, by control of population, they fall into the
power of Peace.

> War and Religion, heavenly pair,
> Twin constellation, fierce and fair,
> Oh cover with your sheltering wings
> The dangerous source where knowledge springs.

Reason's sociologist follows and betrays him. He argues that
war is caused by hunger, and can be prevented by a plentiful
food supply. But his enthusiasm for science leads him up
through Danish eggs and Brazilian coffee to the wireless and
the cinema and the radio-active bomb. This conclusion is

greeted with applause by the assembled nations, and the cause of Reason seems lost. Now comes the crisis. Reason summons his last witness—Passion; the head invokes the heart. Violence exults, for Passion is always on the side of war, and he joins in the dithyrambic invocation, but when the discords resolve it is not into a military march but into the choral movement of Beethoven's Ninth Symphony. Passion has enthroned Peace. What one may call the spiritual construction of the drama is excellent. How it would act is another matter. The prologue was once performed by puppets in Roger Fry's Omega Workshops for the benefit of Belgian refugees, but I did not gain from that any idea of the work as a whole.

There is another mystery play among his MSS. 'The End of Man' which is of the same date as 'War and Peace' and teaches the same lesson. There is also a pleasant unfinished dialogue of post-war date between some statues round a pool, which was suggested to him in the garden of his friends the Morrells, near Oxford. 'It occurred to me at Garsington that spirit and matter are the two sides of the bellows of life' he writes to Lady Ottoline Morrell. 'They blow out the wind but they never touch naturally and they are always moving in different directions.' Was the dreamy fanciful aspect of his character re-emerging? Were his anxieties about civilization at an end?

5

'The Magic Flute', unlike 'War and Peace', ends on a note of interrogation. Reason and Youth have proved their worth, but the victory remains undecided, and it is with a heavy heart that Sarastro retires to his castle. He could give the Queen vision, but she cries, 'I want no vision. I want the night'. This pessimism is significant. For the happier mood of 1919 soon passed and the next few years were the saddest he ever knew—sadder than the war years because they did not provide him with such definite work. His friends were all resuming their old jobs or interesting themselves in new ones. Fry was painting, Schiller at business, McTaggart at philosophy, Wedd and Grant teaching, while as for the young men all they wanted was rest and amusement and they were not the least inclined to rise in their hundreds and demand a new world. He complains to Ashbee (January 14th, 1920):

> Cambridge has resumed precisely as before the war or more so. No change of outlook is visible in young or old. Just tradition reasserting itself, equally the good and the bad. Men are plainly incapable of experience, which, as Oscar Wilde remarked, is an instinct.

With a bad Peace and an unsatisfactory League on his mind, he could not understand such levity, nor always distinguish between levity and resilience. In another letter to Ashbee, dated the following year, he refuses an invitation to Palestine with some tartness; though the 'bar' referred to was soon lifted:

> I find it rather difficult to write to you when every letter of yours treats me as a kind of imbecile needing 'cure' (from Jerusalem of all places!). Perhaps if you were at home you wouldn't think it so foolish to be pre-occupied with the parlous state of Europe. At any rate the difference in our interests is rather a bar to correspondence.

The same feeling of tension appears in this letter to Leonard Woolf:

King's, Cambridge.
April 1923.

Dear Leonard,

> I should like to write for the Nation, if only to get a little money, but I don't know whether I shall be able to. Henderson sent me Papini's book, but really I can't handle such tripe; a sort of sentimental sliming over a quite unreal Jesus. How religious people spoil even their gods! And through the mist one seems to divine in Jesus a really remarkable man. I will do Forster's book however. Only there again is the difficulty of writing on a personal friend, a situation which leads us Cambridge people to underestimate virtues and gifts for fear of being too partial. Oh dear, I wish I could think of *anything* to write on, or any way of writing, but this damned state of Europe keeps my nose on a peculiarly unpleasant grindstone, and the only result is that one's nose wears out, and the grindstone

doesn't. As I am here now, I shall hardly get up to the Labour International Committee. I hope that will not disqualify me, for I particularly wish to continue a member. I have been rereading 'Jacob's Room'. It's full of good stuff, probably better stuff than I know, and beautifully written. But the disjointed effect still worries me, though I realise the point of it. Hope you both enjoyed Spain. I shall in fact be in town next week, for two days, and attending that conference about Europe on the 9th.

G. L. DICKINSON.

To his concern for Europe, he added a more personal melancholy. He had for many years been offering affection where it was not needed, and the knowledge that he had made a mistake and was in a sense blameworthy sank into him and saddened him. He writes to me that he must be 'almost the only man who has ever lived with whom no one has ever been in love': an extraordinary remark, and not the less depressing because it was untrue. Later in his life happier relationships awaited him, but he was now passing through a dubious autumn, when the leaves would not fall from the trees. At moments he felt that nothing except the movements of the heart have any value and that his own had oscillated uselessly between yearning and disappointment.

Worse was to come. While he was in this mood of mistrusting himself and the world, he suffered a terrible blow in the death of his sister Janet. Janet has not often been mentioned in this biography for the reason that few letters were exchanged with her, but she was constantly in his thoughts. She had led an active practical life. Like May, she shared his love of music and his political outlook; all three sisters were in heartfelt agreement with him throughout the war. She was taken seriously ill in the autumn of 1923. Most men are inadequate in the presence of illness and become hysterical and irritable when it continues; Dickinson, so sensitive, might have been expected to react in this way. But his sensitiveness was always at the service of his love. As soon as he realised that it would comfort Janet to see him constantly, he gave up his Cambridge life and came to London, and he visited her every day from November to the following March, when the end came. There is, of course, no external test by which affection can be measured, yet one cannot help comparing this steadiness with the conduct of the so-called 'strong man', and wondering where strength lies. On this account his sister's death has to be mentioned, and also on account of its lasting influence upon him; he had never worried much about his own fate, and now he became still freer from personal fears. He wrote to me the following day:

> Up to the last, she was fully conscious, and one might almost say happy. She had no fear and some kind of unshakeable faith that it was all right.... I think she was an almost perfect spirit. I say 'almost' because those words are so insensitive, after all. She was full of humanity and therefore of the little frictions of humanity. But there was a sort of overshadowing beauty which took charge completely. These last weeks I got very close to her and that I know was a great joy to her, as it must always be happiness to me, so long as I am capable of thought and feeling.

In the 'Recollections' he says:

> I used to read to her, sometimes some of my poems, which it appears, though I did not know it, she had always liked and read and reread....
> Always thinking of other people, her friends....She asked whether she would get better, for she did not want to go through it again. May said 'no that would be too cruel'. She said, 'Oh, nothing is cruel. But I know what you mean'. She spoke of dear God and was sure she was going somewhere safe. No fear, no complaint. She said to me how good it had been to get so close to me. Surely a spirit made perfect. Yet I do not *believe* though I do not *disbelieve* that anything remains.

Can one speak of death without becoming affected? Goldie seems to me to have that rare gift. He can state his grief without exhibiting it, and without the under-statement which is another form of self-consciousness. Janet's death convinced him not of immortality, but of her belief in it. He

felt henceforward that if there is a key to the universe something surprising will be revealed. However, that wasn't the
point. What she had really done for him during those four
months was to reveal additional goodness on earth.

Mrs Lowes' husband had died the previous year. After
Janet's death, she and May decided to live together. They
finally took a flat in Beaufort Street, Chelsea, which was to
be the last of the long series of his London homes.

6

Since he had helped to evoke the League of Nations, he
naturally followed its movements intently—movements so
cumbersome and so involved that they gradually reduced
him to despair. The new machinery installed at Geneva bore
little resemblance to the ardent desires and generous hopes
for a better Europe which he had brought to birth among
humble audiences at home. He did not object to its size, but
had it any purpose? Was it benignant? Might it not be a
'dangerous façade' concealing from ordinary people the indifference and the cynicism of their governments? Above all,
would it work quick enough? 'I should not mind the League
moving slowly if events didn't move fast', he once remarked.
As the end of his own life approached he felt more and more
that civilisation must hasten if it wants to be saved. He had
the impatience and the irritability of the political theorist and
the impression he made on officials at Geneva during his
frequent visits was not altogether favourable. They realised
better than he did the dangers of hurrying. Their perspicuity
has not helped us! He may not have been right, but they
have proved wrong.

His feelings about the League varied. This letter to May
records an early visit.

Geneva,
Sept. 10, 1922.

I am more hustled than I have ever been. To-day, being
Sunday, I have had the morning for an article to the

Manchester Guardian (a little less hasty than one's wires) which I am sending by post. It's an awful business, as there is Assembly in the morning, the committees, and no end of people buzzing round, and no time to reflect or get anything right. Everything in Assembly is repeated both in French and English, which is a waste of time I am not sorry for. But as everything is printed very quickly, one might almost as well not be there! I find Reuter is also reporting to the M. G. which makes it difficult for us to know what to send and what not. I am really impressed by what the League does within its powers, but of course it is mostly complicated and continuous and does not lend itself to quick grasping or reporting. The great thing is that people of different nations have to sit together and give account of their actions or their governments'. When dinner engagements are added to all the work it becomes really desperate. However I suppose I shall get through, and endeavour not to fuss. I have had to take veronal twice, which I don't approve of and must endeavour not to repeat. But if one doesn't sleep one is a rag next day. Moorsom is a great comfort, so helpful as well as so cheerful. He is off however for the week-end walking somewhere, and of course it has come on to rain.

At this date he is definitely hopeful, after 1923 he begins to get sceptical, partly owing to the League's failure over Corfu, and partly owing to an experience of his own. In 1927 he became again hopeful, thanks to the admission of Germany, but then came the aggressive policy of Japan in the Far East and the League's inability, from whatever cause, to protect his beloved China. He did not live to see the withdrawals of Japan and of Germany, but he had witnessed enough to write in his 'Recollections':

Sooner or later a crisis with a great Power is bound to arise and then we shall know whether the League will face the music and win. I think the most likely thing is that there will be no declaration from the Council of who is the aggressor (the British Government by repudiating the Protocol has rejected the only complete definition of an aggressor) and that the members of the League will range themselves on opposite sides.

Only in the case of a comparatively small problem (such as the threatened Greco-Bulgarian conflict) was the Council prepared to act effectively—in other words to act quickly. As soon as powerful interests were involved the machinery slowed up.

To his mind the most urgent question before the League was the treatment of Germany. He held the opinion—and it is an opinion which was once common among Englishmen —that when a war is over it is at all events over for the victors, and that no further punishment need be imposed. Moreover his cultural sympathies were German rather than French; how could he condemn as barbarous the country of Goethe, Hegel and Wagner? He paid a short visit to Berlin in 1920, largely under the auspices of the Quakers, and the misery he saw there among the educated and professional classes made a deep impression on him. So did the sinister atmosphere. 'The most terrible city I ever saw', he writes to May: 'all *planned* (not muddled into like London) and planned without a sign of heart or feeling. It's really typical of the capitalist militarist epoch.' He hoped that the Germans were going to react against the brutality in their tradition, and he knew that they would only react if they were treated in a civilised way by the French and others. Their misery was the most pressing of the evils to be righted at Geneva.

He only once took an official part in League affairs. It was in July 1923, when he served on the 'Committee on Intellectual Co-operation', and a significant incident occurred. This committee had been appointed by the Council of the League. Its chief duties were to examine into the state of learning and culture, and propose measures of relief in distressed areas. Professor Gilbert Murray, the British member, was unable to attend its second session, and Dickinson acted as his deputy. He at once disconcerted his colleagues by raising the question of establishing contact with Germany and of helping the German universities. The name of Germany was mentioned as seldom as possible at

Geneva. She had not yet joined the League, and many of the members had suffered from her during the war and were disposed to withhold relief from her, if possible on high philosophic grounds. And, as if he had not shocked them enough by mentioning her, he went on to suggest that an immediate appeal for funds should be made in America and elsewhere. He urged that the situation was critical, that it concerned not only Germany but civilisation as a whole; clearly he felt that here was a test as to whether people were willing to meet a human need in a field which ought to be non-controversial.

The president of the committee (Henri Bergson) thereupon rose with his accustomed tact and said that there was no question yet of appealing for funds: the committee must continue to examine into the state of learning, and he particularly deprecated any appeal to America; it was without precedent, and might lead to criticism both of the League and of the committee. Dickinson replied that if the appeal was an innovation it was one which he would welcome. He was next told that it would be very difficult to help the German universities because they were state-owned, but this did not wipe out from his memory the starvation he had seen in Berlin. Unable to silence him, the committee then became every inch a committee and set to work to draft a set of alternative resolutions on the lines of his own, but less drastic and more open to interpretation. These he accepted, confident that at all events something would be done for Germany. He took little further part in the debates of the session.

The incident had a sequel. After his return to England he received in due course a list of the national committees which had been set up in the various countries under the auspices of the League for the purpose of intellectual co-operation. Nearly every country, distressed or not distressed, was on the list: Austria, Belgium, Brazil, Bulgaria, &c. But Germany was absent. He was furious and believed he had been tricked. Gilbert Murray shared his indignation and wrote a strongly worded letter to 'The Times' pointing out that the omission of Germany was bound to bring discredit on the League. He himself wrote to 'The Manchester Guardian' and also corresponded with M. de Halecki, the secretary of the committee on which he had served. M. de Halecki apparently rebuked him for writing to the press and asserted that though Germany was omitted from the list there was no intention of discriminating against her. Dickinson was always at the top of his form when rebuked, and he replied: 'I do not of course question that you had no intention your circular should produce the effect it does produce, and if public correspondence should bring out clearly the fact that funds for Germany will be accepted by the Committee, nothing but good will have been done to your objects'. The episode left him with the suspicion that ill faith, as well as timidity, lay entrenched at Geneva.

In spite of his growing doubts he continued to support the League. He saw no other alternative to anarchy, and he felt that if men like Lord Robert Cecil and Sir Arthur Salter believed in it, it must be good. Also he realised, during his frequent visits, that the permanent secretariat was almost unconsciously acquiring an international attitude, and this cheered him. He usually stopped with Elliott Felkin of King's, who was working in the Secretariat with Salter. Occasionally Dickinson acted as correspondent to 'The Nation' and to 'The Manchester Guardian'. Between his visits he was constantly writing to Felkin on points connected with the League. One of these letters shall be quoted in full, to illustrate the closeness with which he followed events. The document on which it comments is 'the Protocol for the pacific settlement of International disputes of 1924'. This Protocol had attempted to close what is known as 'the gap in the Covenant' by providing an automatic test for defining aggression. It was rendered useless by the refusal of the British to sign it—a refusal to which reference has already been made (p. 185).

King's,
Nov. 5th, 1924.

Dear Elliott,

Many thanks for your letter and enclosures. It's really extraordinary how difficult it is to ascertain what any official document means. You say, e.g., and it seems to be borne out by the resolutions of the Assembly 1921, that 'it is the duty of each member of the League to decide for itself whether a breach of the Covenant has been committed'. But on turning to the amendments supposed to carry out these resolutions of the Assembly one reads 'it is for the *Council* to give an opinion whether or not a breach of the Covenant has taken place', which seems flatly to contradict the other. However, that is not the immediate point. So far as I can see, the Protocol is *formally* watertight in its provisions for preventing war: for apparently, even in the case of 'domestic questions', if one Power seems inclined to attack, or does attack, the Council can instantly impose an armistice and then the party not acceding becomes the aggressor. The argument that the Protocol would not *work* therefore seems really to amount in fact to saying that some states would break their agreement. I am far from disputing this. But it strikes at the Covenant as much as at the Protocol. I see, now that we have a Tory Government, that this blessed country, after affirming its love of peace, etc., will be the one to wreck the Protocol, to which even the small states opposed to the treaty of mutual guarantee and the incorrigible France have come round. Truth is, the British really can't bear not to be able to make war when they want it—adding, of course, that they never could want it, and never have wanted it, except for the sake of 'justice', 'liberty', 'right', et hoc genus omne. If Curzon is to be Foreign Minister, I should prophecy war with both Turkey and Russia in a very near future. If on the other hand—quod est impossible—they were to make Cecil Foreign Minister? But no, they couldn't....

I work continuously at my book on pre-war diplomacy, but without any idea that it is much use. No one will read it, and if they do no one will profit. However it keeps me occupied, and in an odd kind of way (rather morbid) interested. There are some nice young men here as usual, and

I am contented enough, though rapidly approaching old age and losing my memory.

Yours,

G. L. D.

The book referred to is 'The International Anarchy' at which he was working during his Geneva period. Perhaps the sense that history was repeating itself helped to disillusion him with the League. But he remained at the service of the League of Nations Union. Here is a letter telling May about a lecture at Cambridge in 1926.

My lecture went off all right. There were about 150 people including an admiral and two generals. The admiral was charming, the breezy kind. I having remarked that no doubt most soldiers and sailors regarded the League as 'tommy rot' (the nearest I dared approach to the probable language) he said 'the phrase "tommy rot" does injustice to the British Navy. The real language is of a kind I can't repeat, but infinitely stronger'. He dotted all my eyes [sic], and said afterwards he could not think how I had discovered so much of the truth! The general, or one of them (the 'junior service' as he remarked bowing to the admiral) was less candid and made an effort to pretend soldiers were pacifists. Of course he could cite one or two. I asked him if he personally knew any who were, and the answer was silence. The other general didn't talk, but asked intelligent questions I didn't know the answer to.

This pleasant letter reminds me of the mess room at Peshawar fourteen years before, when the delighted officers made him swallow the prairie oyster. The date of it is significant; in this year 'The International Anarchy' is published and the final period of his life begins.

CHAPTER XIII

'THE INTERNATIONAL ANARCHY'
1926

THE war, for Dickinson, ended not with the Treaty of Versailles but with the publication of 'The International Anarchy'. That was the date when he established a truce in his own heart. He could do no more against the powers of evil, he had no new weapon in his armoury, he knew that if he attacked again he would become mechanical, hysterical, non-human, an automaton repeating arguments without waiting for the replies, and shrieking peace peace through a megaphone. Some critics will say that he had worn himself out with worry. Others, more discriminating, will say that he had worked the poison of the war out of his system by producing a big book on it, and could now settle down to a cheerful old age. Both are wrong—the first because they ignore the vitality of his last years, the second because they ignore the melancholy mingled with the vitality. He had not come to the end of his powers, but he had with merciless honesty surveyed them. He had always been clear sighted. In his youth he had settled down to be a don because it was the best career of which he felt himself capable. In his old age he forced tragedy into the background because he could not handle it fruitfully any more. He was not complacent, and it would be an error to round off his career complacently. Churchill, Mussolini, Hitler, Gandhi and other menaces to peace still exist and he never forgot them.

'The International Anarchy' is important both in itself and because it initiates this truce. At the time he began to write it he was in the deepest gloom, which he has recorded in a long manuscript note, dated October 30th, 1921:

In all this chaotic horror I find one thread running through which seems to me true and beautiful; that is the

activity of the Quakers. Wherever in Europe is trouble—
and where is there not?—these few men and women are
to be found, talking little, doing much, bringing relief to
Germany, Austria, now to Russia, while the big guns talk
and do nothing. That is one way of life, which is clearly
good. But it is not my way. I set myself at the beginning
to discover all the truth I could, and to state it. The result
is meagre enough, perhaps it is less than nothing, but I have
no other path.

I do not know whether this frame of mind will persist
to the end, which may still be several years, or whether it
will lighten and clarify. Meantime, since I can do nothing
else, I have settled down once more to the pre-war diplomacy, with the idea that I might yet write something that
might be of use. For the last few days I have spent most
of my time reading despatches. It is dreary work enough,
but there is a kind of dramatic interest in it, to see this
catastrophe approaching, to see everyone afraid of it yet
everyone hoping to profit by it, to see how inevitable it is
while the European system prevails, how necessary a complete change of system is, if mankind is not to move quickly
to the final destruction. Every one around me, all my best
friends even, seem to have settled down to live as before,
pleasantly, cynically, or whatever may be their attitude.
I almost alone arise and go to bed with the constant
obsession, is there to be a continuance of the old to the
new war, or a radical transformation? The pain becomes
almost unendurable, and I can only stave it off by plunging
into some kind of work, which yet must bear upon it.

The work of preparation was formidable. Some pre-
liminaries had been done in 'The European Anarchy', but
now he read all the diplomatic documents, including the new
matter published by the Soviet Government. He tried out
some of the material in lectures at King's and at the London
School of Economics, and found it rather intractable. He writes
from Cambridge to Elliott Felkin (February 10th, 1922):

I'm lecturing here on pre-war diplomacy, badly I fear,
and with much labour to myself. The stuff of course is
damned complicated and it's very difficult to arrange and
make clear and interesting to the ignorant. Besides why

does one? This little fly, shaking a remote corner of the spider web of the universe, must look absurd to an onlooking Spinoza-god, who likes to feed the spider. So long, and may what we call society last long enough for you to run a happy course.

This is an unusual mood in which to settle down to four or five years' research. The book produced at the end is remarkable from two points of view. Remarkable in the first place for its learning, logic and lucidity. It has mastered and digested all the available facts, has given an account of the pre-war diplomacy which will never be superseded, has shown how that diplomacy was bound to produce war, and will produce war. Remarkable in the second place because it contains no exhibition of emotion. The violent feelings which agitated the writer, the indignation and irritation, the sorrow and despair, are suppressed, lest they endanger his appeal. He refuses to show his readers how much he suffers, in case they are diverted from the facts and discount the argument. And so, paradoxically enough, 'The International Anarchy' ranks high as a work of art. It is supported by an intense emotion which is never allowed to ruffle the surface. It has the quality which, working through another temperament and in another medium, has produced Bach's fugues.

This quality becomes plainer if we compare it with a book which seems more artistic at the first glance: 'The Magic Flute'. 'The Magic Flute' deserves the praise given to it in a previous chapter. It is serious, profound, inventive, fanciful, beautifully written. But it has one defect; as soon as it describes war the writer's emotions get out of control, and we have him lamenting or denouncing instead of creating. He wrote it too near the events he was trying to exorcise. The war had to sink deeper into him, its causes and its consequences had to penetrate more elaborately before he could attain the agony which is serenity and write 'The International Anarchy'.

The writing of the book is contemporaneous with his visits to Geneva and the League. At last it was accomplished, and on June 2nd, 1927, he concludes another remarkable work, the main version of his 'Recollections', with the following words:

I have published (last November) my big book on the origins of the War. I know that this is a good book. I believe it to be possibly the best book on the subject, because it is the only one I know which stresses the only important fact—that it is not this or that nation nor its policy, but the anarchy that causes wars. The book was considerably and favourably reviewed, but it has not sold as much as a thousand copies, another testimony to the general truth that truth is the last thing people care about. Meantime I have been occupying myself largely with the translation of 'Faust' which Miss Stawell and myself have been working at, and which is now complete. It has been, and is, an infinite relief to me to deal with a mind so sane and so great as Goethe's. But we have not yet found a publisher for our book, and I anticipate the usual fate for it. I don't seem to care much now. I am getting very old and have little left to do but to keep myself innocently occupied so long as I can and must. I still enjoy myself much and often. This term in particular Cambridge has been so lovely in the almost perpetual sunshine that it has been enough to be alive and look at it. And still the young men exercise their perennial fascination, the few I know who are also fit.

He has written a book which he knows to be good and which might save Europe if its lessons were heeded, and under a thousand copies of it have been sold. As in the business of the Boxer indemnity, two years previously, he has been brushed aside. Practical men don't want him. He retires without bitterness and without self-consciousness into his castle, and the Queen of the Night continues her genderings beyond mind.

CHAPTER XIV

THE TRUCE
1926–1932

I

THE rooms in Gibbs's Building, G staircase, which Dickinson occupied for the last twenty years of his life, had been decorated under the advice of Roger Fry, and I remember them as the most beautiful college set I knew as well as the best beloved. They were above the arch of that Jumbo House which has previously been described. One room, crimson papered, looked into the front court, through the great semicircular window. There were two of Fry's pictures here—an early portrait of Ferdinand Schiller, and a landscape of Taormina, ridge beyond ridge and Etna behind. The second main room looked over the Backs. Its walls had a grass-paper of grey-green, and on the floor was a Chinese carpet, featuring four thin pale-purple dragons on a biscuit-coloured ground. Besides the bedroom, there was also an attic, with a little circular window up in the middle of the pediment. Here Dickinson sometimes slept, and anyone who came into college late could see the small round eye of his light—the highest habitable point in King's.

Almost a century earlier another eminent Kingsman had occupied the set—Charles Simeon, the evangelical divine. Simeon's elderly friends had found the climb to the second floor tiring, so a handrail had been placed for their convenience on the staircase, and it is still called 'The Saint's Rest'. Painted chocolate, it leads upwards, through ghosts and draughts. The staircase looks built for eternity, so solidly it stands, but a few years back the death-watch beetle was discovered throughout Gibbs, and there was a fear that the upper dons might fall through on to the heads of the lower.

This was averted, and during the repairs the colour of Dickinson's front wall-paper was changed. For me, however, it remains crimson.

Though he had occupied the set for so long, it seemed to become his own in this final period, when he had done what he could for peace and might retire to his castle and wait. In the vestibule, like weapons at rest, lay the documents he had used in 'The International Anarchy': 'books more for gentlemen really' as a bedmaker rightly remarked. Books were everywhere, but he had a serviceable rather than a valuable library, and was never a bibliophile. The pictures, the Chinese objects, the honourable family furniture, made a stronger impression than the books. The atmosphere was hot: gas, electricity, cosey-stoves, valor-perfection lamps, sizzled and roared. He was determined to get comfortable, why not? and his plaintive appeals mingled with those of other dons bent on a similar ideal and poured into the ears of the Bursar. He succeeded. There was even a bath which had, in the end, no need to be filled with kettles off the ring: there was even that rarest of all academic birds, a W.C. The mixture of luxury and hardship so characteristic of Cambridge retains no charm for a man who is approaching seventy. It is the privilege of the young.

But was he approaching seventy? When his friends argued as they sometimes did, whether he was very old or very young, they had no doubt about the superlative: he was certainly neither rather old nor rather young and he might be approaching seventeen. His appearance at a distance; his air of discouragement and fatigue; his bad memory; his occasional petulance; the garrulity which would pour out an account of the book last read, the play just seen—all these suggested a man at the term of life. Then, in a flash, he seemed younger than anyone, his mind more elastic, his gestures more natural. His sympathy, in particular, had the quickness of youth—that was what made it so precious. And his judgment—thank goodness!—was sometimes at fault. He never acquired that canniness about character which is so depressing in the mature. Although he was shrewd about historical evidence he could blunder over his acquaintances, because he accepted them at their own valuation. If you went up to him in his rooms and told him you were virtuous and able and poor, he would for a time believe you; your merits would be extolled, your qualifications advertised, your wants relieved. And even when he found you out, you retained the right to be a bore. He was generous—in every sense of the word—and as the years passed his generosity got more instinctive. Heaven knows what he gave away in cash; and his other gifts which could be more easily discerned were so spontaneous, they fell on to the recipients before they knew where they were.

One hesitates to call him 'a popular don', for the words suggest some cheery empty creature. He never tried to ingratiate himself with the young: he was too modest and also too proud. When they returned to Cambridge after the war, he felt out of sympathy with them, and when the change took place and both young and old wanted his company, it would have annoyed him to be told he was a success. I remember watching a perky undergraduate ferreting about in his books and him saying to me gently 'I don't know his name —he calls me Goldie'. This expressed a general relationship. The younger generation entered, scarcely knocking at the door, and called him Goldie because they forgot his age and their own.

Another undergraduate, whom he came to know well, has written an impressionistic sketch of a first visit. I will quote from it. Date about 1930. I compare it with my own early memories of Winchester cutlets, and find it in every way superior to them. 'Liebling', as he calls himself, is pounding up G staircase with no thought of 'The Saint's Rest'. He bursts in and:

> a musty smell as of a world silted up with unwanted books met him at the door and a hot air rushed past him down the staircase and out into the cold strenuous winter

world where it perished quickly, and Liebling rubbed his feet cautiously according to directions then paused uncertain which of a variety of doors to choose. 'Come in' cried a distant voice and through tobacco smoke past seated figures stiff and monumental past a large table eager with knives forks tumblers wine glasses he went up to an old mandarin or perhaps it was the holy Larmah seated on a large padded chair with a book rest and a great iron stove in front of him which was roasting everyone in the room except the mandarin who seemed accustomed to the most intense heat and heard a quiet kind voice that never flowed exactly in periods yet was never harsh or frightening say 'So glad to meet your father's son, how do you like King's?'

I don't quite catch the words of greeting, but the heat, the big table, the doubts on arrival are all authentic, as is the banquet which develops:

Food was carried in in large silver plates the mandarin grew nervous and excited as to whether it had really all come could so little food possibly feed so many guests and with his gesture he indicated vast hungry hordes hanging on the outskirts of the table, more silver dishes were brought in, more sausages floating, no reposing on soft beds of mincemeat, like a cockney in his bath, were uncovered steaming, what are they drinking the Larmah asked, and obediently guests became unstuck, moveable, manly, corks popped cider frothed over even the Chinese student began giving advice sausages and mincemeat were conveyed to their final destination the Larmah seemed satisfied somehow the hungry were fed only a miracle could really explain it, the tension relaxed the conversation began.

Various topics occur, such as birth control, do reformed sinners make the best schoolmasters, are there compulsory chapels in China. Finally:

They don't mind dying much in China, do they? shouted Liebling to the Chinaman, hoping to introduce a story he had heard about how one could buy a substitute to be accepted for one. 'Always dying' said the Larmah 'millions by starvation flood plague at this moment so thick on the ground.' That explains why they believe in metamorphosis don't you think said the clever student confidentially to the Larmah. 'May be its true for all I know' said the Larmah shaking his hands towards the two remaining sausages reposing on their cold beds of mincemeat, and just for a moment Liebling was quite certain that in the whole world there was only this funny old man sitting in front of two cold sausages saying I don't know my dear boy, and feeding the starving.

Then the second course comes in—an enormous apple pie with cream—and Dickinson characteristically tries to change all the plates himself. Every one jumps up to help him, and the vision closes.

Besides undergraduates, dons, and constant visitors male and female from London, my own vision of those rooms includes some college servants—more particularly his bedmakers Mrs Newman and Mrs Richardson, Mrs Asplin, and his gyps Rose and Fuller. It surprised him that people who went to and fro and had not even a permanency of masters should be so loyal to the College; among his Cambridges, the Cambridge of dependents was never forgotten, and he was always active on its behalf at College meetings. Not that he was always tactful with his entourage. His innocency bordered on social rashness. He would call out 'Again no slop basin? your memory's as bad as mine!' or he would use up all his tea, forget he had done so, and enquire 'Wherever can it have gone to?' The entourage on its side, had to do a good deal of clearing up and searching. He was not practical, and I can still hear him damning his sleeve links in the morning because they wouldn't go in, or his hot water bottle at night because it puffed in his face when he filled it. He swore constantly, and no wonder. For he was unhandy with 'so called inanimate objects'. They were always splashing or scalding him, or beating a merry retreat at the moment he needed them most. 'Here you are, yes of course' he would say, lifting a sheet of paper, and there beneath it, after the locksmith had been sent for, would be the bunch of keys.

It surprised us after his death that all his papers should be in perfect order, until we remembered his unselfishness and independence; he had spent the last weeks sorting and docketing, so that if the end did come his executors should have the minimum of trouble with his affairs. His will was both thoughtful and affectionate, and the names mentioned earlier in this paragraph are recorded in it among his other friends.

As regards College administration, he was conscientious rather than active. He was diffident at meetings, and he put what he had to say clearly, but not forcibly. Besides being a member of the Congregation, the governing body to which all Fellows of King's belong, he was sometimes elected to the Council, and he was invariably chosen to be a Fellowship Elector, and a member of the Tribunal. He had strong opinions about the development of the College estates, and when it involved the destruction of natural beauty, as it sometimes did, he was not easily appeased. Nor did he favour throwing open the grounds of the College for military parades.

Outside King's he had various interests, as was natural in view of his long residence. He was a vigorous member of the Cambridge Preservation Society, and he was for a time President of the Council for the entertainment of foreign students at Cambridge. In London he was a Fellow of the Royal Society of Literature. The list of his little honours might be extended, but I am unwilling to make it sound important, for he was not interested in posts or in having letters after his name. What he cared for was love and truth. What he hoped for was a change in the human heart. He did not see how the civilisation which he had tried to help could be saved unless the human heart changed, and he meant by 'saved' not some vague apotheosis but salvation from aerial bombing and poison gas.

Let us follow him now from his rooms, down the sloping lawn, over the bridge, through the avenue, across the Backs, and let us leave him in his outdoor home.

In Fellows Gardens, May 4th, 1928:

Yesterday and to day sunshine and lovely May weather.
A great thunderstorm Wednesday cleared away the clouds
at last. I have been sitting in the garden this morning
browsing partly on Goethe partly on Ryland's book,
Words and Poetry, partly on the flowers—the cherries past
their best but scattering white snow on the grass, tulips
yellow red and white, irises, bushes of pyrus japonica, all
dazzling in the sun. Beauty becomes more precious as it
is more precarious for me. One takes the moment—'ver-
weile doch du bist so schön'. I saw clearly this morning that
Goethe is a seer rather than a poet. Never I think has
he the magic of words as Shakespeare had and so many
English poets (any German?). But he sees everything and
sticks it down. . .and what clearness of visual impression. . .
and good songs and good ballads, where simplicity is everything and freshness and genuineness. . .and how profound
and human, e.g. Gott und die Bajadere, also read this
morning. How brave and unmorbid, how Chrĭst-ian (not
chrĭstian), how continually and persistently wise! And at
times how great in lyrics—as in the close of the classical
Walpurgisnacht.—The young men in the orchard yesterday at tea apple blossom everywhere—and on the river,
as lazy and lovely as ever—also, being English, as unconscious and unimaginative. This too happens in the world,
and I take off my hat to it.

2

The books written during these years of respite all have roots
in a pre-war world. The studies on Goethe and on Plato both
go back to the innocent and unblockaded Germany of 1884
and to the Heidelberg pine woods. The life of McTaggart
evokes the Cambridge of the 'eighties and 'nineties where he
had found McTaggart, Fry, Wedd, Schiller. The dialogue
'After Two Thousand Years' goes back to the same Cambridge, city of friendship and truth, Elysian Field where
the old man who is eternally young converses with himself
under the semblances of Plato and Philalaethes, and it also
goes back to Mistra, Greece visible, birthplace of Euphorion,

where the inspiration of writing in the dialogue form first came. It was not until his political work had been concluded by the 'International Anarchy' that he resumed his earlier allegiance to imagination and poetry. His last books do not by any means retreat into fairy land, but they do escape from the struggle with facts and from the enumeration of facts which had occupied him since 1914.

'Goethe and Faust, an Interpretation' (1928), was written in collaboration with Miss Melian Stawell. It is mainly Miss Stawell's work, and he would have had this stated on the title-page but for her resistance. She had finished a rough draft with which she was dissatisfied and had asked for his help, since she knew that he had returned to 'Faust' after the war. His function was mainly that of a critic and a condenser, though they discussed every point and attempted a common style. Miss Stawell has given me a list of about forty passages in the book which are entirely his: they include the description of the opening of the Second Part (pp. 118–22), and the comparison between the final heavenly joy and the Final of the Fourth Act of Shelley's 'Prometheus' (pp. 256–7). The translations are hers—except for some of the Mephistopheles items. The book is a competent sensitive guide, and it should become popular if an interest in Goethe ever revives in this country. Miss Stawell and he also completed a translation of both parts of 'Faust', which remains in manuscript. Furthermore he broadcast on Goethe. His idea was that a renewed study of Goethe at this crisis of our history might lead to a new advance, and he was delighted when men of the younger generation—Robert Nichols for instance—encouraged him. On the whole he received little encouragement. The British public remains cold to the colossus, however tactfully and enthusiastically he is presented. Possibly now that Germany has raised the cry of 'Deutschland ohne Goethe' we shall begin to read him, but not in the spirit which Dickinson enjoined.

'After Two Thousand Years: a dialogue between Plato and

a modern young man' (1930) is one of his finest books. It
pays its double tribute to Plato and to Cambridge, and the
superb passage of prose with which it ends has an oratorical
splendour which shuts out daily life. But it is coloured by
recent experience, for it is the result of his friendship with
the post-war generation. It reveals his ability to learn from
the young. We can all like the young, envy them, and fear
them, but to learn from them is more difficult. The conceit
of experience, the pride of established position, get in our
way, and if we do learn we hope they don't notice it in case
it makes them uppish. Dickinson was above all such pettiness,
because he was in a state where the years do not count:
Plato enters into the young man's outlook in order to develop
his own, and he himself is as much the young man as he is
Plato. The book—which incorporates part of a manuscript
dialogue—is more intimate and frank than most of his publications. He seems to be liberated from conventions which have
hampered him, and can discuss easily and quietly such subjects as love between people of the same sex, or the artificial
control of population. The first half of the dialogue is concerned with the means towards a good life, the second with
the good life itself. 'Yes, the book is my testament and I can
now say "Nunc Dimittis"', he writes to Robin Mayor. He
hopes 'to clear off the memoir of McTaggart and I should
like if there were time to do something about my father for
our own satisfaction', but the serious work of his life is over.

Next year the loyal and affectionate tribute to McTaggart
duly appeared. He was not well satisfied with it. Various
friends had contributed chapters or paragraphs at his request,
and these, however excellent in themselves, blurred the main
outline. Moreover, the complexity of his own emotions may
have confused him. His intense admiration for McTaggart,
their war differences (which McTaggart chose to regard as
mystically non-existent) and their tacit reunion after the war
did not make for literary detachment. McTaggart was a
remarkable figure, possibly a great man, certainly a very

strange one, and, biographically speaking, such a man needs rather ruthless handling if he is to come alive. Dickinson only brought sensitiveness and piety. It is a pity that he could not go on to the projected memoir of his father. The relationship there, though less intimate, was probably more amenable to his treatment.

The other two books, 'Plato and his Dialogues' (1931) and 'The Contribution of Ancient Greece to Modern Life' (1932) were offshoots from other activities. The 'Plato' enlarges some excellent broadcast talks. He was a good broadcaster and his gentle husky voice came through well. Besides the talks on Plato and Goethe, he introduced and closed a series called 'Points of View'; and contributed to the series called 'What I would do with the World'. The interest he aroused showed that a larger public was awaiting him. One day I came across a man in a train who had been listening to 'Points of View'—a series which included Wells, Shaw, etc. He was half clerk, half sailor, and wholly unacademic, and he said that the speaker he really did like was the one he had never heard of before—someone called Low Dickens. I was not surprised. I had always known that Low Dickens existed inside the lengthier designations of the don.

The pamphlet on Ancient Greece in its relation to modern life was a reprint of a lecture delivered to a Summer School. It was published a few days after his death. He was due to broadcast on the same subject in the autumn of the year, and one of his anxieties when he went into hospital was that he might be inconveniencing the B.B.C. officials who had engaged him.

3

I end with several letters. Letters have to pass two tests before they can be classed as good: they must express the personality both of the writer and of the recipient. Dickinson's letters pass the first test but not the second. When he writes, he is always himself—interesting, thoughtful, sympathetic, never failing in comfort or counsel. But there is not the final touch of magic in virtue of which the recipient, as it were, shines through the paper upon which the words are written. It is a magic commoner in talk than in writing, and even in talk many people fail to achieve it, and say their how d'ye do or yes in tones unvarying. And one would not even look for it in his letters, were he not so sensitive and selfless. He, if anyone, might be expected to reflect the unseen features of his correspondents and to echo their inaudible heart-beats. I do not think that he does; to be precise, the personalities of his two great women friends, Mrs Webb and Mrs Moor, have not come out clearly through what he writes to them. Except for the differences in the subject-matter, what is addressed to the one might have been addressed to the other. When he spoke to his friends or spoke of them all altered at once; he vibrated to wave after wave, and as he turned his head from guest to guest at one of his lunch parties one felt that a new universe was seated on every chair. That was his strength, that was his glory, and if that could be communicated in a biography, he would appear for what he was; one of the rarest creatures of our generation. His letters are a misleading substitute; they tend to exhibit him as merely sympathetic and kind.

These later letters are much the best. They are fresher and more translucent, the meditative whirlpools are fewer and they have a quickness of movement unusual in a writer of his age. Moreover, many of them are written to the young, so that they show what he signified when he was in his sixties to correspondents who were still in their twenties and thirties. Their manners are perfect. They don't condescend or chirrup or instruct, nor have they that uneasy ingratiating note which spoils the communications of many well-meaning old men.

They are typed; and the typing is even more remarkable than the handwriting which it superseded. He is said to be the only man who could make a Corona type upside down. He struck the keys rapidly and violently, thinking of what he thought and not of what he did, with the result that he doubled lines, halved them, threw capitals in the air, buried numerals in the earth, broke out into orgies of ?????? or %%%%%, and hammered his ribbon to shreds. George becomes 'Geroge', Gerald 'Gerlad', perhaps 'perhpas', and there are even happier transformations such as husband into 'humsband', and soul into 'soup'. A semicolon in the middle of a word means '1'. When the page was finished he had by no means done with it. He seized his pen and frantically coursed to and fro, correcting, connecting, obscuring, exclaiming 'oh dear!' or 'damn' in the margin. So charming was the result that his friends could scarcely believe it was unintentional. The whimsicality and gaiety in his nature seemed to have found a new outlet and machinery to be of some use after all.

I have arranged the letters in alphabetical order of recipients, and added notes in square brackets.

To Clifford Allen. [Lord Allen of Hurtwood; they discuss the manuscript of 'After Two Thousand Years'.]

Dear Clifford,

King's Coll. Camb.
Aug. 4th (1929?).

I have long thought you the most intelligent and helpful of critics and I think so now more than ever. What you say is exactly the kind of thing that helps, and it seems to me all perfectly true. Writing is the devil, especially as one has to write into a void, not knowing who will read. Over simplifications sometimes seem necessary, if one is to make any effect at all. But it is true that they exasperate. It is also curiously true that a single word may lead to exasperation. I occasionally feel inclined to say that it is better to exasperate, since people won't attend at all otherwise. But I know that really that isn't my game because I never want to do it in conversation. I shall lay your comments aside with my MS. and rewrite at leisure, if I am allowed either leisure or time at all. It's so queer how one suddenly drops out without warning, and one naturally considers that at my age. I do hope my dear Clifford that you will have continual opportunity for that face-to-face verbal persuasion of people actually in politics which seems to me both so important and so difficult, and for which you have such gifts. For aught I know to the contrary, you have gifts of writing too and will use them. But the other seems to me a remarkable speciality, yours, and I hope and expect that health and circumstances will always allow it. I am glad to think of you enjoying that place and I hope better in health. It is true, I think, anyhow, and you and me apart, that the whole order of society which made it possible is vanishing. So perhaps is all English country, inevitably. I hate the thought, but see no way of doing more than save a few bits.

Did you see in the 'Nation' a really interesting article— as I thought—on youth and the war?

An upset has occurred in my plans not worth writing about, which may mean that I have to change them—plans for the summer, I mean. By the bye, I'm reading Shaw's book. He really *is* a writer! And as full of blind spots as men of genius usually are, and apparently must be.

Yours,

G. D.

To Julian Bell. [In a previous letter, partly reproduced at p. 208, he discusses Bell's 'Winter Movement', and greets him as 'the one man who might be a poet among those of the younger generation'. 'Arms and the Man', the Satire here criticised, has appeared in a shortened form in the Anthology 'New Signatures'.]

King's College, Cambridge.

Dear Julian,   July 17, 1931.

Dadie handed me the other day your poem. It was charming of you to dedicate it to me, and I am rejoiced to think that there is at least one young man who hates war. But—these buts! forgive me I am getting an old man and venture to take an old man's offensive liberties. I feel that your poem will be nothing but provocative and offensive to every kind of man that reads it. You will reply that you mean it to be. Yes, but I am thinking of the main thing, what will tend to change opinion about war. I have spent years over this business, not too successfully, and I get more and more convinced that one's only chance is to understand and believe that one is up against an extraordinary complex of atavistic feelings genuinely held by quite good people. (I grant you the others, but I think it is the mass opinions, fears, devotions, despairs, boredoms, poverty, which are the real obstacle.) I regret now every escape of irritation satire and rage which I have let escape, and, to be honest, I feel that, if I accept this dedication from you, I shall be supposed to endorse your methods. Will you understand and forgive my dear, and perhaps reconsider the whole poem? For I feel it in my bones that if you publish it you may regret it later, and that it may do you harm in a way which you yourself will regret. I would not say this latter if I did not feel that you have the chance to write good poetry (which I don't feel about many of the young, though that may be only the imperception of old age) and I would like you not to throw unnecessary obstacles in your own way. Write and forgive me anyhow.   Yours always,

                                        G. LOWES DICKINSON.

To Bernhard Berenson. [The opening reference is to the 'Letters from Italy' of Mr Lowes Dickinson which had been privately printed. 'Tomcat copulation' was then on his mind for the same month he writes to another correspondent, Mrs E. B. C. Lucas: 'The sexual goings on of the present young seem to me very disastrous and very sordid, and I don't think this is a matter of mere silly Victorianism. I think that some of our best intellectuals are simply throwing themselves into the mud till they can savour nothing else'. These strictures are not characteristic; he spent but little time in being shocked by the young. The T.L.S. article on Goethe, was, he believed, by Middleton Murry.]

                                        King's Coll. Camb.
Dear B. B.   March 27th, 1932.

I am very glad to get your letter and that you found my fathers' interesting. They have always been very interesting to me and I think he had a very good vivid Victorian style of letter writing. He was a most charming and delightful

Kings Coll Camb Dec 8

Dear Julian

I ve been reading your poems I have always thought
that you were the oneman who might be a Pote among theose of
the younger generation I happen to have read   certainly

ta nk so the more now There is one poem towards he end in
particular marsh birds pass over Lndo , which impressed and
moved me very much. But they are all interesting and there I
expect one should stop.But I will ne ertheless asd that I th
thin k you try to much to do in petyr what only painting
cando However all this close observatio and record is no
doubt much more hopeful and promising than the usual outpour
ing of immature emoti s Sympathetic thoug I am to this lat
ter.And Shakespeare certainly b&gen like that.The other
sway point s that I thin k yo are to fond of the device o

Letter to Julian Bell, 1930

man, as I am discerning more and more as I read through a number of old family letters. His marriage with my mother was as near the perfect as anything can be in this world, deepening affection on both sides to the end. As I observe from the outside the ways of the modern young, it sometimes seems to me that they are losing everything in a kind of tomcat copulation of the most miscellaneous kind—but I know it is an old and perhaps inevitable vice of the old to growse at the young.

I was very sorry to hear how ill Mary has been. Please give her my kindest remembrances and sympathy. I am glad to see that she is better, and I shall look forward to the possibility of seeing you both in the autumn. To you old age is only a threat, to me it begins to be a reality and of course an unpleasant one. Among other things I have almost lost what little memory I ever had. Still when one is well, and one's mind active, there is something soothing about old age. It's no use fussing any more. I wonder whether you read an article on Goethe in this week's Literary Supplement, of 'The Times', I think it most remarkable and am anxious to know who could have written it. It seems to me just right. For years I have felt Goethe to be more important than any other man and now I see more clearly why.

As to the world about one, I have the chronic feeling of living in a lunatic asylum and I can hardly suppose that a débâcle of unimaginable dimensions is not imminent. If only I could depart before it comes!

Yours sincerely,
G. LOWES DICKINSON.

To Mrs O. W. Campbell. [He much admired her 'Shelley and the Unromantics'. The following passage about religion is suggested by her 'Camilla's Banquet'.]

King's,
March 11, 1932.

I find that my own view or feeling or whatever one should say changes in old age. I have always valued the peculiarly Cambridge attitude about truth and I do so still, and always shall, since it is our only safeguard (if it *be* one) against the wild superstitions always fermenting

below, and always breaking out in times like these. There
is something to be said for supporting the Roman Church
as the only prophylactic against worse evils. But I see
that when it comes to what one is to make of the world
(and many people at any rate have to try to make something of it for practical rather than speculative reasons)
our intellect can't do much for us. We are too ignorant
by the very fact of our little natures and senses, etc. You
put forward a position which was also Goethe's, that all
experience must contribute to anything one may be able
to believe. Of course if one is a little person incapable of
much experience one's thoughts will be little too, and may
easily be (often are) merely imbecile. But if one is a great
person like Goethe then one gets into touch with great things.

To Herbert Corner. [When Dickinson summed up the
'Points of View' series of talks in 1930 he appealed for the
views of the young and received a manuscript which greatly
interested him and which he tried to get broadcast. The
writer was a junior technical engineer in a municipal electricity works in the north. A long correspondence ensued,
from which I have taken the following letter. It shows him
in contact with someone whose upbringing and experiences
had differed from his own, and it shows how little such
differences matter when there is intelligence and sympathy
on both sides, as there is here. It is also of the nature of an
apologia. Corner's visits to Cambridge were a great success.]

King's College, Cambridge.
March 17, 1932.

My dear Corner,

I have several letters of yours which I must make some
attempt to reply to. First as regards Whitsun, I will keep
that week end for you, so make what arrangements you
can and for as long as you can. But if you find some other
time more convenient let me know as soon as you can,
as I am apt to get filled up. Easter is no use as I shall be
away. I expect to leave on Saturday, and shall not be free
again before the 16th April.

No, I doubt whether I shall attempt to 'set down in
book form a simple account of my philosophy of life'.

What is it? It grows and changes, and the more so as I get older, and one can't get such things across to anyone else. For people can only understand and receive what they have lived into. About abattoirs, I was once at Chicago and saw cattle killed by hundreds, an infinite line of them, one blow on the head of each with a hammer and they fall to the ground and are skinned almost before they have ceased to quiver. It's enough to make one hate meat. But there it is—nature's fundamental law, or one of them, that creatures live by preying on one another. Man distinguishes himself only by also murdering his own kind. There are times when I think him the vilest of all creatures and then remember that he is also the finest—as witness the saints and the martyrs of every kind. How could one state diagrammatically or otherwise all the puzzledom of that? No I don't understand relativity and I expect one can't without mathematics; so at least my mathematical friends always tell me. But then of course I don't think mathematics really teaches one much important truth, though it's a useful tool for some purposes, and the relativists themselves seem to be all at sixes and sevens.

I could lend you some day McTaggart's book on 'Some Dogmas of Religion' if you would care about it. But I should say you would not get much out of philosophy. My own view is that what is important in it is the same thing, in a way, as in poetry. Spinoza is a wonderful spirit like Plato, like any philosopher who is a man of genius and not a mere logician. I believe that poetry lets in light; but perhaps only parabolically.

Do you mean that you want to study Greek and Latin in the original tongues? I wonder whether it would be worth your while. I doubt it at your age. I expect it would be more worth your while ('worth whileness') to read the best English writers. But we can discuss that. Anyhow what you need at present is concentration and coherence, the structure of writing before you attempt the ornaments. Or so I think, and McT.'s style is a model of those qualities.

Now your letter of the 7th March, though I don't know that there is much more for me to say about it. I expect you don't know how provocative and irritating your treatment is certain to be to those who fundamentally disagree.

14-2

The question is, whether you do good or harm by stirring
them up even to anger and indignation. And that is a
question hard to answer. I can only say now that I regret
all the provocative things I have said in my books about
the war. It seems as if they only please those who agree
with one, put off the others. And I should think that is
more the case, not less, with the uneducated than the
educated.

As to your question about forgiveness, the literal translation of the passage is 'remit our debts as we have remitted
those we owe to our debtors'. As far as I can see, this does
not mean in *proportion* as etc., but *sheer* remission. Of
course Jesus is using a metaphor. However, I daresay
there is no end of discussion about that, and I am no
scholar in the New Testament. My difficulty about Christianity is and always has been that Christians make the
centre of their faith the historical existence of a man at a
certain age. I daresay he *did* exist, though that has been
doubted. But if he *did*, what was he really like? I cannot
think religion can depend upon such uncertainties, and of
course you agree. Then there is no doubt at all that
Christian theology has been enormously influenced by
Platonism and by many other influences. Dean Inge is
certainly right about that. Only I don't understand how
he connects the Platonism with the historical Jesus. My
main point, however, about all this is that so deeply are
people's religious beliefs entangled in their traditional
church teaching, that one can't tear down the one without
the other. Hence a certain reticence, which I feel more
and more as I get older. When one is actually talking to a
given person one can feel one's way. But when one writes
a book one hardly knows what one is doing. See the
quotation from the Platonic Socrates on p. 55 of my Plato
book. For the rest, I am not a sufficient student of the
history of Christianity to discuss fruitfully your other points.

Yes, that 'running round after your own tail' is really
the gist of my criticism. It seems worth while criticising
you, because you see the point yourself, and therefore can
probably amend it. As to your repetitions I think there
is a great difference between lecturing and writing a book.
In lecturing, it is true that one ought to repeat, and not to
crowd too much into the hour. But the art is to repeat
without people realising you are doing it. But when you

are writing and printing, you assume that the reader has your book in his hands, he can pause and think over what you are saying, and that is what he ought to do. If he is intelligent, he will merely be irritated by constant repetition, especially in the same form of words. That is the essence of your fault as a writer.

But perhaps something too much of all this. On the larger question, I don't expect to find a final philosophy. That, like life itself, is a growth, and in living minds the growth itself never stops. That is why some of the wisest men have held that death is not an extinction but a release to some higher life. Whether it is, I don't know, and don't expect to till it is too late for me to come back and tell any one! You will see, in our book, what Goethe thought. I have been endeavouring the last week to say something about his beliefs for a broadcast talk. He is one of the men I would rather follow than anyone else. But of course I don't know whether he really *knew*. He certainly did not return to tell us! and I doubt if we do much good battering our heads against that wall, though we may try to insinuate ourselves.

I have been much struck lately by reading a book of Lady Welby's correspondence. I met her in the past, and she was a woman of genius, and I keep finding in her echoes of Goethe. Unconscious I think, for there is no evidence that she ever read him. If your librarian is amenable, ask him to get 'Echoes of a larger Life', edited by Mrs Henry Cust. It might interest you. By the way, Goethe is often treated as an egotist, but it is a very inadequate account of him. Besides, it is true what he said, that the value of egotism depends on the value of the egotist!

Let me know about your coming here as soon as you know yourself.   Yours sincerely,

                              G. LOWES DICKINSON.

To Bonamy Dobrée. [About 'After Two Thousand Years'.]

                              King's College, Cambridge.
Dear Dobrée,   July 3, 1930.

Many thanks for your very friendly and perceptive review of my dialogue. It is the only one I have had which goes into the heart of the matter, as is perhaps to be

expected. I think what you say on the most fundamental
issue is true. We are all confined and cribbed by our own
natures; and it would be chimerical to expect to escape
that. I hate conflict and love friendship. However in old
age one begins to emerge from one's burrow and realise
that other people are in theirs, and that theirs are different;
and hence these struggles and horrors. What it's all up to
I don't know; but I have always felt that the view that it
is up to nothing is absurdly inadequate. The creeds, all
alike, seem to me not only guesses but bad ones. There is
more to be got out of the shooting at the stars which is
great poetry and music. I don't think men need to 'create'
their tragedy. It would always be there, even if all I think
possible were achieved. But I don't believe it need be this
hideous tragedy of destruction and war. There I am un-
repentant—that is I am myself. Many thanks again.

Yours sincerely,

Pardon my typing.   G. LOWES DICKINSON

To Elliott Felkin. [Selected from a long correspondence.]

Hotel de l'Abbaye, Talloires.

Dear Elliott,   Sept. 27, 1927.

...I don't quite know how to deal with your many
kindnesses and Joyce's. 'Thank you'? Why, yes, of course.
But that's a word, and one would like to arrive at things.
Anyhow my dear I do thank you and both of you, for all.
I had many thoughts, lying in bed this morning after breakfast—always the best time of day. But they evaporate. You
will not yet realise, nor for many years, how odd it is to
be quite fit and happy yet well aware that at any moment
one may be precipitated—into what? It's idle to speculate,
and Spinoza was right when he said that a wise man never
thought about death. If the human race would have so
done, what might we not have been spared. I have also
been reflecting on Goethe's use of the word 'daemonic'.
It seems to mean the unintelligible irrational element,
which is the world we are caught in. I should translate
it 'energy'. Daemonic men have that, but not at all
necessarily intellect or goodness, e.g. Birkenhead and
Churchill are daemonic, so is Mussolini. Perhaps Caesar

was, but one knows so little about him. However he must
have been. And Bismarck. Goethe himself, having also
intellect and love, may count as one of the few men not
only daemonic but great. Byron of course was daemonic.
What a screed about nothing! But every now and then one
seems to get aperçus about the commonplace. It looks
lovely out to-day, blue sky behind shifting clouds, which
are oddly creeping down the hill opposite. I am glad to
get a feeling of rest. I suppose old age is mostly felt in
getting exhausted more quickly. Otherwise, when one is
well, it's rather pleasant. One takes stock. I don't seem
to myself very different to any other man whom I con-
template—just one more bubble popping up on the stream.
The stream is the thing that matters. But *how* does it
matter? It is the Sphinx. In Goethe I came across yet
another definition of genius—'that power of man which by
its deeds and actions gives laws and rules'. That's an
unusual one! Well, till Sunday. Would you and Joyce care
to come back to dine with us at the Beau Séjour?

To E. M. Forster. [The first letter, referring to 'A Passage
to India', is printed for the reason that it well expresses his
feelings about life as seen through an Indian medium; cf. his
letter to Mrs Moor, p. 140.]

The Shiffolds,
June 2, 1926.

Dear Morgan,

I have now finished your book, I think it is so good that
I havn't much to say about it. For it is always easier to
pick holes. The theme—the incompatibility of Indians and
English—is done as perhaps only you could do it—with
the power of understanding both sides. But then there are
all sorts of behind suggestions; and I have a feeling—rare
for me at my age—that you have lifted a new corner of
the veil. What you see behind it is indeed disquieting
enough; but we cannot shirk it for that reason; at least
I don't want to. But it is one of the puzzling things about
life how 'cheerfulness will break in'. So that in the midst
of my intellect's most hopeless despair and rage I know
that in fact I think there may be some point in the terrible
business, which, *if* one knew, one might approve. Aziz I
think a triumph—so alive and so consistently inconsistent.

You will know well by now, and no doubt knew before, the crux of doubt—what did happen in the caves? why mayn't we know? why mightn't we know all the time? I expect however that you had good reason for your handling of this, and I don't much mind myself. More important is that, whereas in your other books your kind of double vision squints—this world, and a world or worlds behind—here it all comes together. One doesn't know the fate of books. But one would think this should be a classic on the strange and tragic fact of history and life called India. Anyhow you will feel that you have pulled it off, a satisfaction that will abide underneath the never to cease dissatisfaction which belongs to life, and is life if one lives at all.

I can't be made very unhappy now, anyway, because I sort of see all the time the illusion and unimportance of these things. But then 'important—unimportant', as the White Knight meditated. Carpenter is coming over here for the night. I feel a little anxious, wondering how it will go....

Yours,

G. L. D.

[The next letter begins with a display of independence on the part of the typewriter and the marginal lament 'Oh dear!' The stories referred to are in 'The Eternal Moment'.]

London.
April 19, 1928.

Dear Morgan,

I propose to go to Cambridge on Saturday. But this weather rather knocks me. More particularly, looking through my papers, I found a letter of yours of last August, which I was glad to re-read. You will have forgotten it; but you cite Blake and also Vicary re mystic experiences. Which brings me to your stories. I am not well satisfied with them. Your constant pre-occupation to bring realistic life into contact with the background of values (or whatever it is) is very difficult to bring off, and I am apt to feel the cleft. This I say only because we *do* say how we feel about things. I daresay I am wrong, in the sense that you succeed with other people, e.g. Melian Stawell, whom I told to write to you. Not altogether, I gather, with my sister who was delighted that you sent her the book. It was just one of those perceptive things you do. I like best the first and last stories. It is good that someone should take the Wells-Shaw prophecies and turn them inside out. I have just returned from addressing theological students on science. I liked the young men, but I'm not sure it's much good trying these stunts. To begin with, the old can hardly meet the young—really meet I mean—and then theology and 'Jesus'. It all seems to me so 'off' the way they hold it. Why is it 'Jesus' that inspires them—or rather, as they say, is *there alive, directing* them in some way that no one else is. Surely these coils will shuffle off one day for some of them. But meantime that is the way they formulate experience that sometimes at least is genuine if commonly merely traditional and not experience at all. Du reste, most of them seemed fairly open-minded, except the high Anglicans. Romans majestically abstained, but otherwise the gamut ran down (or up) from Anglicans to Quakers. Somebody said you intended to come up this term, and if you do I hope we may meet. In that case perhaps Joe would also come. He called here the day I left for an Easter visit to my brother, so I missed him. I was at Bessie's last week-end in the sleet, but there was no telephoning to you and anyhow you could not have come over, nor I to you.

Well, so long. I must get on with duller things. Furness (J. M.) writes that he much admires and enjoyed your book on the novel. My best remembrances to your mother. I hope she keeps well and warm and enjoys her little tinkle of wireless. What would happen to her if she were obliged to hear a real orchestra in a real Concert Hall!

Yours,

G. D.

K. C. C.

Jan. 17, 1932.

Dear Morgan,

I have been reading Forrest Reid's 'Uncle Stephen', which I picked up at the club and then took out of 'The Times'. It's extraordinary rather, what a curious effect it produces in me. Years ago when I was a boy, I read a book called 'The Boy in Grey', I think, and I think it was by Henry Kingsley. The point was that a prince who wore a ruby met in the courtyard of a palace a boy in grey, with a token, and had to follow him. I have never forgotten the impression of this book, though I have never looked at it since and should hardly care to, for it may be rot. Well, 'Uncle Stephen', at the age of seventy, produces something of the same effect. Not the Uncle Stephen part proper, but the part when he becomes the young Stephen and fascinates Tom. Both the boys are so well done I think. But of course the kind of interest it wakes in me is what they call a wish fulfilment, and I get a whiff of that old feeling 'nothing else would be worth while except that'. I don't know why I should tell you this except that it strikes me as curious and rather ironic. I have no further news. Things here are as usual and I'm rather glad to have got back to my own rooms and to have solitary breakfasts with a book. How odd it is that, with catastrophe waiting round the corner, one can still enjoy Bridge and idle talk. I wonder how long I shall be able, or want, to hold on to life? If only there were no one dependent on one!

G. L. D.

[The next letter was written shortly before he went into hospital. The Goethe poem enclosed in the postscript is 'Sagt er niemand, nur den Weisen' from 'Der West-östliche Divan': it is translated on page 56 of 'Goethe and Faust'. The postscript also quotes 'Vielfach wirken die Pfeile des Amor...' from the third of the Römische Elegien, and recommends 'Goethe's Lebensweisheit' by Emil Ludwig 'if you want to know about Goethe—I daresay you don't'.]

King's Coll. Camb.
July 13, 1932.

Dear Morgan,

Thanks for your letter.... It seems as if one is making a lot of fuss about nothing, but I prefer to make preparations for every alternative. I am quite enjoying myself here, and there is something pleasant in the arrest of time; like I remember feeling years ago between one's tripos exam. and the result.

I don't know whether you know the enclosed poem of Goethe's. It always seems to me profound, and your remarks about sex remind me of it. I think that all forms of love, including the physical, point to something beyond, and I trust Goethe's account of experience, because he had so much and so varied and wrote so much down, and never bothered about being consistent, which indeed it is absurd to be, for one is an oscillating and growing (or declining) creature, and experience too oscillates or grows (or declines). It looks to me as though I might have to wait the full ten days before the room is vacant, and the longer the better so far as I am concerned, because I want to enjoy the warm weather.

G. L. D.

[In connection with the foregoing here is an extract from an earlier letter; I had sent him some remarks on personal immortality which Edward Carpenter had left behind for his friends.]

Many thanks for sending me those words of Edward's. They give all the most beautiful side of his character. I don't know whether what he says is true, except in feeling, and if one begins to think and argue about it there is no end. But it seems to me that love, so understood, is more attainable and better worth having than most things. ...It is I suppose old age that makes me think now that the sex element is rather a disturbance than a consummation. Yet without it, I suppose, love would not attain the height it sometimes does. But I must not chatter.

To Gerald Heard. [Commenting on an early draft chapter of 'The Ascent of Humanity'. When the book was published three years later, he wrote a short introduction to it.]

The Shiffolds,
Holmbury St Mary,
Dorking.
Sept. 15, 1926.

Dear Gerald,

This method of address must be reciprocal, though I observe that some people are naturally called by Christian names and I appear to be one of them. Others, though one becomes very intimate, never are. I suppose there is some psychological ground, but I don't know what it is. My oldest friend, a woman whom I have known for fifty

years nearly, I have never called by anything but her
surname, nor have any of my sisters. 'But to resume' or
rather to commence. Your MS. is a most puzzling proposition. I think, as I did with the former fragment I saw,
that you have got an idea which ought to work out very
interestingly, but must be worked out on a large scale, with
a lot of detail and references, etc. This chapter, like the
former, seems to be a kind of either summary or introduction. I suppose it to be intended so. Your full view seems
to include history (from the anthropologised beginnings),
psychology and mysticism. Your strength should be in the
fact that your mysticism is not shot out of the blue, but
emerges from your science. In fact, it should thereby cease
to be what is properly called mysticism and be rather
psychical research. And that subject also you will have to
include. This large scale, as I understand, is really the
point of your projected book. I feel as if it might really
reorient our thought, if you get the leisure, and command
(as no doubt you will) the patience, to work it out to the
necessary detail. This is for the matter, and is about all
I can say about it.

For the manner, I can say more. Your style is at present
a remarkable combination of epigram (often good epigram)
and pedantry and obscurity. You will have a rather
laborious task, I think, in clarifying it, and no one but
yourself of course can do that. I notice however a few
points [details given].

I see that you have a very difficult problem of style to
write what is scientifically clear and accurate, and yet to
get a literary quality. You will perhaps solve this because,
as I see it, the faults are not those of a man who will never
have a notion of writing, but of one who is struggling with
the medium and will probably emerge into some new
mastery. I *think* you may have to check your epigrams.

The sum of all which is, that I wish you, as soon as may
be, leisure for doing this book which is germinating in you,
which will take I think a long and laborious process to
do, and which might be very important when done.

G. L. D.

To Kingsley Martin. [Addressed to the present editor of the 'New Statesman and Nation', and extracted from their graver correspondence.]

K. C. C.

Dear Kingsley,   Sept. 24, 1925.

On examining my box I find in it the shirt and some collars. There is also a pair of socks, which may be yours, but they are grey and I think you said yours were khaki. I have worn the pair in question, and I rather thought they belonged to Savary. However I send them along, in case. There are no others. I found a pleasant little party here, and had a game of bridge, in which I lost 2s. 6d. and won 2s. 6d., and ended up as you were, a most satisfactory arrangement. Since when I have been strolling in the backs, under a cloudy sky, which just lets through a dim light, showing all the reflections in the river; an owl hooting, otherwise silence and darkness, very beautiful and peaceful. I do hope you will be feeling better for Scarborough, and will endeavour 'nichts bereuen'. I am still vague as to how long I shall stay here, but at latest I leave Saturday for a little round of visits.

Yours,

G. L. D.

To Robert Nichols. [A subsequent letter discusses Goethe and the daemonic (cf. p. 215). The reference here is to R. N.'s 'Fantastica'.]

King's Coll. Cambridge.

Dear Mr Nichols,   Nov. 17, 1928.

Many thanks for your letter and for your book which I have been reading with interest and sympathy. It is always good to find another mind touching one's own even if only in passing, and especially, at my age, a young mind. What you say about myth is very much what I also have felt. Many years ago I tried to say that, in a little book on religion. But the trouble about myths is, that they cannot now become generally credible. I believe men ought to find what they want in poetry and music. But then so many aren't sensitive to those things. My motion is, a little round of light illuminated by science, increasing, one hopes, in illumination and range; and outside, twilight and night, to be filled by art—I mean serious art. Perhaps I should say imagination. What has been the trouble with religion is that it has turned myth into dogma, and out of dogma bred persecution and priestcraft. When you return I hope perhaps we may meet and have a talk, for letters are unsatisfactory, unless one knows the other fellow so well that one can be sure to be rightly understood.

I thought it very nice of you to write, for I have been feeling very isolated.

Yours very truly,

G. LOWES DICKINSON.

To Dennis Proctor. [Selections from a long correspondence. The reference in the first letter is to my friend Frank Vicary (p. 216), who had stayed with Dickinson at Cambridge.]

K. C.
June 14th, 1930.

Dear Dennis,

I meant to show you the enclosed for I know you are interested in Life, and this seems to me to have a singular beauty. The writer (I forget whether I spoke to you about him) has been a miner, fisherman, ship's steward, torpedoed, miner again, pig breeder. I came across him through Morgan Forster, who is a great friend of his and I too feel a great friend now. How people are spread about through all classes, who have the sense of life, and how tiresomely class limits most of us. That is really the principal reason for trying to improve society. Give me this back or send it as I value it. I leave here to-morrow and shall be at Beaufort Mansions till I leave on Saturday. Bless you my dear,

G. D.

Hotel Europäischer Hof (they so call themselves),
München.
7th Aug. 1930.

Dear Dennis,

This in haste, in case I catch you in town. We are staying here until the 15th, and that day expect to move on to Salzburg. There will therefore as I gather be only the 15th that we shall be in Salzburg together. You might communicate with us on the 15th evening. We are staying at Salzburg until the 30th and after that go to France.

Glad to get your letter and news, and know that you are well and happy. I have been for a fortnight odd in the Engadine before joining my sister here. Weather there was better than in most places and I'm the better for it. Here the climate is bad and very unsettled. We were interrupted by a storm of rain at an open air concert yesterday evening which was broken up just as we were beginning to hear Schubert's quartet of Der Tod and das Mädchen. It was all very schwärmerisch and romantic. A song to the harp was sung from the top of a high tower, illuminated for the purpose! Being romantic myself I loved it, but I think your generation could hardly endure it. I find the Germans very pleasant. The young men might be attractive, as they all go about in shorts and open shirts, without ties, but alas they are seldom physically beautiful. I generalise, as I have often done before, that the Germans are the ugliest and least distinguished people God has thought fit to produce. But they are civilised to a degree inconceivable to our English philisterei and insensitive good nature. However I must not run on now. We start the Ring to-night. Wonder if I shall still be an enthusiast. I think I shall. The enchanter always corners me, though I rebel next day. I have now got proofs of my long dialogue through, and suppose it will emerge in the autumn. Nobody of any kind will like it, but I am used to that and imagine myself not to care....I wonder what your mysterious 'triumph' was?

Yours,

G. D.

Montrésor, Indre et Loire.

Dear Dennis,   Sept. 21, 1930.

Owing to the usual muddles and delays of forwarding letters yours of the 27th August reached me only yesterday, hence my delay in replying. I was very glad to hear from you and at such length, the more so as I was not expecting you to write. After you left Salzburg we had a week of wonderful weather. This was during the heat wave, but at Salzburg though it was hot in the day it was fresh and cool at night. We had delightful music of which however I think I wrote; then returned via Innsbruck, my sister to London and I to Paris and thence to Tours, where I met

Roger Fry and his delightful sister Margery, who is as able
as he and more all round. She is at present head of Somer-
ville, but will not be for long. I have enjoyed my stay
with them at this little town, though weather has been
very dicky and the hotel uncomfortable to my aging body.
It's nice country, rather like Suffolk, and full of ruins of
great Abbeys, now turned into farms. There is a castle
inhabited by a Polish countess. Pippa and Pernel Strachey,
sisters of Lytton, have also been here. I have never been
with a trio of such able women. One felt ashamed of one's
sex! Delightful women too, which is not always the case.
What will be my next move, I don't quite know. At the
moment Roger and Margery have determined to fly to the
South of France, but it hardly seems worth while to go there
for a week or so on the chance of sunshine. I may go to
England. At any rate, when I do get there, I will call you
up and hope to visit you in the new house. I'm all in
favour of people writing their autobiography, if they can
do it, and beginning early, but it's a task most people
abandon. My friend at Geneva has kept his most elaborately
for years, with documents, photos, and all the rest of it.
It will be a most interesting document if ever it sees the
light, which I daresay it won't. I have written nothing
and hardly read anything. I play a good deal of chess with
Roger, who usually beats me and I get very sulky about
it, having very bad chess manners. It's really very ridiculous. Then I walk a bit about the rather charming country.
The others have the resource of painting which is inex-
haustible to them. For Margery, who has always been an
executive woman, really likes nothing so much as painting
and playing the flute. She is also an expert on birds.
I was interested to hear of your induced mysticism. There
are very queer things to be learnt and done about oneself.
Your admiration for Proust strikes me as excessive, though
it is shared by so many of your contemporaries. He certainly describes well the little slip of life he deals with.
But what a little slip it is. Parisian society of a rather
snobbish and frivolous character. How much does that
really tell about 'Life'? which extends so infinitely through
time and space, is so incredibly various, even if one con-
fines oneself to humans. And when one takes in also the
animals and insects! not to mention the stuff the physicists
deal with. I can't do much except gape at it now, and

stretch my little imagination as far as it will go before it bursts like a bubble. However that is a matter of age and not for you to bother about.... I append a translation of a queer little poem by Goethe, which rather intrigues me. My love my dear,

G. D.

[The poem which follows occurs in Goethe's posthumous works. It is sometimes printed as two poems, the second, with the title 'Dreifaltigkeit', beginning at the third stanza.]

'The history of the christian church,
What it amounts to I can't conceive.
There's such a lot of stuff to read—
Tell me what you yourself believe.'

'Two champions standing up to box,
The Aryan and the orthodox.
For centuries they kept up the fray,
And will do till the judgment day.

Embodied in creation's riot
The Father is eternal Quiet.

A mighty task the Son assumed
It was to save the world he came;
Much good he taught and much endured,
In our own time it's still the same.

Descended then the Holy Ghost
At Whitsun operative most,
But whence he came and whither goes
For all our efforts no one knows.
Brief was his moment, then it passed,
Although he be the first and last.

And thus repeating faithfully
The ancient creeds we all agree,
Worshipping with unfeigned zeal
The Three in One and One in Three.'

1 Beaufort Mansions, S.W. 3.
Saturday, 4th October, 1930.

I wonder Dennis dear how you got on with the choral symphony. I listened to it on the wireless at Miss Stawell's. Listened to it? No rather to a husky and malicious ghost

parodying it with occasional interpolations of a zany or a
lunatic, perpetual atmospherics, and in all the softer passages the sound of some fool broadcasting on some irrelevant
topic. Moreover it was obvious even so that Wood was
conducting disgracefully, and that the chorus could not
sing the music, but that is invariable and partly Beethoven's
fault for writing the music so high. Nevertheless I listened
all through since even this parody served to recall the
greatest music in existence, unless it be the Mass of Bach.
And you I hope would not realise the defects.... I imagined
you puzzled by the first movement, overwhelmed as I
hoped by the amazing scherzo, deeply moved by the
adagio, and especially by the second theme that comes
in on the cellos. Then comes that queer almost childish-
sublime introduction to the last movement, when all the
previous themes are repeated and rejected by the basses.
And then that amazing theme which is like a bud that
opens and opens into a great rose like the rose at the end
of Dante. I wonder what you did make of it my dear.
I lay awake a long time thinking about you and I am
starting the day telling you what I am thinking, merely
to help me to endure the spectacle of the world with which
one has to occupy most of one's time. Grim and grimmer
it is and will be, but as it becomes more terrible becoming
also more mysterious and perhaps up to something greater
than we can conceive. But such thoughts are not for you,
or for any young man. I am intending to turn up on Friday
(is not it?). I shall be rather like the symphony as heard
on the wireless, and I shall see you only through a mist
of cocktails. So long my dear. By the bye I went yesterday
to have my hair cut at a place in the King's Road. The
barber informed me that he had taken his holiday in
London, investigating the churches and other sights. Of
course he had seen much that I have never seen, or forgotten, among other things the church where Pepys is
buried with a long eulogistic inscription to the wife he was
always deceiving and always quarrelling with. He's (the
barber) a Devonshire man and lives with a Devonshire
family in Fulham where he gets Devonshire dishes such as
soused mackerel. He instructed me firmly and kindly in
history and other things, where certainly I need instruc-
tion. He was inclined to think that the Pepys Library is
at Oxford not Cambridge but there I had to be firm. How

nice the English working people often are with that curious sweetness and kindness. I wonder how long it will last out against the present and future conditions.

Well my dear I must go out from this haven and resume such labour as I have and such thoughts as I cannot escape from.... Sursum corda my dear.

G. D.

[The sonnet referred to in the next letter is in the 1896 Poems and begins:

'Thou knowest, love, of love's immortal tree
Strength is the root and tenderness the flower'.]

K. C. C.
Jan. 21, 1932.

I ought not to be writing to you my dear but to be preparing an address I have to give to-night. Still I want to write because last night I heard the 3rd Act of Siegfried, and so, I think you said, did you. We have a wireless which to my astonishment can give Wagner's orchestration almost as if you were in the Hall. I listened subconscious of the long winded-ness and superficiality of Wagner, but nevertheless in a kind of ecstasy. What a miracle he was! He does not tell you about it, he just *gives* it. And that heroic love, which includes all the other and transcends it, is I expect really the point of life (see my sonnet No. 25). The long years since, and especially the last fifteen, have pretty well killed me. But I see that the 'thing', whatever it is, persists underneath. However, as usual, I begin writing to myself and not to you; so indestructible is egotism (or would you say egoism). I think we ought to make a distinction. One is suffering from the ego, and the other is loving it. You won't and should not feel now what I do about love, but everything must proceed by stages. But there's always something on before, so follow the gleam!

Dein,
G. D.

To D. H. Robertson. [The economist. References to IT are frequent in later letters and talks. The implication is usually sinister.]

King's Coll.
July 29 (1930 ?)

Dear Denys? Dennis?

I have now read a good part of your book, all the latter part, I think. It seems to have all the best qualities of the Cambridge mind so rare, so exasperating to so many people, and as I think so precious and indispensable. I have enough of it to sympathise. But I have also another devil in me who becomes more insistent as my time draws to an end. He says 'nothing important can be proved' and adds 'what I want to know is what *you* stand for in this chaos of different standpoints'. You no doubt have that devil too, but you never let him speak in this book so I don't know what he would say. Mine says 'I hate fighting and all the fine coverings under which it defends itself. I hate empire. I hate nationalism. I hate war. I would rather see the whole of mankind finally destroyed than see it proceed as it is now proceeding'. I reply—that is the other devil replies—'well what's the good of that? You won't stop any of that by hating it'. And the second devil says 'well then, you ought at least to have the guts to be a martyr'. All this is not very relevant to your book, but perhaps it's all I can say. For in the subjects you deal with you are the expert and I the mere amateur. And I find you an admirable exponent, with humour, candour and common sense. The last word lies with what I am in the habit to myself of calling *IT*. IT is probably up to something though perhaps to nothing that interests us ephemerals. It can only be confronted by ? plus Poetry.

Yours,

G. L. D.

To D. K. Roy. [This important reply to an Indian enquirer may be compared with his letter to Corner. He again explains himself to someone whose experience of life differs, but he is here more aware of the difference.]

King's College, Cambridge.
Jan. 18, 1931.

Dear Mr Roy,

I shall find it very hard to say in a brief space, or indeed to say at all, what I feel about the mystical question you ask. This is not merely reserve; it is my sense of the gulf which lies between an Englishman and an Indian, in all these matters, even when on both sides there is good will. When I was a young man I became much absorbed first in Plato, and then Plotinus. I am one of the few Englishmen who have studied Plotinus from cover to cover, though that was years ago. I thought then that there must be some way of reaching ultimate truth (or perhaps I should say ultimate experience) by some short cut. I suppose the principal thing that happened to me, in the course of my life, was the disappearance of this idea. *I feel now that we are all very ignorant and quite incredibly and unimaginably inadequate to deal with the kind of questions we ask about ultimate things.* I know however that there do exist what are called mystic states and I am interested when I come across any one genuine who claims to have had them. But what they signify really, when had, I cannot of course pretend to judge. I am now pretty near to death and naturally my mind moves in that direction. What death really means no one can tell, perhaps it means different things to different people. I am content and indeed obliged to 'wait and see'. You say that you have read the book on Goethe which I wrote. The attitude he had towards all these things is very much my own. I 'wait' hoping and expecting to 'see' if there is any thing to see. Meantime 'Alles Vergängliche ist nur ein Gleichnis' etc. may be a guess at truth. I expect that yoga comes in in this connection and I am quite ready to believe that in your country men have discovered much in the way of the control of the body by the mind, and the engendering of conditions which most Europeans know nothing about. But how important that may be I cannot judge; I have never, since I was a young man, been interested in those things, and have always had the fear that there may be much danger and delusion there, even if there be possible achievement.

To turn from those things to more 'practical' ones, as Englishmen are apt to say (I am not defending our natural attitude), my own instinct or judgment, or whatever it is, is all against attempting to deal with political questions as if they were religious or mystical, etc. When one enters into politics one enters the region of passion, interest, prejudice, and at last, fighting, which, however it begins, always ends in the destruction of all that was best and most generous in those who perhaps inaugurated it. I have heard, of course, from every side the kind of criticism you bring against the League of Nations: it *is* a most imperfect document. But its imperfection represents that of the nations and peoples who framed it, or, by their mere presence in the background, caused it to be framed as it is, and not otherwise. To say it is *bad* is to say what is true: that political mankind is bad. But political mankind will not be much better by scrapping all the poor stuff it tries to do, and crying for the moon—that is for a different humanity. If one is working for that latter, it must be by other than political means, or, if one adopts political methods, one must cut them according to the cloth of the *now* existing mankind. I have written you all this that you may know where I stand, since it is these things you ask me about.   Yours sincerely,

G. LOWES DICKINSON.

To Virginia Woolf. [For 'Jacob's Room', see p. 182. These two letters are about 'The Waves'. The first of them is a sort of critical rhapsody of which I know no other example from his pen. I have inserted some punctuation but not standardised it otherwise. Bernard etc. are all characters in the novel.]

King's College, Cambridge.
Oct. 23, 1931.

Dear Virginia,

I have been living the last week almost entirely in your company whether I have been actually reading you or not and I have kept up such a conversation with you that I am urged to try to put some of it down. But there is such a lot of it, and what one puts down is dead as it touches the paper.

Your book is a poem, and as I think a great poem. Nothing that I know of has ever been written like it. It could I suppose only be written in this moment of time. And now I understand or think I do to what you have been leading up all these years. The beauty of it is almost incredible. Such prose has never been written and it also belongs to here and now though it is dealing also with a theme that is perpetual and universal.

Oh dear what words, and even so only touching the least essential. For there is throbbing under it the mystery which all the poets and philosophers worth mentioning have felt and had their little shot at. I have only read it once and I see and know that it ought to be read often though I don't know whether I shall do that since I brood more and more and read less and less except to get information which is not reading but mugging up. I am an old man now and find age curious. My mind is all right though I suppose it may go tomorrow as my memory is going fast. But oddly enough the imagination functions as never before and about things one can't write down. The world is incomprehensible and must remain so to us animalcules, though the best thing about it is our shots to comprehend it. You make no shots because you will not make the shallow and the stale ones. Possibly though you agree with me (though very likely you don't) in this. The universe (or universes) is not without significance. It is apparently indifferent to our values it is certainly indifferent to our happiness our well being our goodness or badness our morals our loves. 'Our.' But what are we? Waves, yes? but waves in the sea part of the sea inseparable from the sea bound too each of us to be this wave and not that (whence much if not all of our trouble) but able and increasingly able as we get older to perceive that the other waves have their life too and that while we are clashing with them we are somehow they. Those sort of things, which I find in your book (I don't think I merely put them in, though that is the most common thing we do with other people's thoughts and makes us recalcitrant to new truth)....Anyhow I feel it like that. Also life seems like a dream as one comes to the end of it. One's separate individual skin ceases to hold one, it cracks all over, nightmares come in and visions and terrors and ecstacies till finally one rides at death, like your Bernard at the end. Oh dear, words words words as you also so vividly feel.

To change the tone, I walked down the river the other day. The eights were thick over the water and the fours a kind of inextricable tangle, and to every eight and every four a young man (what children they look now) shouting to them from bicycles and horses in every kind of tone, hortatory abusive encouraging desperately earnest. Among them of course Percival. Firmly but kindly he was saying

'It isn't one of you, it's all of you that are wrong'. How profoundly and everlastingly true! Then once more firmly and kindly—'Now I'll tell you the best way'. But alas his words fade on the wind and before he knows or we hear the only way the youth who was piloting an aeroplane will have dropped bombs neatly on him and on all the Percivals before he is brought down himself by a machine gun, falling with the proud sense that he is 'doing his bit' for the dear old country. Courses were being done, the coxes yelled, the October sun shone out in the garden by the river, where some don's wife entertains bored boys, and folks gossip about the matrimonial affairs of the fellows of King's, the dahlias and chrysanthemums burned; someone was upset in a whiff (as we used to call them) and came swimming in laughing (he too was Percival), a very old and disreputable man held open a gate and cursed under his breath when he was not tipped, Louis walked along the tow path ashamed because he could not row, and Nevill, looking for new prey, and I, thinking of you and your book, was aware in the back of my mind that I was coming home to a cup of tea, that there was a fraudulent election on and how should I vote; that I ought to call on so and so and so and so, that I might be dead tomorrow and that nothing mattered except to break through this mesh as decently as one could into—what? At which point, as George Meredith says somewhere, my imagination 'tottered in dots'. Oh dear, too much of this. But, my dear Virginia, you will pardon me for it is the best and only tribute I can pay in return for what seems to me a great book. Leonard's book still lies on the table and before I can get to it I have others to at least look into. Why will people send me their books? What do *you* do when they send them to you? Of course the simplest plan is to write at once saying one hopes to read it, and then not read it, but there are a few cases where this is impossible.

I don't think I shall correct this typing. I'm told it only makes it worse.

Yours always,

G. LOWES DICKINSON.

King's Coll. Camb.
Dear Virginia,   Nov. 13.

I have just finished your book for the second time and I feel like beginning it again at once. I cannot and will not try to tell you how much it tells me in my old age—how beautiful and how profound I feel it. But I shall give you a motto which I came across in the paralipomena to Goethe's Faust, which expresses one side of it (one only):

'Des Menschen Leben ist ein ähnliches Gedicht,
 Es hat wohl einen Anfang, hat ein Ende,
 Allein ein Ganzes ist es nicht.'

Don't answer this. It's only a second exclamation. And incidentally this book makes clearer to me what literature really is. It's not (as it is so often in fact) a kind of antithesis to science. It's science made alive. There's a passage about the Old Man on page 317 which says everything about that bit of anthropological psychology (this is the language of science!) and turns it all from a pale ghost, a thing of words, into a living reality. What makes science so awful is its insensitiveness and consequent pedantry. But what heroes some men of science are. I'm beginning to chatter. Forgive me. I ought to be like Bernard in your wonderful passage, page 310.   Yours,

                                                    G. D.

It is a happy chance that these letters about 'The Waves' should close the series and emphasise his interest in contemporary writing and its experiments.

CHAPTER XV

THE LAST MONTHS

June–August, 1932

> thou dost wait
> At the sad city's open gate.
> But though the mark is on thy brow
> No bondman of the flesh art thou.
> And though thou enter, thou dost bear
> This in thy heart for comfort there:
> Only the morning reads aright
> The sombre secret of the night;
> Only the free divine the laws,
> The causeless only know the cause.
>
> G. L. D. (written in 1893).

Body. Wait till the last, the fiercest struggle, wait
Till I invade in force your every gate,
Flow over ev'ry passage ev'ry cell
Of the proud fort you engineered so well,
Till you become a passing registry
Of the triumphant agony that is I.

Soul. All that you can and may, I don't deny it,
You have the power and if you will can try it.
But this I know, up to the bitter end
I to my purpose all my force will bend,
Believing that the passion of the soul
Is rooted in the nature of the whole.

Body. So, last as first, you miss the best of life,
Waging with me this vain and desperate strife.

Soul. That was imposed upon us by our fate.
But listen! Though I fight I do not hate.
For you, my enemy, have been my friend,
Driving me desperate to my proper end.
We enter now the last most tragic scene
That sums in symbolism all that's been.
Do you your worst, as I shall do my best;
What lies behind us both must do the rest.

G. L. D. (written in 1929).

Age 69

Photo by N. Teulon-Porter.

I N the summer of 1932 a group of Cambridge friends dined
together in London. There were informal speeches and
Goldie had been asked to reply to the toast of 'Eternal
Youth'. Well qualified for such a task, he performed it with
the expected insight and wit, but introduced a note of farewell which deeply impressed his audience. Two of them wrote
down afterwards what they remembered of the speech, and
their letters shall be quoted, because they are in a sense a
reply to the letters in the last chapter. Something has been
said about the Cambridge whom he loved; here is the
Cambridge who loved him.

The writer of the first account is a man of about my own
age. He writes to May:

When he, Goldie, got up he told us that he wasn't going
to talk about 'Youth' at all but proposed to tell us what it
was like to grow old. He said that he found he got, as he
grew older, not exactly less and less interested in the world
about him but more and more detached from it, he found
himself more and more in the rôle of spectator rather than
participant—he described how he would lie awake in the
early morning 'watching himself thinking'—detached
from himself, not responsible for himself or his thoughts,
an amused spectator of himself from the outside, less inclined to praise or blame, just watching himself and others.
. . . The proposer had rallied him in his speech giving it
rather as a sign of Goldie's youthful interest in everything,
that Goldie found the society of such very dull people
entertaining. . . . Goldie met this challenge by saying that
he felt more and more that all human creatures were somehow equally important or unimportant in the scheme of
things as we know it now—and it was then in his speech
(if I remember the connection aright) that he said he didn't
know whether he would be with us next year, very possibly
he wouldn't (I had the feeling at the time that he felt he
probably wouldn't) and he went on to suggest (I can't
quote) that the interest of growing old lay in the getting
nearer to the time when this queer universe would be seen
to be less and less queer, when the irrational and seeming
immortal power whom he called 'It' which seems to control events would be seen in its proper perspective, and he

half suggested that some sort of vision of the truth might be given to old age even this side of death.

I have put this very badly in summarising my recollections and I have perhaps made rather more definite what he was putting rather tentatively. He did it of course with much humour and charm—you know his way when he was trying to find words for an elusive thought, lifting his eyebrows, interlocking his fingers, the muscles rather taut, with a steadfast refusal to dogmatise and then laughing at himself for some paradoxical expression of his point.

The writer of the second account is a young man.

I wish to goodness I could remember more of what he said. But I remember very vividly the impression it made on me at the time. I think I was more moved than at any other time in our relationship. I was sitting almost opposite him, and after he had been speaking for some time, I practically did not take in the words at all, but fixed my eyes on his face and felt such a tenderness for him as I had never had before. It was almost as though he was having then and there as he spoke a 'mystical experience', which he had always said he had never had in his life. He had a rapt smile on his face, as though he were in a state of blissful happiness such as he had never known, and obviously his surroundings were completely lost to him. He had been asked to speak to the text of 'Youth', but on the pretext that old age was second childhood he talked about old age and death instead. Ostensibly he was summing up the condition at which he had arrived, but as he talked on, more and more abstractedly, going over the advantages and happinesses of old age, I felt that really he was penetrating at that moment further than he had ever done before in his constant enquiry, and that he was actually experiencing a happiness that transcended the state of resignation and composure which he was describing.

He seemed to assume without any question that it was the last time he would be there, and somehow he made us feel the same thing. Although there was no reason why he should not live for any number of years more, it was somehow quite evident that this was his farewell speech. I think he probably said as much, but I can't remember for certain: the impression was so strong, that everyone must have felt it, whether he said it or not. For me it was the saddest moment of all my time with him, and it came back to me with a shock of recognition when I first learnt that he was dead.

He died two months later (Aug. 3rd), as the result of a severe operation from which, however, he appeared to be recovering. He wrote to me just before that he felt no fear of death, only a sort of excitement, but dreaded pain. Everything seemed to be going well, he had no excessive discomfort, and he was planning to spend his convalescence with the Trevelyans and Elliott Felkin. Whatever he may have felt in June he had no misgivings now, no more had his family and friends. I was with him on the Tuesday: the following evening I had the news through Ferdinand Schiller and could not at first believe it. There is something unreal about it still, probably for the reason that he never staged himself as an invalid. He was chiefly occupied in saving us trouble and in sparing our feelings. Oddly enough he succeeded. A character of his strength manages to sustain those who cling to it and I have 'minded' more the deaths of people I have loved much less. Perhaps he conveyed to us the impression which he himself had received at the death of his sister Janet. There was no self-consciousness or cynicism in his departure, no sentimentality, and no 'message'; it called for no special tone of voice because he had never used one. Yet it was not pagan, unless the music of the priests in 'The Magic Flute' can be given that name. It did not suggest either that he had become one with the universe or that he had gone for ever.

Much could be added. The memorial services in the College Chapel and in London expressed in different ways what had been lost. In London, the words of Spinoza, read by Roger Fry, and his own words, read by Dennis Proctor, reminded us that the free man thinks not of death, nihil minus quam de morte cogitat, and that man stands upon only one step of an infinite ascent. Eulogies, tributes of affection and esteem, sympathetic obituary notices, the extraordinary impression he made upon the doctor and nurses who attended him in their hospital routine—they could be recorded but they throw no more light. The truest words about him were said by his former bedmaker at Cambridge, Mrs Newman: 'He was the best man who ever lived'. That is what I feel about him myself, and it is what those who knew Socrates say of Socrates at the close of the 'Phaedo'.

EPILOGUE

MEPHISTOPHELES, who should inhabit a cranny in every biography, puts his head out at this point, and asks me to set all personal feelings aside and state objectively why a memoir of Goldsworthy Lowes Dickinson need be written. If I say 'Because I want to', the answer is 'Who are you?' If I say 'My friend was beloved, affectionate, unselfish, intelligent, witty, charming, inspiring', the devil will reply, 'Yes, but that is neither here nor there, or rather it was there but it is no longer here. I have your word and the word of others that this once was so, and I do not query it, but is there nothing which will survive when all of you also have vanished?'

I ponder as this bleak question is pressed, and I have to admit that one important item of interest for a reader—external adventure—is absent from Dickinson's life. It is difficult to think of a life where so little happened outwardly. He was never shipwrecked or in peril, he was seldom in great bodily pain, never starved or penniless, he never confronted an angry mob nor went to prison for his opinions, nor sat on the bench as a magistrate, nor held any important administrative post, he was never married, never faced with the problems of parenthood, had no trouble with house-keeping or servants. From the material point of view Fate gave him a very easy time, which he frankly appreciated, and if his biographer tried to romanticise and imply the contrary, it would only move the devil to laughter.

'Was he a great writer?' Mephistopheles continues. 'Do you claim immortality for him on literary grounds?' And here I am constrained to quote from a letter of a friend of Goldie's and of my own, who belongs to a younger generation, and who embodies, like so many of that generation, the spirit of kindly diabolism. Acute, irreverent, light-hearted, he has been appreciating the educational value of 'Plato and his

Dialogues', and then, fearful of praising indiscriminately, he adds:

BUT...you know I always find a 'but' about Goldie's writing. He would be so inclined to clarity in conversation (with me anyway) but so beautifully unclear with his pen. I get mesmerised when I read anything he writes (except 'John Chinaman') and then have to read it all over again. It's so like travelling in a first class compartment. It rolls gently on and I am never certain what has been said— what station I have been carried through. Do you find this? No, I bet you don't. As a literary gent you are beyond hypnosis.

I find it a little. Not in 'John Chinaman', nor 'A Modern Symposium', nor the 'International Anarchy', nor in the best of 'The Magic Flute' and others of his books. But there frequently is this hypnotic effect, although the argument is taut and the language apposite. Something is wrong—or perhaps too right—with the style. Many readers will differ and think Mephistopheles could easily be routed here, but in the keen air which I am trying to breathe it seems to me that the words 'great writer' won't do for Lowes Dickinson except in the low laudatory sense in which all writers of distinction and integrity get called great.

From Parnassus to Pisgah. Heartened by his two victories, Mephistopheles now points towards the Promised Land and says 'Has he brought *that* any nearer? What has this dreamer effected from the humanitarian point of view?'

The answer to this question lies in the future, but the terms in which the answer must be expressed are obvious. The one big practical thing for which Dickinson worked was a League of Nations. Before the war he worked for it unconsciously, his lecturing and writing imply it, though it has not crystallised in his mind. The war instantly brings it to the surface, and he does as much as any one man in England to promote it. After the war, he watches it with misgiving—and he did not live to see the worst. If the League pulls through it will vindicate him as a publicist, and show that his work for civilisation took a practical direction. If it fails he will join Shelley and the other ghosts who have protested vainly against the course of doom and fate—for that is all that an idealist amounts to in the terms of Mephistopheles' brutal question: a ghost.

The fourth question: 'Is he important as a thinker?' must be answered by his fellow thinkers. Some say that he is, but the majority endorse his own verdict, and according to that he ranks as a Cambridge philosopher below either McTaggart, Moore or Bertrand Russell, and takes no place in the philosophic hierarchy of the past.

The case of Mephistopheles would appear to be watertight, and a biography of my friend and master uncalled for.

But two things must have been noticed about the devil from the days of Job to those of Faust. In the first place he is always defeated on ground which he already occupies, in the second place he assumes that two and two must make four. Blinded by arithmetic, deaf to the warnings of poetry, he assumes that a man is only the sum of his qualities, and it is to the qualities named at the beginning of this epilogue, the 'beloved, affectionate, unselfish, intelligent, witty, charming' which were so easily brushed aside, that I return for his overthrow. These qualities in Goldie were fused into such an unusual creature that no one whom one has met with in the flesh or in history the least resembles it, and no words exist in which to define it. He was an indescribably rare being, he was rare without being enigmatic, he was rare in the only direction which seems to be infinite: the direction of the Chorus Mysticus. He did not merely increase our experience: he left us more alert for what has not yet been experienced and more hopeful about other men because he had lived. And a biography of him, if it succeeded, would resemble him; it would achieve the unattainable, express the inexpressible, turn the passing into the everlasting. Have I done that? Das Unbeschreibliche hier ist's getan? No. And perhaps it only could be done through music. But that is what has lured me on.

BIBLIOGRAPHY

NOTE

THOUGH every endeavour has been made to make this bibliography complete, it is probable that some of Dickinson's writings have escaped notice. In particular it has proved impossible to discover more than a very few unsigned articles; some certainly exist, e.g. in the *Saturday Review* and in *The Nation*, though it is not likely that there were many such. Apart from those indicated as anonymous or pseudonymous, all the items in the following list were published under his own name or initials.

Descriptions have been made as concise as possible, but occasionally where the subject of an entry is not clear from its title a few words of explanation have been added in square brackets. It has not seemed necessary to specify when only minor changes were made in reprinting articles, and 'reprinted' must therefore often be interpreted as equivalent to 'reprinted with verbal alterations'. Indication of the various publishers, English and American, are given in the case of each book, but it has not been practicable to give a complete list of editions. The size and pagination quoted normally refer to the earliest English edition.

The bibliography also includes such of Dickinson's letters to the newspapers as have been traced. Many of these are of considerable length—in some cases an entire column or more of the *Manchester Guardian*—and are valuable expressions of his views on current affairs. Only a very few letters of purely ephemeral scope have been omitted, but less important ones have wherever possible been mentioned only as references in connection with articles or other letters dealing with the same subject.

To the numerous persons who have helped me in my search for Dickinson's writings I owe a deep debt of gratitude. Without their help this bibliography would have been far more incomplete—could indeed hardly have been begun. A list of their names would occupy much space and they will know that my thanks are not less sincere for being collectively expressed. I would, however, especially thank the following: Mr E. M. Forster, Mr Roger Fry, and Mr N. Wedd, my professed intention of questioning whom on every possible occasion must have made the prospect of meeting me a recurrent nightmare; the editors of *The New Statesman and Nation*, the *Manchester Guardian*, the *News Chronicle*, and the *Cambridge Review*, who allowed me access to their files; the editors of the *Atlantic Monthly* and *The New Republic*, the Librarian of Congress, and Messrs Doubleday, Doran & Co. who supplied me with invaluable information about American editions; and the officials and staff of the British Museum and the University Library.

R. E. B.

BIBLIOGRAPHY

BY R. E. BALFOUR
FELLOW OF KING'S COLLEGE, CAMBRIDGE

1883

1. Doubt. [Poem]. *The Carthusian*, Feb. p. 214.
2. Ormusd. [Poem]. *Ibid.* April, p. 235.
3. Cyrene. [Poem]. *Ibid.* June, p. 246.
4. 'Comes there a voice to me'. [Poem]. *Cambridge Review*, Nov. 14, p. 77.

1884

5. A Remonstrance. [Poem]. *Cambridge Review*, April 30, p. 301.
6. Pindar. [Sonnet]. *Ibid.* May 7, p. 317.
7. Diana. [Sonnet]. *Ibid.* May 21, p. 348.
8. To the Student of Bohn. [Epigram]. *Ibid.* June 4, p. 381.
9. Hesperus. [Sonnet]. *Ibid.* June 11, p. 399.
10. Savonarola. A Poem which obtained the Chancellor's Medal at the Cambridge Commencement MDCCCLXXXIV. Occupies pp. 7–16 of *Prolusiones Academicae...A.D. mdccclxxxiv.* Cantabrigiae: Typis Academicis. Reprinted in no. 36.
11. Cologne Cathedral. [Sonnet] *Cambridge Review*, Oct. 29, p. 46.

1885

12. Shelley. [Sonnet]. *Cambridge Review*, March 4, p. 253.
13. Vox Desperantibus. [Poem]. *Ibid.* March 11, p. 272.
14. SYLLABUS OF A COURSE OF LECTURES ON CARLYLE, EMERSON, BROWNING, AND TENNYSON. [University Extension Lectures delivered at Chesterfield, Mansfield and Stamford in the Michaelmas Term 1885, and at Chester in the Lent Term 1886]. Derby: Bemrose & Sons. Demy 8vo. pp. 30.
15. Emerson. [Unsigned article]. *The Church Reformer*, Nov. 16, pp. 248–50.

1886

16. SYLLABUS OF A COURSE OF LECTURES...POETRY, MODERN AND ANCIENT. [University Extension Lectures delivered in conjunction with R. G. Moulton at Preston and Southport in the Lent Term 1886]. Sheffield: Leader & Sons. Demy 8vo. pp. 20. Dickinson delivered the first six lectures on Browning and Tennyson, Moulton the remainder on classical drama.

1887

17. JACOB's LADDER. [Poem]. Privately Printed by the 'Mono-
type' Printing Company, Clement's Inn. Pott 4to. pp. 22.
18. Carmen Mysticum. [Poem signed D]. *The Spectator*, Dec. 3,
p. 1653.

1888

19. 'My love I saw the roses glow'. [Poem signed D]. *Cambridge
Fortnightly*, Feb. 7, p. 8. Reprinted in no. 38.
20. Tynemouth. [Sonnet signed D]. *Ibid.* Feb. 21, p. 56.
21. Sunrise. [Poem signed D]. *Ibid.* March 6, pp. 74–5. Reprinted with the omission of two stanzas in no. 38.
22. The Burning of the Books. [A dream signed D]. *Ibid.*
March 6, pp. 76–8.
23. The Professor. [Unsigned short story]. *Ibid.* March 13,
pp. 92–7.
24. 'Across the waves I saw their purple die'. [Poem signed D].
Ibid. March 13, p. 99.
25. Hymn from the Prologue to 'Faust'. [Poem signed D]. *The
Spectator*, Oct. 13, p. 1392.
26. THE SEEKERS. [Manifesto for an informal society of his
friends]. Privately Printed. Demy 16mo. pp. 8.

1889

27. SYLLABUS OF A COURSE OF LECTURES ON 'MILTON AND HIS
TIMES'. [University Extension Lectures delivered at Newcastle and Sunderland in the Lent Term 1889, Blackburn
and Leicester in the Michaelmas Term 1889, and Ipswich
in the Lent Term 1890]. Cambridge: Fabb & Tyler.
Demy 8vo. pp. 18.
28. The Later Plays of Björnson. [Unsigned article]. *Macmillan's
Magazine*, Dec. pp. 130–5.

1891

29. FROM KING TO KING. The Tragedy of the Puritan Revolu-
tion. [Dialogues in prose and verse]. London: George
Allen. Cr. 8vo. pp. vii, 127. For revised American edition
see no. 78.
30. SYLLABUS OF A COURSE OF LECTURES ON MODERN FRANCE.
[University Local Lectures delivered at Norwich in the
Michaelmas Term 1891]. Cambridge University Press.
Demy 8vo. pp. 19.

1892

31. Plato's Later Theory of Ideas. A criticism of Dr Jackson's articles [in preceding issues]. *Journal of Philology*, xx, pp. 121–33.

32. Peer Gynt. *Cambridge Observer*, Nov. 1, pp. 2–3.

33. REVOLUTION AND REACTION IN MODERN FRANCE. [1789–1875]. London: George Allen. Cr. 8vo. pp. xii, 300. For revised edition see no. 289.

1893

34. 'The Empty Purse' by George Meredith. *Cambridge Observer*, Feb. 14, pp. 3–4.

1894

35. Progress. *Free Review*, April, pp. 47–63.

36. Savonarola. Reprint of no. 10 on pp. 177–84 of *A Complete Collection of the English Poems which have obtained the Chancellor's Gold Medal in the University of Cambridge*, vol. 2. London: Gibbings & Co.

1895

37. THE DEVELOPMENT OF PARLIAMENT DURING THE NINETEENTH CENTURY. London: Longmans, Green & Co. Demy 8vo. pp. viii, 183. For French translation see no. 70.

1896

38. POEMS. Privately Printed at the Chiswick Press. Imp. 16mo. pp. 67. Cf. nos. 19 & 21.

39. THE GREEK VIEW OF LIFE. [A volume in the 'University Extension Series' edited by J. E. Symes]. London: Methuen & Co. Sm. Cr. 8vo. pp. xii, 236. (New York: Scribners; republished by the Chatauqua Press, 1903; McClure, Phillips & Co. 1905; Doubleday, Page & Co. 1908). For revised edition see no. 90.

1897

40. Edition of Carlyle's *French Revolution* in 'The Temple Classics'. 3 vols. London: J. M. Dent & Co.

1898

41. Edition of Shelley's *Prometheus Unbound* in 'The Temple Dramatists'. London: J. M. Dent & Co.

42. Edition of Carlyle's *Sartor Resartus* in 'The Temple Classics'. London: J. M. Dent & Co.

1899

43. Edition of Browning's *Paracelsus* in 'The Temple Classics'. London: J. M. Dent & Co.

1900

44. Edition of Carlyle's *On Heroes, Hero-Worship and the Heroic in History* in 'The Temple Classics'. London: J. M. Dent & Co.

45. Recent Political Theory and Practice. [Unsigned article]. *Quarterly Review*, Oct. pp. 359–80.

1901

46. THE MEANING OF GOOD. A Dialogue. Glasgow: James Maclehose & Sons. Fcap. 8vo. pp. xvi, 231. [2nd ed. London: R. Brimley Johnson, 1902; 4th ed. J. M. Dent & Co. 1907; sheets of 6th ed. transferred to Allen & Unwin, 1930]. (New York: The Macmillan Co.; re-issued by McClure, Phillips & Co. 1906; transferred to Doubleday, Page & Co. 1908).

47. From the Chinese Point of View. Four Letters, signed John Chinaman, to the *Saturday Review*, Jan. 12, 19, 26, and Feb. 2. Reprinted as the first half of no. 48.

48. LETTERS FROM JOHN CHINAMAN. [Anonymous till 1907]. London: R. Brimley Johnson. Fcap. 8vo. pp. 63. [7th impr. J. M. Dent & Co. 1907; 12th impr. Allen & Unwin, 1932]. An enlarged reprint of no. 47. For American edition see nos. 50 & 344, for German, Japanese and Gujarati translations nos. 268, 340 & 341.

1902

49. 'As Others See Us'. [Letter signed Haji Mirza Ali Asghar Kirmanshahi]. *Cambridge Review*, April 24, pp. 265–7.

1903

50. LETTERS FROM A CHINESE OFFICIAL. Being an eastern view of western civilisation. [Anonymous]. New York: McClure, Phillips & Co. Fcap. 8vo. pp. xiv, 76. [Transferred to Doubleday, Page & Co. 1908]. The American edition of no. 48, with a new Introduction, pp. vii–xiv. Reissued as no. 344.

51. Optimism and Immortality. *Hibbert Journal*, April, pp. 425–40. Reprinted as ch. 2 of no. 102.

52. Ecclesiasticism. *Independent Review*, Oct. pp. 115–31. Reprinted as ch. 1 of no. 60.

1904

53. Motoring. *Independent Review*, Jan. pp. 578–89.

54. Tammany. [Review of Alfred Hodder: A Fight for the City]. *Independent Review*, March, pp. 333–6.

55. Religion and Revelation. *Ibid.* May, pp. 530–41, & June, pp. 26–39. Reprinted as chs. 2 & 3 of no. 60.

56. Noise that you pay for. [Music]. *Ibid.* Aug. pp. 377–90. Reprinted in *The Living Age*, Oct. 1, pp. 45–53.

57. Faith and Knowledge. *Independent Review.* Nov. pp. 274–81. Reprinted as ch. 4 of no. 60.

1905
58. The Art of Creation. [Review of Edward Carpenter's book]. *Independent Review*, Jan. pp. 634–40.

59. 'How Long Halt Ye?' [Christianity and Paganism]. *Ibid.* Feb. pp. 27–36.

60. RELIGION. A CRITICISM AND A FORECAST. London: Brimley Johnson & Ince, Ltd. Fcap. 8vo. pp. xi, 93. [3rd impr. J. M. Dent & Co. 1911; sheets of 5th impr. transferred to Allen & Unwin, 1930]. (New York: McClure, Phillips & Co.; transferred to Doubleday, Page & Co. 1908). A reprint of nos. 52, 55, & 57.

61. De Profundis. [Review of Oscar Wilde's book]. *Independent Review*, April, pp. 375–7.

62. Frenzied Finance. [Review of T. Lawson: The Chapters that have gone before of 'Frenzied Finance']. *Ibid.* July, pp. 115–20.

63. The Newest Philosophy. [Santayana's Life of Reason, vols. 1 & 2]. *Ibid.* Aug. pp. 177–90.

64. Some Wagner Letters. [Review of Richard Wagner an Mathilde Wesendonck: Tagebuchblätter und Briefe, 1853–1891]. *Ibid.* Nov. pp. 352–6.

65. A MODERN SYMPOSIUM. London: Brimley, Johnson & Ince, Ltd. Large Fcap. 8vo. pp. 160. [Re-issued J. M. Dent & Co. 1907; Allen & Unwin, 1930]. (New York: McClure, Phillips & Co.; transferred to Doubleday, Page & Co. 1908). For German, Danish, Swedish and Chinese translations see nos. 87, 94, 122 & 343.

66. Euthanasia: From the Note-Book of an Alpinist. *Independent Review*, Dec. pp. 476–80. Reprinted in *The Living Age*, Feb. 17, 1906, pp. 445–7, and as ch. 4 of no. 102.

1906
67. Dickinson was General Editor with H. O. Meredith of 'The Temple Greek and Latin Classics'. 5 vols. London: J. M. Dent & Co.

68. Quo Vadis? [The relation of ideals to practice, & of liberty to property]. *Independent Review*, Feb. pp. 148–57.

69. Ibsen's Letters. [Review of The Correspondence of Henrik Ibsen, edited by Mary Morison]. *Independent Review*, March, pp. 345–8.

70. LE DÉVELOPPEMENT DU PARLEMENT PENDANT LE DIX-NEUVIÈME SIÈCLE. Paris: V. Giard & E. Brière. Translation of no. 37 by M. Deslandres, with a new preface by Dickinson, pp. lxiii–lxxiii.

71. Shakespeare, Ibsen, and Mr Bernard Shaw. *Independent Review*, July, pp. 83–8. Reprinted in *The Living Age*, Aug. 18, pp. 437–40.

72. War and Peace. [Review of The Arbiter in Council]. *Ibid.* July, pp. 113–20.

73. The Motor Tyranny. *Ibid.* Oct. pp. 15–22.

74. Free-thought and Religion. [Review of J. M. Robertson: A Short History of Free-Thought]. *Ibid.* Oct. pp. 111–17.

75. Eastern and Western Ideals: being a rejoinder to William Jennings Bryan. *The Century Magazine*, Dec. pp. 313–16.

76. The American Sphinx. [Review of H. G. Wells: The Future in America]. *The Speaker*, Dec. 1, pp. 261–2.

77. Leslie Stephen. [In connection with F. W. Maitland's Life and Letters of Sir Leslie Stephen]. *Cambridge Review*, Dec. 6, pp. 139–41.

1907

78. FROM KING TO KING. The Tragedy of the Puritan Revolution. New York: McClure, Phillips & Co. Large Fcap. 8vo. pp. vii, 129. [Stock taken over by Doubleday, Page & Co. 1908]. A revised edition of no. 29.

79. A Wild Rose. [Poem]. *Albany Review*, June, p. 250. Reprinted in *The Living Age*, Aug. 17, p. 386, and in no. 99.

80. Christianity and Civilisation. [In connection with J. McCabe: The Bible in Europe]. *The Nation*, Aug. 24, p. 934.

81. Peace or War? *Albany Review*, Nov. pp. 130–9. Reprinted in *The Living Age*, Oct. 14, pp. 668–74.

1908

82. A New Poet. [Review of Lascelles Abercrombie: Interludes and Poems]. *Albany Review*, March, pp. 642–8.

83. Sociology and Ethics. [In connection with a new edition of Leslie Stephen's Science of Ethics]. *Sociological Review*, April, pp. 175–7.

84. Knowledge and Faith. *Hibbert Journal*, April, pp. 515–29. Reprinted as ch. 1 of no. 102.

85. The Social Ideal. [Lecture delivered March 21]. *Working Men's College Journal*, May, pp. 334–9.

86. Machiavellianism. [In connection with the fourth series of Lord Morley's Miscellanies]. *Albany Review*, Aug. pp. 552–8.

87. Ein modernes Symposion. *Oesterreichische Rundschau*, Aug. 15, pp. 245–59; Sept. 1, pp. 285–99; Sept. 15, pp. 380–92; Oct. 1, pp. 47–55. Translation of no. 65, by Mrs J. E. Jacob. The last three speeches of the original were omitted in this translation from lack of space, and the projected issue of the whole in volume form was never carried out.

88. JUSTICE AND LIBERTY. A Political Dialogue. London: J. M. Dent & Co. Cr. 8vo. pp. vi, 229. [Sheets of 2nd impr. transferred to Allen & Unwin, 1930]. (New York: The McClure Company; transferred to Doubleday, Page & Co.). For Japanese and Chinese translations see nos. 339 & 342.

1909

89. Cross-Correspondences [between automatic scripts]. [Paper read Dec. 14, 1908]. *Journal of the Society for Psychical Research*, Jan. pp. 10–15.

90. THE GREEK VIEW OF LIFE. London: Methuen & Co. 7th ed. Cr. 8vo. pp. xii, 250. (New York: Doubleday, Page & Co.). Revised edition of no. 39, with a new preface, pp. v–vi. [17th edition, in 'The Gateway Library', 1932. Fcap. 8vo. pp. xiii, 261].

91. Is Immortality Desirable? *Atlantic Monthly*, May, pp. 586–95. Reprinted as no. 93, and as ch. 3 of no. 102.

92. The Socialised Millionaire. [Review of G. S. Lee: Inspired Millionaires]. *The Nation*, May 8, pp. 204–6. Reprinted in *The Living Age*, June 12, pp. 686–8.

93. Is IMMORTALITY DESIRABLE? The Ingersoll Lecture, 1908. Boston & New York: Houghton Mifflin Co. Large Fcap. 8vo. pp. 63. Cf. nos. 91 & 102.

94. ET MODERNE SYMPOSIUM. Copenhagen: Gyldendalske Boghandel. Translation of no. 65 by D. Grünbaum.

95. Culture. *Cambridge Review*, Nov. 18, pp. 110–11. Reprinted as ch. 10 of Part 4 of no. 130.

96. Letters from America. *English Review*, Nov. pp. 574–86; Dec. pp. 33–46; Jan. pp. 198–207. Reprinted in *The Living Age*, Feb. 12, pp. 387–95; Feb. 26, pp. 526–35; March 12, pp. 651–8; and in Part 4 of no. 130.

1910

97. The Issue with the Lords. [Four letters]. *The Nation*, May 7, pp. 205–6; May 21, pp. 277–8; May 28, p. 312; June 4, pp. 348–9. Cf. an earlier letter on 'The Lords and a Referendum', March 5.

98. The Stream. [Poem]. *Basileon*, p. 14. Reprinted in no. 99.

99. A WILD ROSE AND OTHER POEMS. Privately Printed at the L.C.C. Central School of Arts and Crafts. Sm. Demy 4to. pp. 8. Also an edition in Demy 16mo. pp. 8. Cf. nos. 79 & 98.

100. The Social Ideal of Democracy. [Lecture delivered Nov. 12]. *Working Men's College Journal*, Dec. pp. 430–3, & Jan. pp. 18–19.

1911

101. Ideals and Facts. *Hibbert Journal*, Jan. pp. 263–74. Reprinted in *The Living Age*, March 4, pp. 526–32.

102. RELIGION AND IMMORTALITY. London: J. M. Dent & Co. Fcap. 8vo. pp. 88. [Sheets transferred to Allen & Unwin, 1930]. (Boston & New York: Houghton Mifflin Co.). A reprint of nos. 84, 51, 91, & 66.

103. A Case of Emergence of Latent Memory under Hypnosis. *Proceedings of the Society for Psychical Research*, Aug. pp. 455–67.

1912

104. Demoralising Literature. [The dangers of police censorship]. Letter to *The Nation*, Feb. 3.

105. Five articles, signed Don, in the *Manchester Guardian.* April 12, Aetas Parentum. May 2, 'Women and Children First'. May 7, Travelling, Old Style. May 14, Intellectualism. May 29, Greek and the Spring.

106. πάντα κόνις. [Unsigned poem on the wreck of the 'Titanic']. *Cambridge Magazine*, May 25, p. 361.

107. 'The Crime of being Inefficient'. [Criticism of a leading article on mental deficiency]. Letter to *The Nation*, June 1. Cf. a further letter, June 22.

108. The Man versus The Thing. [Culture the aim of education]. *The Highway*, Aug. pp. 162–3.

109. The Illusion of War. [Review of J. W. Graham: Evolution and Empire]. *The Nation*, Aug. 10, p. 702.

110. Travellers' Tales. A series of articles, signed Don, in the *Manchester Guardian.* 1. Dec. 20, Cairo. The series continued in nos. 111, 112, 115 & 116.

1913

111. Travellers' Tales. [See no. 110]. 2. Jan. 8, In the Red Sea. 3. Jan. 14, A Junta [*sic*]. 4. Jan. 17, Ulster in India. 5. Jan. 21, Anglo-India. 6. Jan. 29, A Mystery Play. 7. Feb. 10, An Indian Saint. 8. Feb. 18, 'Civis Britannicus sum'. 9. March 10, A Village in Bengal. 10. March 14, Sri Ramakrishna. 11. March 24, 'The

Monstrous Regimen of Women'. 12. March 28, Indian Art: a question. 13. April 21, Buddha at Burupudur. 14. May 5, A Malay Theatre. Reprinted, except nos. 8 & 12, as Part 1 of no. 130.

112. Travellers' Tales. [See no. 110]. 15. May 8, Nanking. 16. May 27, Impressions of China. Reprinted in Part 2 of no. 130.

113. The Englishman. [Article signed Don]. *Manchester Guardian*, June 3. Reprinted as ch. 5 of Part 2 of no. 130.

114. The Chances of the Chinese Republic. [Letter written from China]. *The Nation*, June 28, pp. 491–2.

115. Travellers' Tales. [See no. 110]. 17. June 17, In the Yangtse Gorge. 18. June 30, China Today. 19. Aug. 7, Pekin. 20. Aug. 21, The Most Sacred Mountain. Reprinted in Part 2 of no. 130.

116. Travellers' Tales. [See no. 110]. 21. Sept. 4, First Impressions of Japan. 22. Sept. 8, A 'No' Dance. 23. Sept. 12, Nikko. 24. Oct. 2, Divine Right in Japan. 25. Oct. 7, Fuji. 26. Oct. 14, Japan and America. Oct. 22, Epilogue. Reprinted as Part 3 of no. 130.

117. ALBERT KAHN TRAVELLING FELLOWSHIPS. REPORT TO THE TRUSTEES. London University Press. Demy 8vo. pp. 58. Reprinted as no. 132.

118. Japan and the West. [Unsigned review of E. B. Mitford: Japan's Inheritance]. *Manchester Guardian*, Nov. 13.

1914

119. Japan and the West. [Review of Yoshio Markino: My Recollections and Reflections; & Okakura-Yoshisaburo: The Life and Thought of Japan]. *Manchester Guardian*, Jan. 5.

120. Greek Again. [Letter in favour of the abolition of compulsory Greek]. *Cambridge Review*, Feb. 11, pp. 273–4.

121. History as Progress. [Review of F. S. Marvin: The Living Past]. *Cambridge Review*, April 29, p. 395.

122. POLITIK OCH SANNING. Ett modernt Symposion. Stockholm: P. A. Norstedt & Söner. Translation of no. 65 by K. I. Anderberg.

123. Crime and Punishment. [Review of G. Ives: A History of Penal Methods]. *Cambridge Review*, May 6, pp. 409–10.

124. Is War Inevitable? *War and Peace*, May, pp. 221–3, & June, pp. 252–3.

125. A Soul in Trouble. [A conversation in India]. *Basileon*, pp. 2–3.

126. The Holy War. *The Nation*, Aug. 8, pp. 699–700. For Italian and German translations see nos. 133 & 147.

127. The Way Out. *War and Peace*, Sept. pp. 345–6.

128. The War and the Way Out. Preparing the Path to Peace. *Labour Leader*, Sept. 17, p. 3. For German translation see no. 147.

129. A Peace that will end War. The False Moral and the True One. Letter to the *Daily News*, Sept. 17. For German translation see no. 147.

130. APPEARANCES. Being Notes of Travel. London: J. M. Dent & Co. Cr. 8vo. pp. x, 234. [Sheets transferred to Allen & Unwin, 1930]. (New York: Doubleday, Page & Co.). A reprint of nos. 111, 112, 113, 115, 116, together with 95 & 96.

131. 'The Enemy in our midst'. Letter to the *Daily News*, Nov. 3.

132. AN ESSAY ON THE CIVILISATIONS OF INDIA, CHINA & JAPAN. London: J. M. Dent & Co. Fcap. 8vo. pp. 86. [Sheets transferred to Allen & Unwin, 1930]. (New York: Doubleday, Page & Co.). A slightly revised reprint of no. 117. For German translation see no. 269.

133. Il patriotismo di Caino. Translation of no. 126, published as a broadsheet by the Comitato Pro Umanità.

134. The War and the Way Out. *Atlantic Monthly*, Dec. pp. 820–37. Reprinted in the *New York Times*, Dec. 20. Also as nos. 135, 144 & 337. For German, Japanese, Swedish and Italian translations see nos. 139, 338, 140 & 175.

135. THE WAR AND THE WAY OUT. London: The Chancery Lane Press. Sm. Cr. 8vo. pp. 47. A reprint of no. 134.

136. Introduction, pp. 3–4, to Romain Rolland's *Above the Battle-field*. Cambridge: Published for 'The Heretics' by Bowes and Bowes.

1915

137. After the War. *Atlantic Monthly*, Jan. pp. 111–16. Reprinted under the title 'How to end militarism' in the *New York Times*, Jan. 10.

138. The War and the Way Out. [Letter in reply to criticisms made in a leading article]. *The New Republic*, Feb. 13, pp. 49–50. Cf. a letter to the *Cambridge Review*, Feb. 24, p. 223.

139. Ein Ausweg für den Krieg. *Milwaukee-Sonntagspost*, Feb. 14, 21, 28 & March 7. A slightly abbreviated translation of no. 134 by H. Hayssen.

140. KRIGET OCH VÄGEN TILL FRED. Malmö: A–B Framtidens Bokförlag. Translation by A. Jacobsson-Undén of no. 134.

141. The War and the Way Out. A Further Consideration. *Atlantic Monthly*, April, pp. 516–24. Reprinted in nos. 143 & 144.

142. The War and the Way Out. A Positive Plan. *Atlantic Monthly*, May, pp. 691–700. Reprinted in nos. 143, 144 & 145.

143. AFTER THE WAR. London: A. C. Fifield. Demy 8vo. pp. 44. A reprint of nos. 141 & 142.

144. THE WAR AND THE WAY OUT. Boston: Atlantic Monthly Co. Sm. Roy. 8vo. pp. 39. An offprint of nos. 134, 141, & 142, published as a pamphlet.

145. THE FOUNDATIONS OF A LEAGUE OF PEACE. Boston: The World Peace Foundation. [Pamphlet Series, vol. v, no. 2]. Large Cr. 8vo. pp. 20. A reprint of no. 142.

146. On 'Punishing Germany'. *War and Peace*, May, pp. 121–2.

147. Der Heilige Krieg. Ein Friede, der den Krieg beenden wird. Der Krieg und der Weg aus dem Krieg. Translations of nos. 126, 129 & 128, on pp. 1–3, 16–22 of *Kriegsgegner in England*. Munich: G. Birk & Co.

148. The German Socialists and the War. *War and Peace*, Aug. pp. 168–9.

149. Die einzige Lösung. Letter to the *Blätter für zwischenstaatliche Organisation*, pp. 202–4.

150. How can America best contribute to the maintenance of the world's peace? *Annals of the American Academy of Political and Social Science*, Sept. pp. 235–8.

151. A German on the war. [Dr F. W. Förster's Deutschlands Jugend und der Weltkrieg]. *Hibbert Journal*, Oct. pp. 30–6.

152. Approaches to Peace. Two letters to *The Nation*, Nov. 27 & Dec. 11.

153. The Basis of Permanent Peace. An essay, pp. 11–36, in *Towards a Lasting Settlement*, edited by C. R. Buxton. London: Allen & Unwin.

1916

154. The Freedom of the Seas. *War and Peace*, Jan. pp. 56–9.

155. THE EUROPEAN ANARCHY. London: Allen & Unwin. Cr. 8vo. pp. 153. (New York: The Macmillan Co.).

156. The American 'League to Enforce Peace'. *War and Peace*, June, pp. 134–5.

157. De Profundis. [Anonymous poem]. *Cambridge Magazine*, June 10, p. 560. Reprinted as no. 167.

158. The Paris Conference and the Future of Europe. Letter to the *Manchester Guardian*, June 26.

159. Democratic Control of Foreign Policy. *Atlantic Monthly*, Aug. pp. 145–52.

160. Economic Policy after the War. *War and Peace*, Aug. pp. 167–9.

161. After the War. A series of letters to the *Manchester Guardian*. Aug. 1, The Choice before us. Aug. 3, Nationalism and Internationalism. Aug. 5, A Proposed League of Nations. Aug. 7, The Problem of Nationalities. Aug. 9, The Problem of International Trade. Cf. a further letter in reply to criticism, Aug. 16.

162. ECONOMIC WAR AFTER THE WAR. [A criticism of the resolutions of the Allied Economic Conference held in Paris during June]. London: Union of Democratic Control. Demy 8vo. pp. 20.

163. The Law and the Conscientious Objector. Letter to *The Nation*, Aug. 26. Cf. a further letter on 'The Treatment of Conscientious Objectors', Sept. 9.

164. Views of Settlement. Letter to *The Nation*, Sept. 16. Cf. a second letter, Sept. 30.

165. Freedom of Speech. [In relation to Bertrand Russell's dismissal from Trinity]. *War and Peace*, Oct. p. 8. Cf. a letter to *The Nation*, July 29.

166. The Conditions of a Durable Peace. Four articles in the *Cambridge Magazine*, Nov. 11, pp. 103–4; Nov. 18, p. 130; Nov. 25, pp. 158–9; Dec. 2, p. 201.

167. DE PROFUNDIS. [Anonymous reprint of no. 157 as no. 4 of a series of 'Reprints from the *Cambridge Magazine*'.] London: The Morland Press, & Cambridge: Galloway & Porter. Large Demy 8vo. pp. 4.

1917

168. The League to Enforce Peace. *War and Peace*, Jan. pp. 64–7.

169. Articles in the *Cambridge Magazine* continuing no. 166 but under separate titles. Jan. 20, The Significance of the American Note, pp. 213–14; Jan. 27, The Allies' Note, p. 244; Feb. 3, President Wilson's Speech to the Senate, p. 271; Feb. 10, Nationality and the Settlement, p. 300; Feb. 17, Rival Imperialisms, pp. 326–7; Feb. 24, The Choice before us, pp. 357–8.

170. The 'Fight for Right'. [An article in reply to an attack upon himself by the 'Fight for Right' Society in a letter to the *Morning Post*]. *Cambridge Magazine*, March 3, pp. 382–3.

171. Introduction, pp. 5–7, to *The American League to Enforce Peace. An English Interpretation* by C. R. Ashbee. London: Allen & Unwin.

172. The Problem of Armaments and a League of Nations. *Friends' Quarterly Examiner*, Fourth Month, pp. 193–7.

173. THE CHOICE BEFORE US. London: Allen & Unwin. Demy
8vo. pp. xi, 274. (New York: Dodd, Mead & Co.).

174. A New German State of Mind. Letter to *The Nation*,
June 30.

175. LA GUERRA E IL MODO DI USCIRNE. Milan: Libreria
Editrice Avanti! Translation by A. Calabi of no. 134.

176. The Case against Persecution. Letter on the imprisonment
of conscientious objectors to the *Manchester Guardian*, July
26. Cf. another letter on 'The Death of C.O.'s in prison'.
Jan. 28, 1918.

177. World Peace or World's End. The Solemn Choice before
the Nations. *Sunday Pictorial*, Sept. 2.

178. If Germany does not repent. The after-war problem of the
allied nations. *Sunday Pictorial*, Nov. 25.

179. The Destruction of Liberty. Letter on the disfranchisement
of conscientious objectors to the *Manchester Guardian*,
Nov. 28.

1918

180. Is it possible to abolish war? Permanent Peace not a
Utopian dream. *Sunday Pictorial*, Jan. 13.

181. Education and Patriotism. Letter to the *Morning Post*, Jan. 15,
in reply to criticism in a leading article of a lecture on
'The Educational Basis of Internationalism' reported in
the issue of Jan. 8.

182. A League of Nations now? [Contribution to a symposium].
War and Peace, Sept. pp. 327–8.

183. Amnesty for political prisoners. Letter in favour of the
immediate release of conscientious objectors to the *Manchester Guardian*, Nov. 18. An abbreviated version was
published in the *Daily News*, Nov. 18, under the title
'Victory and Amnesty'.

184. Introduction, pp. v–xix, to *Problems of the International Settlement*. London: Published for the National Peace Council
by Allen & Unwin.

1919

185. Disarmament. *The League of Nations Journal*, Jan. pp. 16–17.
Cf. a letter on 'The One Thing Needful' to *The Nation*,
Nov. 30, 1918.

186. 'Saul, Saul, why persecutest thou me?' [Unsigned article
on the continued imprisonment of conscientious objectors].
The Nation, Feb. 8, pp. 539–40.

187. Introduction, pp. xi–xxvii, to *Documents and Statements relating to Peace Proposals and War Aims*. London: Allen
& Unwin.

258   BIBLIOGRAPHY

188. The Peace Terms. Letter to the *Manchester Guardian,* May 19.

189. Review of J. L. Garvin: The Economic Foundation of Peace. The *League of Nations Journal,* June, pp. 230–1.

190. Bolshevism. [Review of L. Trotsky: History of the Russian Revolution to Brest-Litovsk; J. Reed: Ten Days that Shook the World; E. Buisson: Les Bolsheviki, 1917–1919; and A. Ransome: Six Weeks in Russia in 1919]. *The International Review,* July, pp. 544–8.

191. From Big Three to Big Four. Letter to *The Nation,* Sept. 6.

192. The [Railway] Strike and some Morals. Letter to *The Nation,* Oct. 11.

193. Either the League or the Doom of Mankind. *The Star,* Nov. 11.

1920

194. The Choice Before Us. *The Covenant,* Jan. pp. 182–95.

195. The U.D.C. Meeting. Letter to the *Cambridge Review,* March 12, protesting against the breaking-up of a meeting.

196. Letter from Hungary. The Red Regime and the White. [Anonymous article purporting to be from a Hungarian correspondent]. *Manchester Guardian,* March 23.

197. Review of L. Woolf: Empire and Commerce in Africa. *The Covenant,* April, pp. 439–41.

198. Review of Lord Eustace Percy: The Responsibilities of the League. *Ibid.* April, pp. 441–2.

199. The Future of British Liberalism. *Atlantic Monthly,* April, pp. 550–5.

200. Rousseau Up To Date. [Review of G. D. H. Cole: Social Theory]. *The Athenaeum,* April 9, pp. 476–7.

201. An Episode in a Free Empire. [Unsigned article on native labour in British East Africa]. *The Nation,* April 17, pp. 62–3.

202. The Pilgrimage of Peace. [Review of C. L. Lange: Histoire de l'Internationalisme, tome 1]. *The Athenaeum,* April 30, pp. 586–7.

203. THE FUTURE OF THE COVENANT. [In a series of Study Circle Pamphlets]. London: The League of Nations Union. Demy 8vo. pp. 20. Some copies were published by British Periodicals, Ltd.

204. The Religion of Progress. [Review of Professor Bury's Idea of Progress and Dean Inge's Romanes Lecture]. *The Athenaeum,* June 18, pp. 791–2.

205. 'Justum et Tenacem'. [Review of G. P. Gooch's Life of Lord Courtney]. *The Athenaeum,* July 23, pp. 105–7.

206. CAUSES OF INTERNATIONAL WAR. [No. 1 of the Swarthmore International Handbooks—a series of 8 volumes edited by Dickinson]. London: The Swarthmore Press Ltd. Cr. 8vo. pp. 110. (New York: Harcourt, Brace & Howe).

207. Germany under the Treaty. Four articles in the *Manchester Guardian*. Nov. 29, The Tragedy of the Children. Dec. 1, The Destitution of the Worker. Dec. 3, The Plight of the Middle Class. Dec. 4, The Moral and a Remedy. A controversy arising out of these articles led to two letters on 'The "Round Table" and Germany', Dec. 4 & 8. Cf. also an earlier letter written from Berlin, on 'The Allies and Germany's Milk Shortage', Oct. 23.

208. The Plight of Germany. *The Nation*, Dec. 11, pp. 380–1.

209. THE MAGIC FLUTE. A Fantasia. London: Allen & Unwin. Sm. Cr. 8vo. pp. 128. (New York: The Macmillan Co.).

1921

210. Opinion in Germany. *Common Sense*, Jan. 8, p. 136.

211. Goethe. [Review of P. Hume Brown's Life of Goethe]. *The Athenaeum*, Jan. 14, pp. 37–8, & 21, p. 68.

212. S.O.S.—Europe to America. *Atlantic Monthly*, Feb. pp. 244–9.

213. The Allies and Germany. Letter to the *Manchester Guardian*, March 31.

214. Review of J. A. Hobson: Problems of a New World. *Sociological Review*, April, pp. 111–12.

215. The Internationalism of the Seas. [Review of J. A. Salter: Allied Shipping Control]. *The Nation and the Athenaeum*, July 30, pp. 251–2.

216. The Disease of War. [Review of R. Rolland: Clerambault, Histoire d'une conscience libre pendant la guerre]. *Foreign Affairs*, Aug. pp. i–ii.

217. The Russian Famine. Letter to the *Manchester Guardian*, Oct. 7. Cf. a second letter, Oct. 17.

218. A German looks at the League. [Review of W. Schucking & H. Wehberg: Die Satzung des Völkerbundes]. *Headway*, Nov. p. 38.

1922

219. Anglo-French Relations. Letter to the *Manchester Guardian*, May 26.

220. Hofmannsthal's Mystery Play. ['Das grosse Welttheater' in the Kollegien-Kirche at Salzburg]. *Manchester Guardian*, Aug. 28.

221. Dickinson went to Geneva as *Manchester Guardian* correspondent at the Third Assembly of the League of Nations.

He wrote a preliminary survey of 'The Work before the
Assembly', Sept. 4; a daily despatch Sept. 7–Oct. 2; and
articles entitled 'A week of the League of Nations',
Sept. 14, and 'Final Impressions', Oct. 5. 'A Week of
the League of Nations' was reprinted in *The Living Age*,
Oct. 28, pp. 199–202, under the title 'At the League
Assembly'.

222. Science and Goodwill. Letter to *The New Leader*, Oct. 27.

223. On Sovereignty. *Youth*, Dec. pp. 178–9.

224. 'British Mandates in the Pacific'. Letter to the *Manchester
Guardian*, Dec. 5.

225. The Problem of the Straits [with reference to the Lausanne
Conference]. Letters to the *Manchester Guardian*, Dec.
9 & 30.

1923

226. Peace. *Manchester Guardian Commercial*. *Reconstruction in
Europe, section* 12. Jan. 4, pp. 739–40.

227. 'Smashing Up Germany'. Letter to the *Manchester Guardian*,
Jan. 6.

228. The French in the Ruhr. Letters to the *Manchester Guardian*,
Jan. 30, Feb. 5 & 12.

229. France on organising peace. [Review of Les français à la
recherche d'une Société des Nations depuis le roi
Henri IV jusqu'aux combattants de 1914]. *Headway*,
Feb. p. 276.

230. Mr Bonar Law and the League of Nations. Letter to the
Manchester Guardian, Feb. 22.

231. A Personal Impression of Tagore. *The New Leader*, Feb. 23,
pp. 11–12.

232. Der Krieg, der Frieden und die Ruhrbesetzung. *Friedens-
Warte*, March, pp. 68–70.

233. Causes of the Great War. *Foreign Affairs*, March, pp. 195–6.
Reprinted as pp. 58–65 of no. 235.

234. 'The European Outlook'. Letter to the *Manchester Guardian*,
March 2.

235. WAR: ITS NATURE, CAUSE AND CURE. London: Allen &
Unwin. Cr. 8vo. pp. 155. (New York: The Macmillan
Co.). Cf. no. 233. For Danish and Swedish translations
see nos. 243 & 260.

236. Mr Forster's New Book. [Review of E. M. Forster: Pharos
and Pharillon]. *The Nation and the Athenaeum*, May 26, p. 273.

237. Goethe Once More. [In connection with E. Ludwig:
Goethe, Geschichte eines Menschen]. *Ibid*. June 23,
pp. 390–2. Reprinted in *The Living Age*, Aug. 4, pp. 230–2.

238. 'It is not to be thought of'. [Review of Clive Bell: On British Freedom]. *The Nation and the Athenaeum*, July 7, pp. 457–8.

239. The Native, the Boer, and the Englishman. [Review of Olive Schreiner: Thoughts on South Africa]. *Ibid.* July 21, pp. 522–3.

240. Entente Diplomacy before the War. [Review of G. A. Schreiner: Entente Diplomacy and the World]. *Ibid.* Aug. 11, p. 613.

241. What the Issues are at Geneva. [Article about the Corfu incident written from Geneva]. *Daily Herald*, Sept. 8.

242. Three articles in *The Nation and the Athenaeum* written from Geneva. Sept. 15, Italy and the League, pp. 738–9; Sept. 22, The Competence of the League, pp. 769–70; Sept. 29, Can these bones live? pp. 800–2. The third article was reprinted in *The New Republic*, Oct. 24, pp. 228–30.

243. KRIGEN, FREDEN OG FREMTIDEN. Copenhagen: P. Haase & Sons. Translation of no. 235 by D. Grünbaum.

244. Vale. [Review of Sir Walter Raleigh: Some Authors]. *The Nation and the Athenaeum*, Nov. 3, p. 189.

245. Goethe. [Review of B. Croce: Goethe]. *Ibid.* Dec. 1, p. 347.

246. The Perfect Friend. [Review of Some New Letters of Edward Fitzgerald, edited by F. R. Barton]. *Ibid.* Dec. 8, p. 378.

1924

247. The [Proposed] Treaty of Mutual Assistance. Two letters to *The Nation and the Athenaeum*, Jan. 5 & 19.

248. Shelley and Science. [Review of O. W. Campbell: Shelley and the Unromantics]. *The Nation and the Athenaeum*, Feb. 16, p. 703.

249. The League and German Universities. Letter to the *Manchester Guardian*, Feb. 22. Cf. a second letter, March 1.

250. The Making of the Treaty of Versailles. [Review of R. S. Baker: Woodrow Wilson and World Settlement]. *Foreign Affairs*, March, pp. i–iv.

251. Distress in Germany. The Facts. Letter to the *Manchester Guardian*, March 7.

252. A Vision of England. [Review of E. L. Grant Watson: English Country]. *The Nation and the Athenaeum*, March 8, p. 802.

253. M. Poincaré. [In connection with Sisley Huddleston: Poincaré, a Biographical Portrait]. *Ibid.* March 29, pp. 913–14.

254. A Woman of Genius. [Review of S. C. Cronwright-Schreiner's Life of Olive Schreiner]. *The Nation and the Athenaeum*, April 26, p. 116. Reprinted in *The Living Age*, June 21, pp. 1203–5.

255. The Modern Caligula. [Review of Count R. Zedlitz-Trützschler: Twelve Years at the Imperial German Court]. *Ibid.* June 28, p. 414.

256. Review of F. C. S. Schiller: Problems of Belief. *Proceedings of the Society for Psychical Research*, July, pp. 196–9. Cf. a letter to the *Journal of the S.P.R.* Oct. p. 324.

257. An Appeal to British Fair Play. [In connection with a pamphlet issued by a number of German intellectuals on the question of the origin of the War]. *The Nation and the Athenaeum*, Aug. 30, pp. 660–1.

258. Europe: 1890–1898. [According to the *Grosse Politik*, vols. 8–12]. *Contemporary Review*, Sept. pp. 316–22.

259. Disarmament and Security. Letter to the *Manchester Guardian*, Sept. 8.

260. KRIGET, FREDEN OCH FRAMTIDEN. Upsala: J. A. Lindblad. Translation of no. 235 by E. Lundquist.

261. 'Victory'. [Review of A. Fabre-Luce: La Victoire]. *The Nation and the Athenaeum*, Oct. 4, pp. 19–20.

262. A Field Marshal's Memoirs. [Review of F. Whyte: A Field-Marshal's Memoirs, from the Diary, Correspondence and Reminiscences of Alfred, Count von Waldersee]. *Ibid.* Nov. 1, p. 188.

263. Life after Death. Do we Desire Immortality? [In connection with Sir James Marchant's symposium on Immortality]. *The New Leader*, Nov. 14, p. 8.

264. Exporting Munitions. Letter to the *Manchester Guardian*, Nov. 21.

265. A short contribution to a symposium on 'E. D. Morel: the Man and his Work'. *Foreign Affairs*, Dec. p. 124.

1925

266. Mr Wells Prophesies. [Review of H. G. Wells: A year of Prophesying]. *The Nation and the Athenaeum*, Jan. 17, p. 554.

267. Egypt and the League. [A criticism of British action after the assassination of the Sirdar]. *Headway*, Feb. p. 25. Cf. a letter to the *Manchester Guardian*, Nov. 27, 1924.

268. BRIEFE EINES CHINESISCHEN GELEHRTEN. Celle: N. Kampmann. Translation of no. 48 by A. Malata.

269. INDIEN, CHINA UND JAPAN. Celle: N. Kampmann. Translation of no. 132 by A. Malata.

270. The League under Fire. [Review of F. Kellor: Security against War]. *Foreign Affairs*, May, pp. 262–3.

271. The Perfect Militarist. [Review of Politische Dokumente von A. von Tirpitz, vol. 1]. *The Nation and the Athenaeum*, May 16, pp. 208–9.

272. The Export of Arms. Letter to the *Manchester Guardian*, May 20.

273. The Situation in China. Letter to the *Manchester Guardian*, July 14.

274. Mr Santayana's Dialogue. [Review of G. Santayana: Dialogues in Limbo]. *The Nation and the Athenaeum*, Aug. 29, pp. 650–1.

275. The Bombardment of Damascus. Letter to the *Manchester Guardian*, Oct. 31.

276. The Serajevo Murder. [Review of M. E. Durham: The Serajevo Crime]. *The Nation and the Athenaeum*, Dec. 26, pp. 471–2.

1926

277. THE INTERNATIONAL ANARCHY, 1904–1914. London: Allen & Unwin. Demy 8vo. pp. xiv, 516. (New York: The Century Co.). Cf. no. 280.

278. The Failure at Geneva. Letter to the *Manchester Guardian*, March 29.

279. 'Who is on our side, who?' [In connection with Mr D. A. Peat's 'Arbitrate First' Bureau]. *The Nation and Athenaeum*, Aug. 28, p. 605. Cf. a letter on 'Personal Service for Peace' to the *Manchester Guardian*, Aug. 24.

280. Die wirkliche Moral der Ereignisse. *Europäische Gespräche*, Sept. pp. 463–72. Translation of pp. 472–81 of no. 277 by A. H. R. Wach.

1927

281. Review of vol. 11 of the British Documents on the Origins of the War. *Journal of the Royal Institute of International Affairs*, Jan. pp. 52–3.

282. 'British Hypocrisy'. [Review of H. Luz: Lord Grey und der Weltkrieg]. *The Nation and Athenaeum*, April 16, p. 52.

283. French and British Disarmament Plans. *Foreign Affairs*, May, pp. 299–300.

284. Oscar Browning. [In connection with H. E. Wortham's biography]. *Cambridge Review*, May 20, pp. 425–6.

285. Macchiavelli. [On the occasion of the quatercentenary of his death]. *The Nation and the Athenaeum*, June 18, pp. 366–7.

286. Review of A. Ebray: A Frenchman looks at the Peace; O. Hammann: The World Policy of Germany 1890–1912; & E. Brandenburg: From Bismarck to the World War. *Journal of the Royal Institute of International Affairs*, July, pp. 253–5.

287. Contribution, pp. 40–42, to *Russell Hillard Loines, 1874–1922. A Selection from his letters and poems with biographical sketch and recollections by his friends*. New York: privately printed.

288. Two articles in *The Nation and Athenaeum* written from Geneva. Sept. 3, The Eighth Assembly, pp. 712–13; Sept. 24, The Debate in the Assembly, pp. 796–7.

289. REVOLUTION AND REACTION IN MODERN FRANCE. London: Allen and Unwin. Cr. 8vo. pp. 256. (New York: Brentano). Revised edition of no. 33, with a new preface and conclusion.

290. East and West. [Review of Hwuy-ung: A Chinaman's Opinion of Us and of His Own Country]. *The Nation and Athenaeum*, Nov. 26, p. 322.

291. Introduction, pp. v–xxii, to *A Project of Perpetual Peace. Rousseau's Essay*. Translated by Edith M. Nuttall. London: R. Cobden-Sanderson.

292. Armed Anarchy. [In connection with vol. 1 of the British Documents on the Origin of the War]. *Foreign Affairs*, Dec. pp. 173–4.

1928

293. Bismarck. [In connection with E. Ludwig: Bismarck, the Story of a Fighter]. *Foreign Affairs*, Jan. p. 217.

294. Goethe's View of Nature. [In collaboration with Miss F. M. Stawell]. *Hibbert Journal*, April, pp. 399–409. Reprinted as ch. 2 of no. 297.

295. The Real Moral. [Review of P. Renouvin: The Immediate Origins of the War]. *The Nation and Athenaeum*, April 28, pp. 111–12.

296. On the Discovery of Good—a Dialogue. *Journal of Philosophical Studies*, July, pp. 279–84. Partly incorporated in nos. 309 & 315.

297. GOETHE AND FAUST. An Interpretation. With Passages newly translated into English Verse. [In collaboration with Miss F. M. Stawell]. London: G. Bell and Sons, Ltd. Demy 8vo. pp. 291. (New York: The Dial Press). Cf. no. 294.

298. Goethe Again. [Review of E. Ludwig: Goethe, the History of a Man]. *The Nation and Athenaeum*, Oct. 27, pp. 146–8.

299. Anglo-American Relations. A Very Real Danger [of hostility through naval competition]. Letter to the *Manchester Guardian*, Nov. 29.

300. Obscene Books and the Law. [The dangers of police censorship]. Letter to the *Manchester Guardian*, Dec. 29.

1929

301. Reviews of F. Stieve: Germany and Europe; & of The Memoirs of Prince Max of Baden. *Journal of the Royal Institute of International Affairs*, Jan. pp. 52–4.

302. 'All Quiet on the Western Front'. [Review of E. M. Remarque's book]. *Cambridge Review*, May 3, p. 412.

303. Our Knowledge of Other People. *Ibid.* June 5, pp. 515–17.

304. Goethe's View of Nature. *The Realist*, Aug. pp. 97–106.

305. Introduction, pp. xi–xiv, to *The Ascent of Humanity* by Gerald Heard. London: Jonathan Cape.

306. Points of View. [A series of broadcast talks of which Dickinson gave the first and last]. *The Listener*, Oct. 9, pp. 465–6 & 490, and Nov. 20, pp. 679–81. Reprinted as no. 313.

307. Arthur Berry. [Obituary]. *Cambridge Review*, Oct. 11, p. 10.

308. On Translation. [In connection with Tu Fu: the Autobiography of a Chinese Poet, A.D. 712–70, arranged and translated by F. Ayscough]. *The Nation and Athenaeum*, Nov. 23, pp. 282–3.

1930

309. A Political Dialogue. *The Political Quarterly*, Jan. pp. 70–85, & April, pp. 248–64. Reprinted as pp. 11–54 of no. 315. Cf. also no. 296.

310. C. P. Sanger. [Obituary]. *The Nation and Athenaeum*, Feb. 22, p. 701.

311. Euripides and the 'Bacchae'. *Cambridge Review*, Feb. 28, pp. 298–9.

312. The Ascent of Humanity. [In connection with Gerald Heard's book]. *Antiquity*, March, pp. 5–11.

313. Introduction, pp. 9–18, and two talks, pp. 21–32 & 129–43, in *Points of View. A Series of Broadcast Addresses.* London: Allen and Unwin. A Reprint of no. 306, with the addition of the introduction.

314. Goethe. [Broadcast talk]. *The Listener*, April 23, pp. 713–14.

315. AFTER TWO THOUSAND YEARS. A Dialogue between Plato and a Modern Young Man. London: Allen & Unwin. Cr. 8vo. pp. 213. (New York: W. W. Norton & Co.). Cf. nos. 296 & 309.

316. The Abyss. [Review of K. A. Bratt: That Next War]. *The Nation and Athenaeum*, Nov. 8, pp. 211–12.

1931

317. Then and Now. [A broadcast discussion with John Maud on the ideas of young men in the early eighties and today]. *The Listener*, Jan. 7, pp. 23–4.

318. We hear a great deal about Plato. *The Radio Times*, Feb. 13, pp. 349 & 398.

319. The Dialogues of Plato. [A series of six broadcast talks]. *The Listener*, Feb. 18, pp. 264–5 & 286; Feb. 25, pp. 320–1; March 4, pp. 369–70; March 11, pp. 422–3; March 18, pp. 464–5; March 25, pp. 511–12 & April 1, pp. 559–60. Reprinted in an expanded form as no. 329.

320. Russian Foreign Policy. [Review of L. Fischer: The Soviet in World Affairs]. *The Political Quarterly*, April, pp. 278–83.

321. Edward Carpenter as a Friend. An essay, pp. 34–46, in *Edward Carpenter in Appreciation*, edited by G. Beith. London: Allen & Unwin.

322. Would *You* Fight for the League? *The Clarion*, June, pp. 167–8.

323. Reflections of Spiritualism. [Review of G. O. Leonard: My Life in Two Worlds]. *The New Statesman and Nation*, Sept. 26, p. 376.

324. The Essential Issue. [Contribution to a symposium of 'Reflections on the Crisis']. *The Political Quarterly*, Oct. pp. 470–2.

325. The Issue. [Socialism and Capitalism]. *The Highway*, Nov. pp. 5–7.

326. J. McT. E. McTaggart. [With chapters by Basil Williams and S. V. Keeling]. Cambridge University Press. Cr. 8vo. pp. viii, 160. (New York: The Macmillan Co.).

327. Mr Nevinson on Goethe. [Review of H. W. Nevinson: Goethe, Man and Poet]. *The New Statesman and Nation*, Nov. 14, p. vii.

328. If I were Dictator. [One of a series of articles under this title]. *The (New York) Nation*, Nov. 25, pp. 567–8.

329. PLATO AND HIS DIALOGUES. London: Allen & Unwin. Cr. 8vo. pp. 228. (New York: W. W. Norton & Co.). An expanded version of No. 319.

330. What I would do with the world. [The last of a series of broadcast talks under this title]. *The Listener*, Dec. 16, pp. 1048–9.

331. B.B.C. Talks. [Dissent from the proposed policy of attempting to avoid all possible offence]. Letter to *The Times*, Dec. 23.

1932

332. Dialogue as a Literary Form. A paper read on Feb. 17 and published posthumously in *Essays by Divers Hands, being the Transactions of the Royal Society of Literature of the United Kingdom*, New Series, vol. XI, pp. 1–19.

333. Goethe—the Man. Goethe revealed in 'Faust'. [Two broadcast talks]. *The Listener*, April 6, pp. 481–4 & 513, and April 13, pp. 519–20 & 552.

334. The Political Background. *Scrutiny*, May, pp. 40–6. Reprinted under the title 'Two Issues' in *The Living Age*, Aug. pp. 539–43.

335. Mencius. [Review of A. Lyall's translation of Mencius; I. A. Richards: Mencius on the Mind; & L. S. Hsü: The Political Philosophy of Confucianism]. *The New Statesman and Nation*, June 18, pp. 801–2.

336. THE CONTRIBUTION OF ANCIENT GREECE TO MODERN LIFE. Being the Inaugural Lecture delivered at the Local Lectures Summer Meeting of the University of Cambridge, 1932. London: Allen & Unwin. Fcap. 8vo. pp. 32.

ADDENDA

337. THE WAR AND A WAY OUT. Reprint of no. 134. The Hague: Belinfante Brothers. 1915.

338. SENSŌ ZEHI. Translation of no. 134 by S. Koizumi & K. Minabe. Tokyo: Keiogijuku University Press. 1915.

339. GENDAI EIKOKU NO SANGYO KAKUMEI. Translation of no. 88 by I. Uyehara. Tokyo: Seikyosha. 1916.

340. SHINA NO ICHI KANRI YORI ŌBEIJIN NI ATŌRU SHO. Translation of no. 48 by J. Nakura. Tokyo: Hokuseidō. 1925.

341. CHINNO AVAJ. Translation of no. 48 by Chandrashankar Shukla. Ahmedabad: D. B. Kalelkar. 1927.

342. CHÊNG I YÜ TZŬ YU. Translation of no. 88 by Ch'êng Chên-chi. Shanghai: The Commercial Press. 1927.

343. CHIN TAI LUN T'AN. Translation of no. 65 by Liang Yü-ch'un. Shanghai: The Spring Tide Bookshop. 1929.

344. HANDS OFF CHINA! The Letters of a Chinese Official. [Anon.] Reprint of no. 50. New York: W. Faro. 1932.

345. Article on Oscar Browning in the *Dictionary of National Biography. Twentieth Century, 1922–1930*. Oxford University Press. Forthcoming.

Obituary Notices

This list contains only such obituary notices as were written by friends who knew Dickinson personally and who are therefore able to give original impressions of his character.

The Times, Aug. 4. Followed by short appreciations from E. M. Forster, Aug. 6, and Syed Ross Masood, Aug. 9.

Manchester Guardian, Aug. 4. With an appreciation by Professor Ernest Barker.

The New Statesman and Nation, Aug. 6, editorial paragraph. Also a paragraph by 'Critic', Aug. 13.

The Week-End Review, Aug. 13. Letter from Gerald Heard.

The Spectator, Aug. 13. A tribute by E. M. Forster. Reprinted in *The Living Age*, Oct.

The (New York) Nation, Aug. 17. Editorial paragraph.

The New Clarion, Aug. 27. Article by H. M. Tomlinson.

Sunday Times, Aug. 28. Review of no. 336 by Desmond MacCarthy, under the title 'Liberal Culture'.

Headway, Sept. Paragraph by Professor Gilbert Murray.

Cambridge Review, Oct. 14. Obituary by J. T. Sheppard.

The Listener, Oct. 19. Broadcast talk by E. M. Forster.

The Political Quarterly, Oct.–Dec. Article on 'Graham Wallas and Lowes Dickinson' by Professor H. J. Laski.

The Journal of Education, Nov. Letter from a former pupil at the London School of Economics.

Journal of the S.P.R. Nov. Obituary by Miss F. M. Stawell.

The Criterion, Jan. Article on 'Goldie Dickinson: the latest Cambridge Platonist' by N. Wedd.

Goldsworthy Lowes Dickinson. A Memoir by Roger Fry. Privately printed (together with J. T. Sheppard's obituary) for distribution to members of King's College, Cambridge. pp. 28.

INDEX

INDEX

(Works by G. L. D. are in italics)